The Responsibility to Protect and Counter-terrorism

The Responsibility to Protect and Counter-terrorism

Contradictions and Congruences

Edited by

Shannon Zimmerman

BRILL | NIJHOFF

LEIDEN | BOSTON

This collection of essays was first published in the journal *Global Responsibility to Protect* (vols. 14 and 15, 2022 and 2023).

Cover illustration: Photograph by Levi Meir Clancy, 2021.

The Library of Congress Cataloging-in-Publication Data is available online at https://catalog.loc.gov
LC record available at https://lccn.loc.gov/2023015893

Typeface for the Latin, Greek, and Cyrillic scripts: "Brill". See and download: brill.com/brill-typeface.

ISBN 978-90-04-54811-4 (paperback)

This book is printed on acid-free paper and produced in a sustainable manner.

Contents

Acknowledgements

Much scholarship is a collaborative endeavour and none more so than an edited volume. I would first like to thank the contributors for being willing to wrestle with the complex and vexing issues surrounding counter-terrorism and R2P and being so open to working with me to craft a cohesive volume. Next, I must thank the phenomenal editors of the journal *Global Responsibility to Protect*: Cecilia Jacob, Adrian Gallagher, and Charles T. Hunt. It was with Charlie's encouragement that I first pitched the idea of a special issue on this theme, and the editors have been unwavering in their support as these works have been shepherded through the process of becoming this edited volume. Lastly, I thank my support network, all the wonderful people in my life who support me as I take on new challenges such as my first edited volume.

Notes on Contributors

Adrian Gallagher
is Professor in the School of Politics and International Studies at the University of Leeds. He is Co-director of the European Centre for the Responsibility to Protect. He is author of *Genocide and Its Threat to Contemporary International Order* (Palgrave Macmillan, 2013) and has published in peer reviewed journals such as *International Affairs*, *International Theory*, *Review of International Studies*, *Politics*, and *Journal of Global Security Studies*. In 2021 he began an Economic and Social Research Council-funded project on non-state armed groups perpetrating mass atrocities in Democratic Republic of Congo, Central African Republic, Iraq, Nigeria, Syria, and Somalia which runs till mid-2023.

Josie Hornung
is a PhD candidate at the University of Queensland, Australia, under the supervision of Professors Christian Reus-Smit and Alex Bellamy. During her candidacy she has spent time at the European University Institute as the Australian European University Institute Fellowships Association postgraduate fellow, and at Oxford University as a visiting PhD fellow. She holds a Bachelor of Arts, and a Master of International Relations (Advanced) with honours, both from the Australian National University. Her research focuses on the prevention of imminent mass atrocities and draws on both historical and contemporary case studies to examine the forces and factors affecting decision-making.

Charles T. Hunt
is Associate Professor of International Security in the School of Global, Urban & Social Studies at RMIT University, Senior Fellow (non-resident) at the United Nations University's Centre for Policy Research and honorary Senior Research Fellow at the Asia Pacific Centre for the Responsibility to Protect. His research is focused on the prevention of and responses to atrocity crimes, the protection of civilians through UN peace operations and peacebuilding in conflict-affected societies with recent articles published in *Survival*, *Conflict and Cooperation*, *International Affairs*, *International Peacekeeping*, and *Global Governance*.

Wisdom Oghosa Iyekekpolo
is a staff of the Academic Services arm of the University of Auckland, New Zealand. He obtained a PhD in Politics and International Relations at the University of Auckland after his Bachelor's and Master's degrees in the same

course from the University of Benin, Nigeria. He has published extensively on armed group emergence, trajectory, and how to end their activities in Africa and around the world. His current book project explores the political process that enables the rise of armed groups.

Blake Lawrinson
is a Teaching Fellow in International Relations in the School of Politics and International Studies at the University of Leeds. As an early career researcher, his research focuses on norms and human protection with publications in the *British Journal of Politics and International Relations* on UK norm entrepreneurship (2022) and *Global Responsibility to Protect* on norm clusters in Mali (with Adrian Gallagher and Charles T. Hunt, 2022).

Sascha Nanlohy
is a Sessional Academic at the University of Sydney's School of Social and Political Sciences. His research focuses on external influence on genocide. He is also a Research Associate with Atrocity Forecasting Project. He holds PhD, Master's, and Bachelor's degrees from the University of Sydney.

Isaac Taylor
is an Associate Senior Lecturer in Practical Philosophy at Stockholm University. He works primarily in applied ethics and political philosophy. His current research investigates how states can provide security both effectively and ethically, especially in light of the increased use of private companies and AI systems in the defence and security sectors. His book, *The Ethics of Counterterrorism*, explores what moral principles apply to government agents in their pursuit of terrorists, and was published by Routledge in 2018.

Shannon Zimmerman
is a Lecturer in Strategic Studies at Deakin University at the Australian War College. Prior to that she was a postdoctoral research fellow at the RMIT University in Melbourne, Australia. Her research focuses on how UN peace operations protect civilians in conflict environments characterised by asymmetric threats. She also studies misogyny motivated terrorism, looking at the online groups in the 'Manosphere'. Shannon received her PhD from the University of Queensland in 2019 and her Master's in Conflict Resolution from Georgetown University in 2012.

Introduction: The Responsibility to Protect and Counter-terrorism

Shannon Zimmerman
Lecturer in Strategic Studies, Deakin University at the Australian War College, Weston, ACT, Australia
s.zimmerman@deakin.edu.au

The norms of Responsibility to Protect and counter-terrorism emerged from the tumultuous 1990s, where the post-Cold War collapse of weak states saw the proliferation of intrastate conflicts. At first glance, they are rather strange bedfellows; the former seemingly emphasizing human rights while the latter appears devoted to state preservation. Because of this, these two concepts have routinely been understood as contradictory, a dichotomy where actors must make a choice between prioritizing individual human rights or the security of the state. The two concepts, however, are far more closely related than they first appear. First, both R2P and counter-terrorism are state-centric, prioritizing the role, rights and responsibilities of the state and designed to support state sovereignty. Second, both norms are rooted in international law and are more the solidification or escalation of existing practices than new concepts. Their contradictions, when present, are more the result of the different interpretation and implementation by specific actors than the inevitable outcome of conflicting norms.

This introduction provides the genesis of the Responsibility to Protect and counter-terrorism, including how these two concepts have evolved alongside each other, have variously been interpreted and implemented, and have now come to overlap in important and problematic ways. This chapter then identifies these two concepts as norms and lays out a theoretical framework which explains and illustrates their malleable nature. It then engages with the key debates around where and how R2P and counter-terrorism intersect. With the stage set, it will introduce the chapters in this edited volume, each of which looks at different areas of congruence or conflict between R2P and counter-terrorism in an effort to provide much needed insights into how these two major norms are being used to shape how we go about and understand the role of the state, sovereignty and international interventions.

 | DOI:10.1163/9789004548114_002

1 The Responsibility to Protect and Counter-terrorism Emerge on the Global Stage

Both R2P and counter-terrorism 'came of age' at the turn of the millennium as the international community was grappling with the challenges emerging from the end of the Cold War. The withdrawal of great power support for weak state regimes resulted in multiple state collapse. This, in turn, led to human atrocities and the proliferation of non-state actors who engaged terrorist tactics to achieve their political goals. Crimes that had previously been hidden by Cold War regimes or overlooked in the tense Cold War environment, were made visible.

Leveraging human rights conventions passed near the end of the Cold War,[1] the United Nations articulated a concept of 'human security', which emphasized the importance of protecting individual citizens.[2] Francis Deng, in his role as the first UN Special Representative on Internally Displaced Persons (IDP), reiterated that the primary responsibility for protecting individuals (citizens or otherwise) lay with the state.[3] Failure to uphold this 'Sovereignty as Responsibility' would damage a state's legitimacy in international society. This position underpinned the Guiding Principles presented by the Secretary-General to the UN Commission on Human Rights in 1998.[4] The Principles endorsed the idea that legitimate sovereignty was premised on the responsibility to protect populations and, when that was beyond the capacity of the state, to accept international assistance in doing so.

These debates about sovereignty as responsibly occurred over the backdrop of the ethnic cleansing in Bosnia from 1992–1995 where large numbers of Bosnian Muslims and Croats were forced to flee or be murdered by Serbian military forces.[5] This atrocity, in turn, was punctuated by the 1994 genocide

1 Charter of Paris. (1991). Charter of Paris for a New Europe. *Current History, 90*(553), 78.

2 Human security was officially coined in 1994 in the United Nations Human Development Report and refined security to include economic security, food security, health security, environmental security, personal security, community security, and political security, p. 24–33.

3 United Nations Commission on Human Rights. (1998). *Report of the Representative of the Secretary-General, Mr. Francis M. Deng, submitted pursuant to Commission resolution 1997/39. Addendum: Guiding Principles on Internal Displacement. E/CT.4/1998/53/add. 11 February 1998.* New York: United Nations.

4 United Nations High Commissioner for Refugees (UNHCR). (1998). *Guiding Principles on Internal Displacement.* (ADM 1.1,PRL 12.1, PROO/98/109). New York: United Nations Retrieved from http://www.refworld.org/docid/3c3da07f7.html.

5 United Nations Security Council. (1994). *Final Report of the Commission of Experts Established Pursuant to Security Council Resolution 780 (1992). S/1994/674.* United

in Rwanda where an estimated 800,000 Tutsis and moderate Hutu where slaughtered in just three months.[6] In both cases, state actors played key roles in committing atrocity crimes against their own civilians. At the same time, the international community was present on the ground but unwilling, unable, or unprepared to intervene.

Confronted with the UN's failure to act to stop these atrocities, then UN Secretary-General Kofi Annan called for an investigation into the responsibilities of states and the international community in cases of mass atrocities. The response was the International Commission on Intervention and State Sovereignty (ICISS), which concluded that it was a state's responsibility to protect its population and formally re-characterized sovereignty away from *sovereignty as control* over a population to *sovereignty as responsibility* towards that population.[7] If the state struggled or failed to do this, the international community had a responsibility to support state efforts at protection, or even intervene to stop atrocities.[8] Thus, the responsibility to protect was born.

The emergence of R2P as a defined principle was overshadowed by the international community's scramble to respond to transnational terrorism. Mere weeks before the ICISS report was released, the world was shaken by the terrorist attacks of 11 September 2001, which killed 2,977 people. The very next day, the UN Security Council declared 'international terrorism as a threat to international peace and security'.[9] A few weeks later they unanimously passed Resolution 1373, a super-legislative resolution with the first binding requirement that states criminalise and respond to terrorist activities.[10] Notably, UNSCR 1373 did not identify respect for human rights and international humanitarian law as integral to the design and implementation of counter-terrorism efforts. Lack of explicit adherence to human rights in counter-terrorism, alongside the upswelling of support for the global 'war on terror', left 'the impression

---

Nations: New York Retrieved from https://documents-dds-ny.un.org/doc/UNDOC/GEN/N94/200/60/PDF/N9420060.pdf?OpenElement.

6 United Nations Security Council. (1999). *Report of the Independent Inquiry into the action of the United Nations during the 1994 genocide in Rwanda, S/1999/1257. 16 December 1999.*

7 ICISS. (2001). *The Responsibility to Protect: Report of the International Commission on Intervention and State Sovereignty.* International Development Research Centre. Ottawa, ON, Canada.

8 Ibid.

9 UNSC Res. 1368 [Threats to International Peace and Security Caused by Terrorist Acts], 12 September 2001.

10 UNSC Res. 1373, 28 September 2001; Fionnuala Ní Aoláin, 'Human Rights and Counterterrorism: A Sisyphean Tale', 16 June 2021, Retrieved from https://theglobalobservatory.org/2021/06/human-rights-and-counterterrorism-a-sisyphean-tale/, accessed 07 January 2022 2021.

that human rights protection is a secondary consideration in the campaign against terrorism, instead of an essential component of any counterterrorism strategy'.[11]

In its immediate post-9/11 form, counter-terrorism relied on heavily realist approaches to security which emphasised security for the state and the primacy of force and military control of the population. The prevailing state-led approaches also flaunted international legal norms by prioritising enforcement and using torture, arbitrary detention, and excessive force which, at times, verged on atrocity crimes.[12] While such approaches were initially effective, the securitization of the population and human rights violations alienated the domestic population from their governments and were leveraged by terrorist groups as recruitment material.[13] Such was the negative impact of counter-terrorism efforts on human rights that, by 2003, UN Special Rapporteurs and independent experts expressed 'profound concern at the multiplication of policies, laws and practices increasingly being adopted by many countries in the struggle against terrorism which in their view were negatively affecting the enjoyment of virtually all human rights – civil, cultural, economic, political and social'.[14] Subsequent UN Resolution 1456 (2003) on counter-terrorism finally connected effective counter-terrorism to actions 'in accordance with the Charter of the United Nations and international law', but by then the damage had been done.[15]

---

11 International Helsinki Federation for Human Rights (IHF), 'Anti-Terrorism Measures, Security and Human Rights: Developments in Europe, Central Asia and North America in the Aftermath of September 11', (International Helsinki Federation for Human Rights, 2003), 42.

12 Elin Miller, 'The Use of Targeted Sanctions in the Fight against International Terrorism – What About Human Rights?', *Proceedings of the Annual Meeting (American Society of International Law)*, 97, 46–51 (2003); David Cole, *Enemy Aliens: Double Standards and Constitutional Freedoms in the War on Terrorism* (New York: The New Press, 2005); Rebecca Sanders, 'Human Rights Abuses at the Limits of the Law: Legal Instabilities and Vulnerabilities in the "Global War on Terror,"' *Review of International Studies* 44(1) 2–23 (2018).

13 Byman, D. L. (2007). *Iraq and the Global War on Terrorism.* Brookings Institution. Washington, D. C. Retrieved from https://www.brookings.edu/articles/iraq-and-the-global-war-on-terrorism/ Drash, W. (2009, 20 May 2009). Abu Ghraib photos were 'big shock,' undermined U.S. ideals. *CNN*. Retrieved from http://edition.cnn.com/2009/WORLD/meast/05/18/detainee.abuse.lookback/index.html.

14 United Nations Economic and Social Council, *Report of the United Nations High Commissioner for Human Rights and Follow-up to the World Conference on Human Rights*, E/CN.4/2004/4, 5 August 2003.

15 United Nations Security Council. (2003). *Security Council resolution 1456 (2003), S/RES/1456. 20 January 2003*. New York: United Nations.

To re-align counter-terrorism efforts with human rights and civilian protection, the UN emphasized their mutual relationship. The 2004 High-Level Panel on Threats, Challenges and Change made it clear that some actions undertaken in the 'war on terrorism…corroded the very values that terrorists target: human rights and the rule of law'.[16] Effective counter-terror responses then needed to strengthen 'responsible states and the rule of law and fundamental human rights'.[17] This was reaffirmed by the UN Secretary-General who argued that '[e]ffective counter-terrorism measures and the protection of human rights are not conflicting goals, but complementary and mutually reinforcing ones' alluding to the mounting evidence that violations of human rights actually fostered radicalisation.[18]

The 2005 World Summit, convened with over 170 heads of state and government to address pressing global problems, called for more clarity on both R2P and counter-terrorism. The resulting World Summit Outcome Document codified (but narrowed) R2P, affirming both state and international responsibilities to protect their populations from four specific atrocity crimes: genocide, war crimes, ethnic cleansing, and crimes against humanity.[19] The UN Secretary-General's report on implementing the Responsibility to Protect followed a few years later in 2009 and broke R2P into pillars for implementation.[20] The World Summit Outcome Document also laid the groundwork for a more unified and human-rights focused approach to counter-terrorism by requesting that the UN Secretary-General strengthen the UN's role in counter-terrorism.[21] His subsequent report, *Uniting against Terrorism: Recommendations for Global Counterterrorism Strategy*,[22] became the basis for the UN's Global Counter-Terrorism Strategy (GCTS) which was adopted by consensus in 2006 and forms the basis for the UN's work on counter-terrorism.[23] The GCTS specifically noted that states must take '[m]easures to ensure respect for human rights for all and

16 United Nations. (2004). *Report of the Secretary-General's High-Level Panel on Threats, Challenges and Change: A More Secure World: Our Shared Responsibility. A/59/565.*

17 Ibid.

18 United Nations. (2006). *Uniting Against Terrorism: Recommendations for a global counter-terrorism strategy. Report of the Secretary-General. A/60/825, 27 April 2006.* New York: United Nations.

19 '2005 World Summit Outcome', UNGA Res. 60/1, 24 October 2005, paras. 138–140.

20 United Nations General Assembly. (2009). *Implementing the Responsibility to Protect. Report of the Secretary General. A/63/677. 12 January 2009.* New York: United Nations.

21 *ibid.*, paras. 81–91.

22 UN Secretary-General, *Uniting against Terrorism: Recommendations for a Global Counter-Terrorism Strategy*, A/60/825, 27 April 2006.

23 'The United Nations Global Counter-Terrorism Strategy', A/RES/60/288, 20 September 2006.

the rule of law as the fundamental basis for the fight against terrorism'.[24] With the GCTS, the UN Secretary-General made it clear that '[e]ffective counter-terrorism measures and the protection of human rights are not conflicting goals, but complementary and mutually reinforcing ones'.[25]

2 The Challenges of Conceptual Ambiguity

The congruences between R2P and counter-terrorism have only grown over the past twenty years as R2P advocates have emphasised the role of the state as the 'first responder' over external intervention.[26] Simultaneously, lessons from counterinsurgency and counter-terrorism efforts in Iraq and Afghanistan made it clear that securitised and heavy-handed approaches to counter-terrorism often exacerbated rather the reduced terrorist threats and a more population-centric approach was necessary.[27] With their shared basis in international and customary law, and emphasis on the role and rights of the state, counter-terror and R2P efforts now significantly overlap (Table 1).[28] So much, in fact, that the UN Security Council now often considers efforts to counter terrorism and prevent atrocities concurrently. Despite this, these two norms continue to be implemented not just differently but in ways that directly contradict each other. This variation can be explained by the fact that, as norms, R2P and counter-terrorism are open a level of 'social reconstruction' by their implementors, as they attempt to apply norms in different contexts and according to different values.[29]

The malleable nature of R2P and counter-terrorism has resulted in several lively debates as to their individual nature and content and, more vexingly,

24 *ibid.*, p. 9.

25 UN Secretary-General, *Uniting against Terrorism*, A/60/825, 27 April 2006, para. 5.

26 Axworthy, L., & Rock, A. (2009). R2P: A New and Unfinished Agenda. *Global Responsibility to Protect*, *1*(1), 54–69. https://doi.org/10.1163/187598409X405479.

27 Owens, P. (2013). From Bismarck to Petraeus: The question of the social and the Social Question in counterinsurgency. *European Journal of International Relations*, *19*(1), 139–161. https://doi.org/10.1177/1354066111425259.

28 Luke Glanville, *Sovereignty and the Responsibility to Protect: A New History* (Chicago: University of Chicago Press, 2014), Introduction; Shannon Zimmerman, 'Strange Bedfellows: Terrorism/Counter-Terrorism and the Responsibility to Protect' in Charles T. Hunt and Phil Orchard (eds.), *Constructing the Responsibility to Protect: Contestation and Consolidation* (Milton, UK: Taylor & Francis Group, 2020).

29 Van Kersbergen, K., & Verbeek, B. (2007). The Politics of International Norms: Subsidiarity and the Imperfect Competence Regime of the European Union. *European Journal of International Relations*, *13*(2), 217–238. https://doi.org/10.1177/1354066107076955.

TABLE 1 Pillars of R2P and GCTS

R2P framework	Global counter-terrorism strategy
1. The state's responsibility to protect its own population from the crimes of genocide, war crimes, ethnic cleansing, and crimes against humanity 2. The role and responsibilities of the international community to assist the state in fulfilling its responsibilities 3. The role of the international community to act when protection by the state is manifestly failing.	1. Addressing the conditions conducive to the spread of terrorism 2. Measures to prevent and combat terrorism 3. Measures to build states' capacity to prevent and combat terrorism and to strengthen the role of the United Nations system in that regard 4. Measures to ensure respect for human rights for all and the rule of law as the fundamental basis for the fight against terrorism.

how they might interact and relate to each other. Some key aspects of these debates are discussed below and revolve around the nature of the norms themselves, the rights and responsibilities of sovereignty; the impact of these norms on gender equality; obligations placed on terrorist actors by R2P; and the potential to misuse R2P and counterterrorism.

2.1 *The Normative Nature of R2P and Counter-terrorism*

Within this edited volume, both R2P and counter-terrorism are broadly considered to be norms. However, the nature, form, strength, and structure of these norms are deeply contested. Finnemore and Sikkink first defined norms as 'standards of appropriate behaviour for actors with a given identity.'[30] In most cases, norms proscribe behaviour and identify prohibited actions i.e., the norm against torture or violating human rights. In other cases, norms are prescriptive, indicating that action must be taken under particular circumstances.[31] Both R2P and counter-terrorism prohibit some behaviours, atrocity crimes for the former and terrorist acts for the latter, however, they also place requirements for

30 Finnemore, M., & Sikkink, K. (1998). International Norm Dynamics and Political Change. *International Organization*, *52*(4), 887–917. https://doi.org/10.1162/002081898550789.

31 Kratochwil, F. (1984). The force of prescriptions. *Internatinal Organization*, *38*(4), 685–708. https://doi.org/10.1017/S0020818300026916.

action on individuals, states, and the international community. What specific actions are required are left to the discretion of the implementing actors.

Variation in norm implementation is common. Norms, specifically international norms, must have some degree of ambiguity to be adopted by a wide range of actors.[32] Individual actors then take broad normative concepts and 'localise' their 'meaning-in-use' to make them contextually acceptable and relevant.[33] Variation in proscriptive norms tends to be limited as they usually specifically identify prohibited actions.[34] The prescriptive aspects of norms, however, are far more susceptible to being both understood and prioritised differently. For example, in counter-terrorism efforts the need to prevent future terrorist attacks against the population in general might be understood to supersede the value of an individual's human rights.[35] Alternatively, the protection of human rights could be understood as a necessary component of effective counterterrorism. The contexts in which norms are implemented, and the culture, values, and political priorities of the implementers means that norms can be interpreted in multiple ways. As both prescriptive and proscriptive norms, this variation in R2P and counter-terrorism implementation can become extreme as subsequent chapters in this edited volume will show.

Adding to the ambiguity of individual norms, many scholars of R2P and counter-terrorism argue that these concepts do not represent individual norms, rather they are made up of multiple norms in different configurations such as 'clusters,'[36] 'bundles,'[37] or 'regimes'.[38] Within these different configurations,

32 Wiener, A. (2014). *A theory of contestation* (1st ed.). Springer.

33 Acharya, A. (2004). How Ideas Spread: Whose Norms Matter? Norm Localization and Institutional Change in Asian Regionalism. *International Organization*, *58*(2), 239–275. https://doi.org/10.1017/S0020818304582024, Acharya, A. (2011). Norm Subsidiarity and Regional Orders: Sovereignty, Regionalism, and Rule-Making in the Third World. *International Studies Quarterly*, *55*(1), 95–123. https://doi.org/10.1111/j.1468-2478.2010.00637.x, Wiener, A. (2009). Enacting meaning-in-use: qualitative research on norms and international relations. *Review of International Studies*, *35*(1), 175–193. https://doi.org/10.1017/S0260210509008377.

34 Though with some notable exceptions. For an example see Heller, R., Kahl, M., & Pisoiu, D. (2012). The 'dark' side of normative argumentation – The case of counterterrorism policy. *Global Constitutionalism*, *1*(2), 278. https://doi.org/10.1017/S2045381711000049.

35 Ibid.

36 Winston, C. (2018). Norm structure, diffusion, and evolution: A conceptual approach. *European Journal of International Relations*, *24*(3), 638–661. https://doi.org/10.1177/1354066117720794.

37 Bloomfield, A., & Scott, S. V. (2016). Norm antipreneurs in world politics.. In A. Bloomfield & S. V. Scott (Eds.), *Norm Antipreneurs and the Politics of Resistance to Global Normative Change* (pp. 16–35). Taylor & Francis Group.

38 Orchard, P. (2020). Contestation, Norms, and the Responsibility to Protect as a regime. In C. T. Hunt & P. Orchard (Eds.), *Constructing the Responsibility to Protect: Contestation and Consolidation* (pp. 28–49). Taylor & Francis Group.

some norms dominate and even influence other norms, changing their implementation. These conceptual ambiguities around R2P and counter-terrorism are explored in this edited volume by two chapters. Adrian Gallagher, Blake Lawrinson and Charles T. Hunt assess how R2P and counter-terrorism engage with the norm of civilian protection – ultimately subjugating it to counter-terrorism. Alternatively, Shannon Zimmerman investigates R2P and Counter-terrorism as they are interpreted through differing understandings of sovereignty and incorporated into distinct sovereign norm regimes.

2.2 *Rights, Responsibilities, and Limits of Sovereignty*

The most controversial aspect of R2P and counterterrorism is the fact that they problematise a cornerstone of the international system, the inviolable nature of sovereignty. International interventions under the auspices of humanitarian assistance have been commonplace since the 1990s but these, with a few notable exceptions, were undertaken with consent of the host state. This is because the UN Charter prohibits intervention 'in matters which are essentially within the domestic jurisdiction of any state'.[39] Postcolonial critiques argue that R2P is simply an imperialist doctrine that can be used to legitimise unilateral military action or foreign interference by a strong state in a weaker state's domestic affairs without the need for consent.[40] The unilateral actions of powerful states in their war on terror, such as the US Coalition intervention into Iraq, which was framed in part as a civilian protection measure to obscure other motivations, only exacerbated these fears.[41] The seemingly neo-imperialist tendencies of R2P, however, have been countered by arguments that R2P is not so much a North-South dichotomy but a question of agency around who gets to interpret and apply the norm.[42]

---

39 United Nations. (1945). *Charter of the United Nations*. New York: United Nations. Retrieved from http://www.refworld.org/docid/3ae6b3930.html [accessed 18 July 2018].

40 Bellamy, A. J. (2005). Responsibility to protect or Trojan horse? The crisis in Darfur and humanitarian intervention after Iraq. *Ethics & International Affairs*, *19*(2), 31–54. Cunliffe, P. (2010). Dangerous duties: power, paternalism and the 'responsibility to protect'. *Review of International Studies*, *36*, 79–96. https://doi.org/10.2307/45301276.

41 Kampmark, B. (2015). Humanitarian Intervention after Iraq: The Politics of Protection and Rescue. In B. Isakhan (Ed.), *The Legacy of Iraq: From the 2003 War to the 'Islamic State'*. Edinburgh University Press.

42 Thakur, R., & Weiss, T. G. (2009). R2P: From Idea to Norm – and Action. *Global Responsibility to Protect*, *1*(1), 22–53. Acharya, A. (2004). How Ideas Spread: Whose Norms Matter? Norm Localization and Institutional Change in Asian Regionalism. *International Organization*,

Theoretically, invoking either R2P or counter-terrorism could justify international interventions into weaker countries where transnational terrorist attacks originate or in cases where the state is failing to prevent or respond to domestic terrorist incidents. Such interventions would, in essence, delegitimise sovereign states that suffer from weak institutions.[43] Al-Qaeda's horrific attack on the United States on September 11, 2001 and the subsequent UN-sanctioned invasion of Afghanistan, demonstrated that one state could intervene in another in order to defend itself from terrorist attacks. Similarly, Kenya evoked Article 61 of the UN Charter, referring to territorial integrity, before it deployed operation Linda Nichi in Somalia in response to al-Shabaab attacks on Kenyan soil and the abduction of foreign tourists.[44] These cases, however, are more the exception than the rule as these interventions were made by states that had experienced significant losses due to terrorism and were conducted in states that were considered unable or unwilling to respond adequately to address the terrorist threat themselves. Outside of these exceptional circumstances, norms which can justify external intervention in other states are viewed with a great deal of suspicion.

The crux of much of this uncertainty lies in the ambiguity around when the state must cede its sovereign protections against external intervention because it has defaulted on its sovereign protection responsibilities, either intentionally, or through lack of action or capacity. Key R2P documents label this point at 'manifestly failing' to protect civilians, but no indicators for determining this have been given except for reference to the prevention of the four atrocity crimes or their incitement.[45] As terrorism can be considered either a crime against humanity or a war crime, depending on context, this ambiguity exists for R2P responses to terrorism as well. For example, Chijioke Egwu Ekumaoko and Kingsley Emeka Ezemenaka (2022) argue that the Nigerian state has manifestly failed to protect civilians from the ravages of the terrorist group Boko

58(2), 239–275. https://doi.org/10.1017/S0020818304582024. Acharya, A. (2014). Who Are the Norm Makers? The Asian-African Conference in Bandung and the Evolution of Norms. *Global Governance, 20*(3), 405–417. https://doi.org/10.1163/19426720-02003006.

43 Chandler, D. (2010). R2P or Not R2P – More Statebuilding, Less Responsibility. *Global Responsibility to Protect, 2*(1–2), 161–166.

44 Africa Research Bulletin. (2011). Operation Linda Nchi (Protect the Nation). *Africa Research Bulletin: Political, Social and Cultural Series, 48*(11).

45 United Nations General Assembly. (2005). *2005 World Summit Outcome Document. A/RES/60/1. 24 October 2005*. New York: United Nations. United Nations General Assembly. (2009). *Implementing the Responsibility to Protect. Report of the Secretary General. A/63/677. 12 January 2009*. New York: United Nations.

Haram.[46] The government's failure to stop the group after ten years of violent insurgency, accompanied by the groups increasingly transnational nature and affiliation with ISIS in 2014, should then make in necessary to consider external intervention under the auspices of R2P. Isaac Taylor engages this debate in his chapter in this volume on the ethics of foreign counter-terrorist interventions.

2.3 *Culpability of Non-state Actors*

The proliferation of non-state terrorist groups such as Boko Haram and ISIS, and their ability to take and hold large quantities of territory, has raised the question of the role and responsibilities of non-states actors. The majority of mass atrocities have been committed by states. When R2P was initially modelled, it was based on the idea of 'bad' governments' committing atrocities against 'good people'.[47] While the World Summit Outcome Document implied that mass atrocities can be committed by actors outside of state structures, the concept remained understood as state-centric.[48] However, the increased use of atrocity tactics by national and transnational terrorist groups have raised the important question of whether such groups have the responsibility to protect populations under their control from atrocity crimes and, if interventions to combat these groups can be triggered by R2P.[49] This need has been exacerbated by the fact that, in some cases of atrocity crimes, state's often have some level of control over non-state actors but deny or obfuscate their command and/or control over these groups to avoid international censure.[50] This includes such cases as Sudan where the Janjaweed were proxies for the

46 Ekumaoko, C. E., & Ezemenaka, K. E. (2020). Responsibility to protect: external intervention on Boko Haram terrorism in Nigeria. *Security Journal, 33*(3), 493–513. https://doi.org/10.1057/s41284-020-00239-1.

47 Luck, E. (2015). *The Responsibility to Protect at Ten: The Challenges Ahead.* The Stanley Foundation. Policy Analysis Brief.

48 United Nations General Assembly. (2005). *2005 World Summit Outcome Document. A/RES/60/1. 24 October 2005.* New York: United Nations.

49 Loyle, C. E. (2018). *Understanding Nonstate Actor behavior.* Simon-Skjodt Center for the Prevention of Genocide. United States Holocaust Memorial Museum. Series of Occasional papers. No. 9. Retrieved from https://www.ushmm.org/m/pdfs/Cyanne_Loyle_02142018.pdf, Luck, E. C. (2015). R2P at ten: A new mindset for a new era. *Global Governance, 21*, 499. Thomas-Jensen, C. (2018). *Fighting Fire with Fire: The Growing Nexus between Atrocity Prevention and Counterterrorism and its Implicatins for the Use of Force to Protect Civilians.* Simon-Skjodt Center for the Prevention of Genocide. United States Holocaust Memorial Museum. Series of Occasional papers. No. 8. Retrieved from https://www.ushmm.org/m/pdfs/Colin_Thomas-Jensen_fellowship_paper_02072018.pdf.

50 Ferguson, K. (2020). *Architectures of Violence: The Command Structures of Modern Mass Atrocities, from Yugoslavia to Syria.* Oxford University Press. https://doi.org/10.1093/oso/9780190949624.001.0001.

Sudanese government.[51] The continuing state-centric emphasis of R2P has limited the creation of atrocity prevention policy which can address the hybrid nature of the actors responsible for atrocities.

The 2009 UN Secretary-General's report on the implementation of R2P introduced the idea that non-state armed groups, including terrorist groups, also have protection responsibilities. This means that the failure of these groups to protect civilians, or their commission of atrocity crimes can trigger R2P assistance to states under pillar two.[52] This position was echoed by a 2015 Report by the Stanley Foundation which concluded that non-state actors who had state-like characteristics, such as control over a defined territory, had obligations towards the population on that territory.[53] This included observing the Geneva Conventions, refraining from committing atrocity crimes, and acting to prevent atrocity crimes when they are happening on their occupied territory.

However, the lower capacity of terrorist actors, their fluid and fractured nature, and the prohibition against engaging with them politically, has made it much more difficult to construct policy and approaches that clarify how R2P might apply to terrorist actors.[54] When looking at the role R2P might play in Nigeria against Boko Haram, Çaglar Açikyildiz noted that '[t]he fact that the main perpetrator of the mass atrocity crimes is an NSAG [non-state armed group] that operates on different territories complicates the process of devising an appropriate response.'[55] In the case of intervention in Syria, both Russia and China made the consequentialist argument that supporting Syrian rebel forces against the regime in the name of R2P would only foster extremism and terrorism and accused supporters of R2P in this case of pursuing regime change.[56] Indeed, The appeal of intervention in Syria waned notably when

51 United Nations High Commissioner for Human Rights. (2004). *Situation of Human Rights in the Darfur Region of the Sudan. E/CN.4/2005/3 (May 7, 2004)*. Geneva: United Nations. Retrieved from https://digitallibrary.un.org/record/521370?ln=en.

52 Luck, E. (2015). *The Responsibility to Protect at Ten: The Challenges Ahead.* The Stanley Foundation. Policy Analysis Brief.

53 The Stanley Foundation. (2015b). *Violent Nonstate actors as perpetrators and Enabelers of Atrocity Crimes. Policy Dialogue Brief. 56th Annual Strategy for Peace Conference 14–16, October 2015, Warrington, VA.*

54 The Stanley Foundation. (2015a). *Nonstate Actors as Perpetrators and Enablers of Mass Atrocity Violence, Policy Memo.*

55 Açikyildiz, Ç. (2022). Boko Haram in Nigeria: R2P and Non-State Armed Groups. In P. Gözen Ercan (Ed.), *The Responsibility to Protect From Twenty Years On: Rhetoric and Implementation.* Palgrave Macmillan.

56 Chen, Z., & Yin, H. (2020). China and Russia in R2P debates at the UN Security Council. *International Affairs, 96*(3), 787–805. https://doi.org/10.1093/ia/iiz229.

both sides were seen to have committed atrocities or when the 'good' side was joined by extremist or terrorist actors.[57]

The UN has been unable to provide much clarity on how R2P might apply to terrorist actors beyond former UN special Adviser to the Secretary-General on the Responsibility to Protect, Jennifer Welsh, noting that R2P's 'initially state-centric focus might be expanded to address the challenge of non-state armed groups (NSAGs) as threats to civilians.'[58] To date, only once has R2P triggered a response against a terrorist group to prevent an immanent attack: when US forces, with Iraq's consent, conducted airstrikes and deployed special operations forces to evacuation civilians facing ISIS atrocities on Mount Sinjar.[59] Josie Hornung explores this exceptional case more in-depth in her chapter in this volume.

Another alternative to state responses are the potential community responses to terrorist actors. While states have been slow to use R2P to protect civilians, populations themselves have begun to call for and implement self-protection strategies to fill this gap.[60] It is often the case the civilians take steps to escape violence and, if necessary, protect themselves and their property – even through armed resistance.[61] Equipped with knowledge of the local contexts and actors, community self-protection initiatives have the potential to be powerful forces for civilian protection, but significant challenges exist and poor implementation could actually result in higher civilian casualties.[62]

---

57 Luck, E. (2015). *The Responsibility to Protect at Ten: The Challenges Ahead.* The Stanley Foundation. Policy Analysis Brief.

58 Welsh, J. (2018). Non-state armed groups and the responsibility to protect. In M. Lattimer & P. Sands (Eds.), *The grey zone: Civilian protection between human rights and the laws of war* (pp. 357–376). Bloomsbury Publishing.

59 Thomas-Jensen, C. (2018). *Fighting Fire with Fire: The Growing Nexus between Atrocity Prevention and Counterterrorism and its Implicatins for the Use of Force to Protect Civilians.* Simon-Skjodt Center for the Prevention of Genocide. United States Holocaust Memorial Museum. Series of Occasional papers. No. 8. Retrieved from https://www.ushmm.org/m/pdfs/Colin_Thomas-Jensen_fellowship_paper_02072018.pdf.

60 Gorur, A., & Carstensen, N. (2016). Community Self-protection. In H. Willmot, R. Mamiya, S. Sheeran, & M. Weller (Eds.), *Protection of Civilians.* Oxford University Press. https://doi.org/10.1093/acprof:oso/9780198729266.003.0020.

61 Sanaullah. (2021). Civilians' survival strategies during the Taliban's insurgency (2007–9), Pakistan: a look at the consequences. *Small Wars & Insurgencies*, *32*(1), 26–52. https://doi.org/10.1080/09592318.2020.1840892 Williams, P. D. (2013). Protection, Resilience and Empowerment: United Nations Peacekeeping and Violence against Civilians in Contemporary War Zones. *Politics*, *33*(4), 287–298. https://doi.org/10.1111/1467-9256.12014.

62 Agbiboa, D. E. (2021). The Precariousness of Protection: Civilian Defense Groups Countering Boko Haram in Northeastern Nigeria. *African Studies Review*, *64*(1), 192–216. https://doi.org/10.1017/asr.2020.47.

Wisdom Oghosa Iyekekpolo explores what this might look like as he examines mechanisms for integrating international, state, and local agency in combatting non-state terrorist groups in Nigeria.

2.4 *Gender as Integral to R2P and Counter-terrorism*

It is impossible to talk about protection, especially protection from terrorist actors, without addressing the pivotal role of gender. The gender dynamics of terrorism and atrocity crimes are well known, but routinely overlooked in R2P and counter-terrorism responses. Feminist critiques of both norms note their militarizing and infantilising nature. R2P has been accused of militarising protection, which undermines non-military and therefore more female accessible approaches to conflict resolution.[63] It also embodies masculine modes of reasoning which privileges male elites and relies on stereotypes of women as victims and/or peacebuilders. These critiques have been leveraged by gender advocates to push for an alignment between R2P and the Women, Peace and Security agenda and more clearly identify sexual and gender-based violence as a war crime or crime against humanity.[64]

When counter-terrorism did acknowledge gender, it routinely cast women as passive victims.[65] It also initially understood women as a single, homogeneous group, overlooking their unique experiences of terrorism and related atrocities.[66] The resulting gender-essentialism excluded women from having a say in what constituted terrorism nor how they engage with it.[67] As counter-terrorism evolved, this perception has shifted to see women as active agents in countering terror, however, this often results in the instrumentalization of women rather than an intersectional approach aimed a building women's

---

63 O'Connell, M. E. (2010). Responsibility to Peace: A Critique of R2P. *Journal of Intervention and Statebuilding*, *4*(1), 39–52. https://doi.org/10.1080/17502970903541671.

64 Davies, S. E., & Stamnes, E. (2012). GR2P Special Issue: The Responsibility to Protect and Sexual and Gender Based Violence (SGBV). *Global Responsibility to Protect*, *4*(2), 127–132. Stamnes, E. (2012).The responsibility to protect: integrating gender perspectives into policies and practices. *Global Responsibility to Protect*, *4*(2), 172–197. Harris-Rimmer, S. (2014). When WPS Met CEDAW (and Broke Up with R2P?). e-International Relations. Retrieved from https://www.e-ir.info/2014/03/13/when-wps-met-cedaw-and-broke-up-with-r2p/

65 Charlesworth, H. (2010). Feminist Reflections on the Responsibility to Protect. *Global Responsibility to Protect*, *2*(3), 232–249.

66 Berlingozzi, L. (2022). O sister, where art thou? Assessing the limits of gender mainstreaming in preventing and countering violent extremism in Mali. *Critical Studies on Terrorism*, *15*(3), 659–680. https://doi.org/10.1080/17539153.2022.2101536.

67 Ní Aoláin, F. (2016). The 'war on terror' and extremism: assessing the relevance of the Women, Peace and Security agenda. *International Affairs*, *92*(2), 275–291. https://doi.org/10.1111/1468-2346.12552.

capacity to counter-terrorism. Women, women's organisations, and gender equality initiatives are leveraged as counter-terrorism tools rather than being support for their inherent value.[68]

2.5 *Misuse of the Norms*

The malleable nature of R2P and counter-terrorism and the mounting pressure placed on states to protect their populations from terrorism and their sovereignty from foreign intervention, has arguably resulted in instances of the misuse of these two norms. The most obvious of these misuses is when counter-terrorism activities have been used to justify the violation of human rights – often of specific groups. This has been done under the broader argument that by doing so, the rights of the majority of individuals will be preserved and protected. For example, China has filtered the R2P norm through its particular cultural and political priorities to find the "right balance between justice and interest".[69] This interpretation of R2P, within a counter-terrorism context, has been used to justify the mass internment of the Uyghur ethnic minority.[70] Inversely, the Sri Lankan government in the final months of its war against the Liberation Tigers of Tamil Eelam (LTTE) used counter-terrorism as justification for atrocities against civilians and the rhetoric of the global war on terrorism to mute criticism of their actions.[71] At the same time, they headed off any discussion of external intervention by re-emphasising their primary responsibility and right of the government to take the actions necessary to protect its own civilians.[72] Sascha Nanlohy uses the cases of Kenya and Sri Lanka to explore how abuses of these two norms come about in his chapter in this volume.

---

68 Aroussi, S. (2021). Strange Bedfellows: Interrogating the Unintended Consequences of Integrating Countering Violent Extremism with the UN's Women, Peace, and Security Agenda in Kenya. *Politics & Gender*, *17*(4), 665–695. https://doi.org/10.1017/S1743923X20000124.

69 Kozyrev, V. (2016). Harmonizing 'Responsibility to Protect': China's vision of a post-sovereign world. *International Relations (London)*, *30*(3), 328–345. https://doi.org/10.1177/0047117816659589.

70 Foot, R. (2021). R2P Sidelined: The International Response to China's Repression of Muslim Minorities in Xinjiang. *Global Responsibility to Protect*, *13*(1), 29–32. https://doi.org/10.1163/1875-984X-13010005.

71 Nackers, K. (2016). Sri Lanka. In A. J. Bellamy & T. Dunne (Eds.), *The Oxford Handbook of the Responsibility to Protect* (1 ed.). Oxford University Press. https://doi.org/10.1093/oxfordhb/9780198753841.001.0001.

72 *Kahona, P. (2011). Protection of Civilians in Armed Conflict. United Nations Security Council Open Debate. 10 May 2011. New York, United Nations.*

3 Summary of Chapters

This edited volume hopes to make intelligible the complex relationship between counter-terrorism and R2P. It does this in three ways: first, by providing possible theoretical frameworks for understanding the overlaps between R2P and counter-terror; second, by exploring the intersections of counter-terror, R2P, and the closely related but much broader concept of protection of civilians; and third, by delving into the conditions necessary to trigger R2P in response to atrocity crimes by non-state actors labelled as terrorists and what these responses, either state or civilian led, might look like.

The first two chapters approach R2P and counter-terrorism from different theoretical perspectives. Shannon Zimmerman explores how R2P and counter-terrorism can act as subsidiary norms within the broader 'norm regime' of sovereignty. As part of this norm regime, R2P and counter-terrorism are interpreted through the diverse lenses of individual states and state self-interests. The result can be norm modification to the extent that the norm's original intent is lost, and even violated, as shown through her case studies of China and the Uyghurs and the Sri Lankan government's battle against the Tamil Tigers.

Using ethics as a starting point, Isaac Taylor's chapter explores whether the ethical imperatives that support humanitarian and R2P driven interventions could also support counter-terrorism interventions. As R2P has helped legitimatise the right for humanitarian intervention, this has raised the possibility that foreign counter-terrorist intervention will come to be viewed as permissible under similar considerations. Taylor goes beyond asking if this can happen to investigate the ethical question of whether or not such parallels should be drawn. To do so he explores arguments put forth by leading thinkers Michael Walzer and David Luban. Walzer's collectivist explanation for interventions does not stretch well to encompass counter-terrorism interventions but Luban's more individualist approach conceivably could include such operations. To find clarity within the multiple views available, Taylor turns to Just War Theory. He notes that to be considered legitimate, humanitarian interventions – including R2P – must not undermine state sovereignty. Additionally, and often overlooked, is the requirement that these interventions do no harm. Taylor finds that, ultimately, foreign counter-terrorist interventions do not necessarily violate sovereignty, but they cannot guarantee that their enaction will not institutionalise norms that can have potentially unacceptable effects. Counter-terrorism is particularly vulnerable to this, as Forester and Taylor note, because it is easily co-opted by international actors to justify particularistic action in the pursuit of self-interest, and often to the detriment of others and in violation of the norms original intent.[73] Overall, Taylor argues for caution when using a norm to legitimate foreign interventions for counter-terrorism. Taylor's conclusions about the complexity of legitimising foreign interventions based on counterterrorism set the stage for Sascha Nanlohy's work, which explores the diverse ways that domestic actors may use the language of counter-terrorism to both pre-empt or prompt interventions under the auspices of R2P.

Sascha Nanlohy's chapter argues that the discursive abuse of counterterrorism has been used by some states as normative cover as they uncritically apply strategies of counter-terrorism to entire populations or use the discourse of terrorism to 'toxify' specific groups to justify securitised responses that can result in atrocity crimes. Such challenging situations hamper the implementation of R2P as it is often the case the terrorist actors are embedded within vulnerable civilian populations. International intervenors then face the dilemma of either protecting both civilians and terrorists or allowing both to be hurt. The result is often a general lack of political will to act except in cases of clear R2P crimes. However, in other cases, the value of countries in broader counterterrorism initiatives has prompted robust international responses, as was the case in Kenya in 2008. Nanlohy investigates R2P 'success' in Kenya (2007–2008) and R2P 'failure' in Sri Lanka (2009) and concludes that terrorism and counter-terrorism narratives can both augment and complicate the application of R2P depending on how they interact with the multitude of other geopolitical dynamics in the conflict.

Also investigating the interactions between R2P and counter-terrorism, Adrian Gallagher, Blake Lawrinson, and Charles Hunt add complexity to these dynamics by including the distinct but closely related concept of civilian protection. To make intelligible the multiple norms present, the authors engage the concept of 'norm clusters' to identify how these three norms interact. In assessing the UN peacekeeping mission in Mali, the authors find that the shared characteristics of these norms have resulted in a 'human protection norm cluster'. However, while all norms embody the value of human protection, the norms themselves are given different respective values and are not mutually reinforcing when applied in practice – such as in a UN peace operation. In particular, the inclusion of the counter-terrorism norm alongside norms designed to protect civilians, despite its more peripheral role, can be counterproductive to civilian protection.

---

73 Forster, E., & Taylor, I. (2022). Asking the fox to guard the chicken coop: In defense of minimalism in the ethics of war and peace. *Journal of International Political Theory*, *18*(1), 91–109. https://doi.org/10.1177/17550882209858 82.

The final two substantive chapters of this volume engage in the grey area of R2P application against non-state terrorist groups. Over the past decade there has been an increase in the number of mass atrocity crimes committed by non-state actors. In his chapter, Wisdom Iyekekpolo explores alternative options for facilitating community resilience to terrorism. Looking at the impact of Boko Haram and other armed groups on local populations in Nigeria, Iyekekpolo argues that people-centric interpretations of R2P and counter-terrorism create space for cooperative action. Civilian protection measures, when combined with localised self-protection measures, economic well-being initiatives and the ideological reorientation of vulnerable communities, can leverage local knowledge and agency to help increase community resilience against violent non-state actors.

Josie Hornung examines the vital but understudied second pillar of R2P, which provides encouragement, capacity building and protection assistance to states which are attempting to uphold their protection responsibilities. This includes military intervention on behalf of the recipient state to prevent or stop atrocity crimes. Hornung assesses the unique circumstances around the successful intervention by US and Iraqi forces in preventing the genocide of the Yazidis on Mount Sinjar by the Islamic State in Iraq and the Levant (ISIL). Using this case, Hornung identifies specific factors, such as the clarity and imminence of the threat, and the interventions alignment with intervening states domestic and political agendas, that made the application of Pillar Two protection assistance both possible and successful in preventing possible atrocity crimes by a terrorist group.

4 Conclusion

R2P and counter-terrorism have undergone constant evolution over the past 20 years, defining and redefining themselves as concepts caught in the struggle to balance national security imperatives with human rights. In this process they have been understood and implemented in a vast array of configurations. In some instances, R2P and counter-terrorism operate in tandem, often focusing on prevention. In the majority of instances, however, R2P and counter-terrorism are placed in opposition, where compromises must be made between protecting human rights and military-centric responses to terrorism. As these two concepts continue to evolve, opportunities arise to leverage the emerging synergies between them to more effectively address both atrocity crimes and terrorism.

Bibliography

Acharya, A. (2004). How Ideas Spread: Whose Norms Matter? Norm Localization and Institutional Change in Asian Regionalism. *International Organization*, *58*(2), 239–275. https://doi.org/10.1017/S0020818304582024.

Acharya, A. (2011). Norm Subsidiarity and Regional Orders: Sovereignty, Regionalism, and Rule-Making in the Third World. *International Studies Quarterly*, *55*(1), 95–123. https://doi.org/10.1111/j.1468-2478.2010.00637.x.

Acharya, A. (2014). Who Are the Norm Makers? The Asian-African Conference in Bandung and the Evolution of Norms. *Global Governance*, *20*(3), 405–417. https://doi.org/10.1163/19426720-02003006.

Açikyildiz, Ç. (2022). Boko Haram in Nigeria: R2P and Non-State Armed Groups. In P. Gözen Ercan (Ed.), *The Responsibility to Protect From Twenty Years On: Rhetoric and Implementation*. Palgrave Macmillan.

Africa Research Bulletin. (2011). Operation Linda Nchi (Protect the Nation). *Africa Research Bulletin: Political, Social and Cultural Series*, *48*(11).

Agbiboa, D. E. (2021). The Precariousness of Protection: Civilian Defense Groups Countering Boko Haram in Northeastern Nigeria. *African Studies Review*, *64*(1), 192–216. https://doi.org/10.1017/asr.2020.47.

Aroussi, S. (2021). Strange Bedfellows: Interrogating the Unintended Consequences of Integrating Countering Violent Extremism with the UN's Women, Peace, and Security Agenda in Kenya. *Politics & Gender*, *17*(4), 665–695. https://doi.org/10.1017/S1743923X20000124.

Axworthy, L., & Rock, A. (2009). R2P: A New and Unfinished Agenda. *Global Responsibility to Protect*, *1*(1), 54–69. https://doi.org/10.1163/187598409X405479.

Bellamy, A. J. (2005). Responsibility to protect or Trojan horse? The crisis in Darfur and humanitarian intervention after Iraq. *Ethics & International Affairs*, *19*(2), 31–54.

Berlingozzi, L. (2022). O sister, where art thou? Assessing the limits of gender mainstreaming in preventing and countering violent extremism in Mali. *Critical Studies on Terrorism*, *15*(3), 659–680. https://doi.org/10.1080/17539153.2022.2101536.

Bloomfield, A., & Scott, S. V. (2016). Norm antipreneurs in world politics. In A. Bloomfield & S. V. Scott (Eds.), *Norm Antipreneurs and the Politics of Resistance to Global Normative Change* (pp. 16–35). Taylor & Francis Group.

Byman, D. L. (2007). *Iraq and the Global War on Terrorism*. Brookings Institution. Washington, D.C. https://www.brookings.edu/articles/iraq-and-the-global-war-on-terrorism/.

Chandler, D. (2010). R2P or Not R2P – More Statebuilding, Less Responsibility. *Global Responsibility to Protect*, *2*(1–2), 161–166.

Charlesworth, H. (2010). Feminist Reflections on the Responsibility to Protect. *Global Responsibility to Protect*, *2*(3), 232–249.

Charter of Paris. (1991). Charter of Paris for a New Europe. *Current History, 90*(553), 78.

Chen, Z., & Yin, H. (2020). China and Russia in R2P debates at the UN Security Council. *International Affairs, 96*(3), 787–805. https://doi.org/10.1093/ia/iiz229.

Cunliffe, P. (2010). Dangerous duties: power, paternalism and the 'responsibility to protect'. *Review of International Studies, 36*, 79–96. https://doi.org/10.2307/45301276.

Davies, S. E., & Stamnes, E. (2012). GR2P Special Issue: The Responsibility to Protect and Sexual and Gender Based Violence (SGBV). *Global Responsibility to Protect, 4*(2), 127–132.

Drash, W. (2009, 20 May 2009). Abu Ghraib photos were 'big shock,' undermined U.S. ideals. *CNN*. Retrieved from http://edition.cnn.com/2009/WORLD/meast/05/18/detainee.abuse.lookback/index.html.

Ekumaoko, C. E., & Ezemenaka, K. E. (2020). Responsibility to protect: external intervention on Boko Haram terrorism in Nigeria. *Security Journal, 33*(3), 493–513. https://doi.org/10.1057/s41284-020-00239-1.

Ferguson, K. (2020). *Architectures of Violence: The Command Structures of Modern Mass Atrocities, from Yugoslavia to Syria*. Oxford University Press. https://doi.org/10.1093/oso/9780190949624.001.0001.

Finnemore, M., & Sikkink, K. (1998). International Norm Dynamics and Political Change. *International Organization, 52*(4), 887–917. https://doi.org/10.1162/002081898550789.

Foot, R. (2021). R2P Sidelined: The International Response to China's Repression of Muslim Minorities in Xinjiang. *Global Responsibility to Protect, 13*(1), 29–32. https://doi.org/10.1163/1875-984X-13010005.

Forster, E., & Taylor, I. (2022). Asking the fox to guard the chicken coop: In defense of minimalism in the ethics of war and peace. *Journal of International Political Theory, 18*(1), 91–109. https://doi.org/10.1177/17550882220985882.

Gorur, A., & Carstensen, N. (2016). Community Self-protection. In H. Willmot, R. Mamiya, S. Sheeran, & M. Weller (Eds.), *Protection of Civilians*. Oxford University Press. https://doi.org/10.1093/acprof:oso/9780198729266.003.0020.

Harris-Rimmer, S. (2014). When WPS Met CEDAW (and Broke Up with R2P?). *e-International Relations*. https://www.e-ir.info/2014/03/13/when-wps-met-cedaw-and-broke-up-with-r2p/.

Heller, R., Kahl, M., & Pisoiu, D. (2012). The 'dark' side of normative argumentation – The case of counterterrorism policy. *Global Constitutionalism, 1*(2), 278. https://doi.org/10.1017/S2045381711000049.

ICISS. (2001). *The Responsibility to Protect: Report of the International Commission on Intervention and State Sovereignty*. International Development Research Centre. Ottawa, ON, Canada.

Kahona, P. (2011). *Protection of Civilians in Armed Conflict*, United Nations Security Council Open Debate. 10 May 2011. New York, United Nations.

Kampmark, B. (2015). Humanitarian Intervention after Iraq: The Politics of Protection and Rescue. In B. Isakhan (Ed.), *The Legacy of Iraq: From the 2003 War to the 'Islamic State'*. Edinburgh University Press.

Kozyrev, V. (2016). Harmonizing 'Responsibility to Protect': China's vision of a post-sovereign world. *International Relations* (*London*), *30*(3), 328–345. https://doi.org/10.1177/0047117816659589.

Kratochwil, F. (1984). The force of prescriptions. *International Organization*, *38*(4), 685–708. https://doi.org/10.1017/S0020818300026916.

Loyle, C. E. (2018). *Understanding Nonstate Actor behavior* Simon-Skjodt Center for the Prevention of Genocide. United States Holocaust Memorial Museum. Series of Occasional papers. No. 9. Retrieved from https://www.ushmm.org/m/pdfs/Cyanne_Loyle_02142018.pdf.

Luck, E. (2015). The Responsibility to Protect at Ten: The Challenges Ahead. The Stanley Foundation. Policy Analysis Brief.

Luck, E. C. (2015). R2P at ten: A new mindset for a new era. *Global Governance*, *21*, 499.

Nackers, K. (2016). Sri Lanka. In A. J. Bellamy & T. Dunne (Eds.), *The Oxford Handbook of the Responsibility to Protect* (1 ed.). Oxford University Press. https://doi.org/10.1093/oxfordhb/9780198753841.001.0001.

Ní Aoláin, F. (2016). The 'war on terror' and extremism: assessing the relevance of the Women, Peace and Security agenda. *International Affairs*, *92*(2), 275–291. https://doi.org/10.1111/1468-2346.12552.

O'Connell, M. E. (2010). Responsibility to Peace: A Critique of R2P. *Journal of Intervention and Statebuilding*, *4*(1), 39–52. https://doi.org/10.1080/17502970903541671.

Orchard, P. (2020). Contestation, Norms, and the Responsibility to Protect as a regime. In C. T. Hunt & P. Orchard (Eds.), *Constructing the Responsibility to Protect: Contestation and Consolidation* (pp. 28–49). Taylor & Francis Group.

Owens, P. (2013). From Bismarck to Petraeus: The question of the social and the Social Question in counterinsurgency. *European Journal of International Relations*, *19*(1), 139–161. https://doi.org/10.1177/1354066111425259.

Sanaullah. (2021). Civilians' survival strategies during the Taliban's insurgency (2007–9), Pakistan: a look at the consequences. *Small Wars & Insurgencies*, *32*(1), 26–52. https://doi.org/10.1080/09592318.2020.1840892.

Stamnes, E. (2012). The responsibility to protect: integrating gender perspectives into policies and practices. *Global Responsibility to Protect*, *4*(2), 172–197.

Thakur, R., & Weiss, T. G. (2009). R2P: From Idea to Norm – and Action. *Global Responsibility to Protect*, *1*(1), 22–53.

The Stanley Foundation. (2015a). *Nonstate Actors as Perpetrators and Enablers of Mass Atrocity Violence*, Policy Memo.

The Stanley Foundation. (2015b). *Violent Nonstate actors as perpetrators and Enabelers of Atrocity Crimes.* Policy Dialogue Brief. 56th Annual Strategy for Peace Conference 14–16, October 2015, Warrington, VA.

Thomas-Jensen, C. (2018). *Fighting Fire with Fire: The Growing Nexus between Atrocity Prevention and Counterterrorism and its Implicatins for the Use of Force to Protect Civilians.* Simon-Skjodt Center for the Prevention of Genocide. United States Holocaust Memorial Museum. Series of Occasional papers. No. 8. Retrieved from https://www.ushmm.org/m/pdfs/Colin_Thomas-Jensen_fellowship_paper_02072018.pdf.

United Nations. (1945). *Charter of the United Nations.* United Nations Retrieved from http://www.refworld.org/docid/3ae6b3930.html [accessed 18 July 2018].

United Nations. (2004). *Report of the Secretary-General's High-Level Panel on Threats, Challenges and Change: A More Secure World: Our Shared Responsibility. A/59/565.* Retrieved from http://www.un.org/en/peacebuilding/pdf/historical/hlp_more_secure_world.pdf.

United Nations. (2006). *Uniting Against Terrorism: Recommendations for a global counter-terrorism strategy. Report of the Secretary-General. A/60/825, 27 April 2006.* New York: United Nations.

United Nations Commission on Human Rights. (1998). *Report of the Representative of the Secretary-General, Mr. Francis M. Deng, submitted pursuant to Commission resolution 1997/39. Addendum: Guiding Principles on Internal Displacement. E/CT.4/1998/53/add. 11 February 1998.* New York: United Nations.

United Nations General Assembly. (2005). *2005 World Summit Outcome Document. A/RES/60/1. 24 October 2005.* New York: United Nations.

United Nations General Assembly. (2009). *Implementing the Responsibility to Protect. Report of the Secretary General. A/63/677. 12 January 2009.* New York: United Nations.

United Nations High Commissioner for Human Rights. (2004). *Situation of Human Rights in the Darfur Region of the Sudan. E/CN.4/2005/3 (May 7, 2004).* Geneva: United Nations Retrieved from https://digitallibrary.un.org/record/521370?ln=en.

United Nations High Commissioner for Refugees (UNHCR). (1998). *Guiding Principles on Internal Displacement.* (ADM 1.1,PRL 12.1, PR00/98/109). New York: United Nations Retrieved from http://www.refworld.org/docid/3c3da07f7.html.

United Nations Security Council. (1994). *Final Report of the Commission of Experts Established Pursuant to Security Council Resolution 780 (1992). S/1994/674.* United Nations: New York Retrieved from https://documents-dds-ny.un.org/doc/UNDOC/GEN/N94/200/60/PDF/N9420060.pdf?OpenElement.

United Nations Security Council. (1999). *Report of the Independent Inquiry into the action of the United Nations during the 1994 genocide in Rwanda, S/1999/1257. 16 December 1999.*

United Nations Security Council. (2003). *Security Council resolution 1456 (2003), S/RES/1456. 20 January 2003*. New York: United Nations.

Van Kersbergen, K., & Verbeek, B. (2007). The Politics of International Norms: Subsidiarity and the Imperfect Competence Regime of the European Union. *European Journal of International Relations, 13*(2), 217–238. https://doi.org/10.1177/1354066107076955.

Welsh, J. (2018). Non-state armed groups and the responsibility to protect. In M. Lattimer & P. Sands (Eds.), *The grey zone: Civilian protection between human rights and the laws of war* (pp. 357–376). Bloomsbury Publishing.

Wiener, A. (2009). Enacting meaning-in-use: qualitative research on norms and international relations. *Review of International Studies, 35*(1), 175–193. https://doi.org/10.1017/S0260210509008377.

Wiener, A. (2014). *A theory of contestation* (1st ed.). Springer.

Williams, P. D. (2013). Protection, Resilience and Empowerment: United Nations Peacekeeping and Violence against Civilians in Contemporary War Zones. *Politics, 33*(4), 287–298. https://doi.org/10.1111/1467-9256.12014.

Winston, C. (2018). Norm structure, diffusion, and evolution: A conceptual approach. *European Journal of International Relations, 24*(3), 638–661. https://doi.org/10.1177/1354066117720794.

CHAPTER 1

R2P and Counter-terrorism: Where Sovereignties Collide

Shannon Zimmerman
Lecturer in Strategic Studies, Deakin University at the Australian War College, Weston, ACT, Australia
s.zimmerman@deakin.edu.au

Abstract

States play the lead role in implementing the norms of the international system. They interpret norms through the lens of their sovereignty, refining and revising them until they are suitable to local interests and context. The complex nature of sovereignty and its diverse manifestations across states means that norms will be interpreted and implemented in different ways. This chapter argues that R2P and counter-terrorism are complex norm regimes which are susceptible to modification as they are interpreted through diverse conceptions of state sovereignty. Using the cases of China's response to the Uyghurs and Sri Lanka's response to the Liberation Tigers of Tamil Eelam, this chapter shows that the malleable prescriptive norms of R2P and counter-terrorism can be reinterpreted by states in ways contingent on their sovereignty that deeply impact, and may even violate, the original intent of the norm.

Keywords

counter-terrorism – responsibility to protect (R2P) – norm regimes – sovereignty

1 Introduction

States play the lead role in implementing norms in the international system. They interpret norms through the lens of their sovereignty, refining and revising them until they are suitable to local interests and context. More than just the physical attributes of territory and military power, sovereignty is a composite concept or norm regime itself that endows the state with political authority both domestically and internationally.[1] It functions as an organising principle

 | DOI:10.1163/9789004548114_003

that 'addresses relations between state at the international level while also addressing the relationship between the state and their society'.[2] The complex nature of sovereignty and its diverse manifestations across states means that norms – particularly those associated directly with sovereignty – will be interpreted and implemented in different ways. This variation can clearly be seen in the implementation of the responsibility to protect (R2P) and counter-terrorism, two norm regimes that specifically prioritise state implementation and have a number of prescriptive aspects which are open for interpretation.

The responsibility to protect (R2P) and counter-terrorism emerged as international priorities at the turn of the millennium. First articulated in the early 1990s, the idea of 'sovereignty as responsibility' was confirmed with the 2001 International Commission on Intervention and State Sovereignty (ICISS) which made the remarkable step of redefining sovereignty away from *sovereignty as control* of a population to *sovereignty as responsibility* towards the population.[3] Supported by the momentum garnered after the failure to stop ethnic cleansing in the former Yugoslavia and genocide in Rwanda, the subjugation of national authority to international standards of 'responsible' sovereignty seemed irreversible.[4] However, mere weeks before the ICISS report was released, terrorists attacked the World Trade Center and the Pentagon, killing almost 3,000 civilians. Deeply shaken, this attack was a 'juncture of normative turbulence' for the international community; conceptions of sovereignty as responsibility collided with the global war on terror's prioritisation of state security.[5] Within days of the attack, the UN Security Council passed Resolution 1373, which took the exceptional step of requiring states to take concrete action to prevent and combat terrorism. For the next few years, counter-terrorism dominated discussions at the United Nations and military approaches to counter-terrorism contributed to limited progress on human rights in general, and R2P specifically. Competing sides emerged over the nature and associated rights of the state; one side championing realist-based sovereignty

1 Christian Reus-Smit, 'Human Rights and the Social Construction of Sovereignty', *Review of International Studies*, 27(4) 519–538 (2001), p. 521.

2 Dominik Zaum, *The Sovereignty Paradox* (Oxford: Oxford University Press, 2007), p. 29.

3 International Commission on Intervention and State Sovereignty (ICISS), *The Responsibility to Protect* (Ottawa: IDRC, 2001).

4 Francis Deng, 'From "Sovereignty as Responsibility" to the "Responsibility to Protect"', *Global Responsibility to Protect*, 2(4) 353–370 (2010), p. 336.

5 Louise Wiuff Moe and Anna Geis, 'From Liberal Interventionism to Stabilisation: A New Consensus on Norm-Downsizing in Interventions in Africa', *Global Constitutionalism*, 9(2) 387–412 (2020), pp. 391, 400.

focused on kinetic counter-terrorism responses and the other promoting liberal ideas of a broader and deeper sovereignty focused on human rights.[6]

The 2005 World Summit Outcome document clarified the parameters of R2P and counter-terrorism at the international level. R2P was distilled to apply to only four atrocity crimes: genocide, ethnic cleansing, war crimes, and crimes against humanity. States were identified as the primary actors responsible for protecting their civilians, supported by the international community with collective action as a last resort.[7] States were advised to act through 'appropriate and necessary means' to prevent atrocities, leaving considerable room for norm interpretation. In the same document, the UN Secretary-General was asked to submit a proposal on a UN-led counter-terrorism effort. The result was the adoption of the UN Global Counter-Terrorism Strategy (GCTS) in 2006 which articulated a plan of action based on four pillars:

- Measures to address the conditions conducive to the spread of terrorism;
- Measures to prevent and combat terrorism;
- Measures to build states' capacity to prevent and combat terrorism and to strengthen the role of the United Nations system in that regard;
- Measures to ensure respect for human rights for all and the rule of law as the fundamental basis for the fight against terrorism.[8]

While several internal and external mechanism have emerged to support implementation of the GCTS by individual states, coordination between them is limited.[9] Additionally, the UN was unable to come to an agreement on a definition of terrorism. As a result, states have had a great deal of latitude in both determining who can be considered a terrorist threat to their sovereignty and what actions they can undertake to address this threat. Some states have gone so far in their responses against perceived terrorist groups that they have found themselves in danger of violating R2P.

Though they were initially considered a pair of 'strange bedfellows', and interpreted in conflicting ways, R2P and counter-terrorism are norm regimes that have key points of overlap.[10] They both have a strong basis in international

6 *ibid.*, pp. 389–390.

7 '2005 World Summit Outcome', UNGA Res. A/RES/60/1, 24 October 2005, paras. 138–140.

8 'The United Nations Global Counter-Terrorism Strategy', A/RES/60/288, 20 September 2006.

9 James Cockayne, Alistair Miller, David Cortright, and Peter Romaniuk, *Reshaping United Nations Counterterrorism Efforts: Blue-Sky Thinking for Global Counterterrorism Cooperation 10 Years after 9/11* (Washington DC: Center on Global Counterterrorism Cooperation, 2012).

10 Shannon Zimmerman, 'Strange Bedfellows: Terrorism/Counter-Terrorism and the Responsibility to Protect' in Charles T. Hunt and Phil Orchard (eds.), *Constructing the Responsibility to Protect: Contestation and Consolidation* (Milton, UK: Taylor & Francis Group, 2020).

law and place primacy on the state. It has also become increasingly clear that the risk factors that promote individual participation in violent extremism, such as state repression, absence of civil liberties, and perception of a threat to religion, are the same factors that predict the commission of atrocity crimes.[11] The continued increase in terrorist threats to international peace and security, their related state responses, and the negative impact this has had on civilian populations, has forced the UN Security Council to consider counter-terrorism and atrocity prevention concurrently. In doing so, this has made visible the interaction of these regimes, both with each other, and the sovereignty regime of the implementing state.

This chapter argues that R2P and counter-terrorism are norm regimes which interact with state-specific conceptions of sovereignty. R2P and counter-terrorism have core proscriptive norms that must be undertaken by the state; these are, respectively, preventing and stopping atrocity crimes and terrorist attacks. These imperatives are complimentary and, in many cases, overlap. However, as norm regimes, the clear proscriptive norms of R2P and counter-terrorism are accompanied by aligned but more malleable prescriptive norms. States interpret these norms through their unique, and historically contingent, conceptions of sovereignty and its associated rights and responsibilities. The results are dramatically different implementations of R2P and counter-terrorism across states, at times making these norms appear complementary and at other times making them contradictory. In some extreme cases, modified prescriptive norms shift the norm regime to the extent that it fails to accomplish its core objective. This indicates the need for further elaboration of these norms at the international level to place limiting parameters on their interpretation and use.

This chapter is divided into three sections. The first section explains the nature of norms and demonstrates how R2P, counter-terrorism, and sovereignty are all norm regimes and engage as such. The second section details the primary role of the state in implementing R2P and counter-terrorism norm regimes and illustrates diverse conceptions of sovereignty and their impact on state approaches to R2P and counter-terrorism. The final section provides two case studies. The first looks at China's reframing of counter-terrorism to justify their internment of ethnic Uyghurs in Xinjiang. The second looks at Sri Lanka's invocation of R2P during the end of their civil war with the Liberation Tigers of Tamil Eelam. These case studies illustrate how states can modify and even change the nature of norms by aligning them with local conceptions of

11 UNDP, *Journey to Extremism in Africa: Drivers, Incentives and the Tipping Point for Recruitment* (New York: United Nations, 2017); United Nations, *Framework of Analysis for Atrocity Crimes: A Tool for Prevention* (New York: United Nations, 2014).

sovereignty and connected self-interests. This chapter concludes with a discussion of the vulnerability of R2P and counter-terrorism norms to radical interpretations by states and the need for further theoretical debate to place limitations on their meaning-in-use.

2 Aligning Norm Regimes

This chapter considers both R2P and counter-terrorism to be norm regimes, which are a group of individual but related norms working together. Individual norms are socially constructed beliefs that make behavioural claims on actors.[12] They indicate 'standards of appropriate behaviour for actors with a given identity'[13] that 'make demands, rally support, justify action, ascribe responsibility, and assess the praiseworthy or blameworthy character of an action'.[14] The majority of norms proscribe behaviour, meaning they indicate actions states should not take. In these cases, norms set the minimum standard for 'good' behaviour and room for norm interpretation is limited. However, norms can also be prescriptive in nature, ascribing responsibility to actors for taking specific actions.[15] For prescriptive norms, variation is far more common as norm interpretation and implementation are contingent on the norm implementor's frames of reference and priorities, as well as their environment and other relevant norms in that context.[16]

With both proscriptions and multiple and varied prescriptions, R2P and counter-terrorism can be understood as multiple norms working together as a norm 'cluster',[17]'bundle',[18] or 'regime'.[19] Alex Bellamy sees R2P as a collection

12 Thomas Risse-Kappen, Stephen C. Ropp, and Katrhyn Sikkink, *The Power of Human Rights: International Norms and Domestic Change*, Cambridge Studies in International Relations, vol. 66 (Cambridge: Cambridge University Press, 1999).

13 Martha Finnemore and Kathryn Sikkink, 'International Norm Dynamics and Political Change', *International Organization*, 52(4) 887–917 (1998), p. 891.

14 Friedrich Kratochwil, 'The Force of Prescriptions', *International Organization*, 38(4) 685–708 (1984), p. 686.

15 Kratochwil, 'The Force of Prescriptions'.

16 Alexander Betts and Phil Orchard (eds.), *Implementation and World Politics: How International Norms Change Practice* (Oxford: Oxford University Press, 2014).

17 Carla Winston, 'Norm Structure, Diffusion, and Evolution: A Conceptual Approach', *European Journal of International Relations*, 24(3) 638–661 (2018).

18 Alan Bloomfield and Shirley V. Scott, 'Norm Antipreneurs in World Politics' in Alan Bloomfield and Shirley V. Scott (eds.), *Norm Antipreneurs and the Politics of Resistance to Global Normative Change* (London: Taylor & Francis Group, 2016), p. 18.

19 Phil Orchard, 'Contestation, Norms, and the Responsibility to Protect as a Regime' in Charles T. Hunt and Phil Orchard (eds.), *Constructing the Responsibility to Protect: Contestation and Consolidation* (Milton: Taylor & Francis Group, 2020).

of norms divided between the responsibilities of the state and the international community.[20] Similarly, Luke Glanville argues that R2P consists of two norms: the uncontroversial expectation that states protect their population from atrocity crimes; and the less accepted expectation that the international community has a similar responsibility.[21] Phil Orchard breaks R2P down even further to argue that R2P is a 'norm regime' which bundles together existing legal and social norms to create norms or sets of norms around the four atrocity crimes of R2P: genocide, war crimes, crimes against humanity, and ethnic cleansing.[22] Two additional prescriptive norms reflect the responsibilities of the state and the international community to act to prevent and protect against atrocity crimes; a final norm, that the UN Security Council would act, would only be enacted when previous actions manifestly fail.[23] For the purposes of this chapter, R2P is understood as a norm regime that has proscriptive norms forbidding genocide, war crimes, crimes against humanity, and ethnic cleansing and prescriptive norms around preventing and responding to such atrocity crimes. The latter, however, can vary in number and content depending on the implementing state.

The evolution of counter-terrorism as a norm regime has been less explored than R2P but can be discerned by observing how the UN has articulated counter-terrorism efforts at the international level. Prior to the global war on terror the prohibition of most terrorist acts was already enshrined in international and customary law through multiple international legal instruments.[24]

---

20 Alex J. Bellamy, 'The Responsibility to Protect Turns Ten', *Ethics & International Affairs*, 29(2) 161–185 (2015), p. 162.

21 Luke Glanville, 'Does R2P Matter? Interpreting the Impact of a Norm', *Cooperation and Conflict*, 51(2) 184–199 (2016), p. 186.

22 Orchard, 'Contestation, Norms, and the Responsibility to Protect as a Regime'.

23 *ibid.*

24 There are now 19 international legal instruments designed to prevent terrorist attacks. These are the 1963 Convention on Offences and Certain Other Acts Committed On Board Aircraft, the 1970 Convention for the Suppression of Unlawful Seizure of Aircraft, the 1971 Convention for the Suppression of Unlawful Acts against the Safety of Civil Aviation, the 1973 Convention on the Prevention and Punishment of Crimes against Internationally Protected Persons, the 1979 International Convention against the Taking of Hostages, the 1980 Convention on the Physical Protection of Nuclear Material, the 1988 Protocol for the Suppression of Unlawful Acts of Violence at Airports Serving International Civil Aviation, supplementary to the Convention for the Suppression of Unlawful Acts against the Safety of Civil Aviation, the 2005 Amendments to the Convention on the Physical Protection of Nuclear Material, the 1988 Convention for the Suppression of Unlawful Acts against the Safety of Maritime Navigation, the 1988 Protocol for the Suppression of Unlawful Acts against the Safety of Fixed Platforms Located on the Continental Shelf, the 1991 Convention on the Marking of Plastic Explosives for the Purpose of Detection, the 1997 International

Terrorism was generally considered a domestic issue and, in the few instances it came to the level of the UN, it was handled in an *ad hoc* basis by the General Assembly with specific action left to concerned states.[25] While the state-centricity of the norm remained, the terrorist attacks of 9/11 made terrorism a global priority. A clear counter-terrorism agenda was formed and efforts to combat terrorism became globalised and standardised.[26] In 2006 the UN General Assembly adopted the Global Counter-Terrorism Strategy (GCTS), indicating the international community's acceptance of a norm against terrorism. Applying Orchard's concept of norm regime to counter-terrorism reveals multiple proscriptive norms against specific terrorist acts stemming from the pre-existing legal frameworks. Also discernible are several prescriptive norms addressing a broad array of political, economic, and social factors which are deemed to contribute to terrorism.[27]

The proscriptive and prescriptive nature of R2P and counter-terrorism present unique implementation challenges. Both norms identify particular acts as wrong – for R2P this is preventing and combating atrocity crimes; for counter-terrorism this is preventing and combating terrorist acts – and demand that action be taken by states to prevent and/or combat these acts but provide minimal guidance on how states might go about doing this.[28] Aiden Hehir has criticised R2P as 'hollow', because it offers no clear behavioural prescriptions

---

Convention for the Suppression of Terrorist Bombings, the 1999 International Convention for the Suppression of the Financing of Terrorism, the 2005 Protocol to the Convention for the Suppression of Unlawful Acts against the Safety of Maritime Navigation, the 2005 Protocol to the Protocol for the Suppression of Unlawful Acts against the Safety of Fixed Platforms located on the Continental Shelf, the 2005 International Convention for the Suppression of Acts of Nuclear Terrorism, the 2010 Convention on the Suppression of Unlawful Acts Relating to International Civil Aviation, the 2010 Protocol Supplementary to the Convention for the Suppression of Unlawful Seizure of Aircraft, and the 2014 Protocol to Amend the Convention on Offences and Certain Acts Committed on Board Aircraft.

25 Edward C. Luck, *UN Security Council: Practice and Promise* (London: Taylor & Francis Group, 2006), pp. 95–101.

26 *ibid.*, p. 102.

27 A/RES/60/288, 20 September 2006.

28 Eglantine Staunton and Jason Ralph, 'The Responsibility to Protect Norm Cluster and the Challenge of Atrocity Prevention: An Analysis of the European Union's Strategy in Myanmar', *European Journal of International Relations*, online (2019), p. 4, https://doi.org/10.1177/1354066119883001; Luke Glanville, 'Norms, Interests and Humanitarian Intervention', *Global Change, Peace & Security*, 18(3) 153–171 (2006), pp. 154–156. Roughly defined, terrorism can be understood as 'any action, in addition to actions already specified by the existing conventions on aspects of terrorism, the Geneva Conventions and Security Council resolution 1566 (2004), that is intended to cause death or serious bodily harm to civilians or non-combatants, when the purpose of such an act, by its nature or context, is to intimidate a population, or to compel a Government or an international organization to do

and is susceptible to co-option.[29] The same argument could be made for counter-terrorism, which has manifested in countless ways from state to state. This is where the variation in norm implementation occurs. While these norm regimes have a 'core' proscriptive norm that must be enacted – preventing atrocity crimes and terrorism – the associated prescriptive norms are contestable. These remaining norms must align with core norms in some way to be justified[30] but they will also inevitably be influenced by the values, expectations, and even formal organisational features of the implementors.[31] In the case of R2P and counter-terrorism, norm implementation falls explicitly to the state so variation will be driven by state interests and attributes. While variation is to be expected, some states have instrumentalised norms so much that they lose their meaning and essentially act as a shield for poor state behaviour.

Here it must be noted that there are limits to how much a norm can be revised to accommodate state-driven actions. As Quentin Skinner argues 'any agent possesses a standard motive for attempting to legitimate his untoward social or political actions'.[32] As such, those actors will claim their actions were motivated by an accepted set of political principles and, regardless of whether or not this is the case, are obliged to behave as though their actions are compatible with the principles they have claimed.[33] Because of this, Nicholas Wheeler argues, once norms are established they can constrain even the strongest of states as they reflect and enforce the prevailing morality rather than underlying distributions of power.[34] When states' 'linguistic sleight-of-hand'[35] becomes too obvious and norms can no longer be 'stretched' to justify their actions, states turn instead to obfuscation, disinformation, and outright denialism as illustrated in the case studies below.

---

or to abstain from doing any act'. Quoted in United Nations,' Report of the High Level Panel on Threats, Challenges and Change on a More Secure World: Our Shared Responsibility [A/59/565]', 2004, para. 164, https://www.un.org/en/peacebuilding/pdf/historical/hlp_more_secure_world.pdf.

29 Aidan Hehir, *Hollow Norms and the Responsibility to Protect* (Cham: Springer, 2019), pp. 72–74.

30 Jeffrey S. Lantis and Carmen Wunderlich, 'Resiliency Dynamics of Norm Clusters: Norm Contestation and International Cooperation', *Review of International Studies*, 44(3) 570–593 (2018), p. 571.

31 Kratochwil, 'The Force of Prescriptions', p. 685.

32 Quentin Skinner, 'Some Problems in the Analysis of Political Thought and Action', *Political Theory*, 2(3) 277–303 (1974), p. 299.

33 *ibid.*

34 Nicholas J. Wheeler, *Saving Strangers: Humanitarian Intervention in International Society* (Oxford: Oxford University Press, 2000), pp. 6–7.

35 Skinner, 'Some Problems in the Analysis of Political Thought and Action', p. 298.

3 The Role of the State in R2P and Counter-terrorism

For both R2P and counter-terrorism the state is the 'first responder'. R2P has been designed not to undermine sovereignty but to reaffirm its importance by anchoring the state as the preferred actor in civilian protection and R2P as the 'ally of sovereignty'.[36] The first principle of R2P is that '[s]tate sovereignty implies responsibility, and the primary responsibility for the protection of its people lies with the state itself'.[37] Counter-terrorism as articulated by the United Nations, is also centred on respect for sovereignty and the primacy of state action.[38] As Edward Luck notes, the UN Security Council takes on the role of 'facilitator, convenor, and legitimator in the longer-term effort' but it is 'up to member states, not the Council, to defend against and respond to individual acts of terrorism'.[39] As the primary responder, the state determines when and how R2P and counter-terrorism will be conducted on their soil. It is in this process that the incongruencies between norm interpretation and implementation become clear and the nature of the implementing regime becomes consequential.[40]

The nature of the state and its institutions play an integral role in how the norm regime is interpreted and implemented. While the state has limited influence on the core norms of R2P or counter-terrorism, it does have a fair amount of latitude to interpret the associated norms that will become part of the regime. Depending on the content of the norm, implementing states can undertake norm localisation, norm subsidiary, or a combination of both. These two concepts, both articulated by Amitav Acharya, explain the processes where local actors interpret and, if necessary, reconstruct, international norms to fit local beliefs and institutions. Localisation occurs when 'norm-takers build

36 United Nations Secretary-General, 'Secretary-General Defends, Clarifies "Responsibility to Protect" at Berlin Event on "Responsible Sovereignty: International Cooperation for a Changed World"', news release, 15 July 2008; UN Secretary-General, *Fulfilling Our Collective Responsibility: International Assistance and the Responsibility to Protect*, A/68/947–S/2014/449, 11 July 2014, p. 4.

37 ICISS, *The Responsibility to Protect*, p. xi.

38 UN Secretary-General, *Uniting against Terrorism: Recommendations for a Global Counter-Terrorism Strategy*, A/60/825, 27 April 2006; A/RES/60/288, 20 September 2006.

39 Luck, *UN Security Council: Practice and Promise*, pp. 109–110.

40 Kees Van Kersbergen and Bertjan Verbeek, 'The Politics of International Norms: Subsidiarity and the Imperfect Competence Regime of the European Union', *European Journal of International Relations*, 13(2) 217–238 (2007), p. 222.

congruence between transnational norms ... and local, beliefs and practices'.[41] As states are inherently self-interested this will involve appropriating norms for a variety of different purposes,[42] including prioritising particular aspects of a norm regime during implementation in an effort to (re)shape norms to suit national interests and cultural contexts. This is an inward process generic to most actors where norms are imported for local usage and need to be justified to domestic audiences.[43]

Alternatively, norm subsidiary is a 'process whereby local actors create rules with a view to preserve their autonomy from dominance, neglect, violation, or abuse by more powerful central actors'.[44] The norm subsidiary process is outward focused, concerned with relations with internal and external powers, specifically 'in terms of the former's fear of domination by the latter'.[45] States often engage in both processes as they implement norms. Powerful states will revise and apply norms to support their national interests. State with more vulnerable sovereignty claims may undertake additional revision to ensure applied norms support their sovereignty domestically and reinforce their sovereign claims internationally. In this process the nature of the state implementing R2P and counter-terrorism norms and how it understands the rights and responsibilities of the state become pivotal. State sovereignty which understands security as civilian-centric will interpret R2P and counter-terrorism as aligned and complimentary with R2P limiting the actions of states. States with sovereignty focused on state preservation will interpret them as conflicting, prioritising counter-terrorism and attempting to reframe R2P in such a way that it either allows or even justifies counter-terror actions.

3.1 *State Sovereignty(ies)*

Sovereignty can be understood as 'the idea that there is a final and absolute political authority in the political community'.[46] Just like R2P and counter-terrorism, sovereignty is a norm regime, containing multiple other norms

41 Amitav Acharya, 'How Ideas Spread: Whose Norms Matter? Norm Localization and Institutional Change in Asian Regionalism', *International Organization*, 58(2) 239–275 (2004), p. 241.

42 Mona Lena Krook and Jacqui True, 'Rethinking the Life Cycles of International Norms: The United Nations and the Global Promotion of Gender Equality', *European Journal of International Relations*, 18(1) 103–127 (2012), p. 104.

43 Amitav Acharya, 'Norm Subsidiarity and Regional Orders: Sovereignty, Regionalism, and Rule-Making in the Third World', *International Studies Quarterly*, 55(1) 95–123 (2011), p. 98.

44 *ibid.*, p. 97.

45 *ibid.*, p. 98.

46 Francis Harry Hinsley, *Sovereignty*, 2nd ed. (Cambridge; New York: Cambridge University Press, 1986), p. 26.

which interact and evolve in unique ways. Traditionally, the purpose of sovereignty was to protect the state from outside interference via 'the principles of autonomy, territory, mutual recognition and control'.[47] These could be considered the core norms of sovereignty. However, over time, the rights and responsibilities of sovereignty have changed, incorporating new norms such as human rights, and limiting sovereign authority.

According to Samuel Makinda, the sources of sovereign authority can be broken down into three schools of thought.[48] The most basic is juridical sovereignty, which stems from the state's recognition by international law. The second is empirical sovereignty, which expands on juridical sovereignty to include the state's capacity to control people, resources, and activities within its borders. This includes some level of state legitimacy through the provision of state services.[49] The final type of sovereignty has emerged only recently, driven by the collapse of the Soviet Union and the emerging power of human and civil rights – popular sovereignty. This sovereignty is marked by the claim that people are entitled to fundamental freedoms and can only be governed with their consent. All recognised states have juridical sovereignty, many have empirical sovereignty, and some have popular sovereignty. These strains of sovereignty are prioritised and perpetuated in different ways by different political regimes. Which sovereignties they embody, and to what extent, will dictate how they will incorporate the norms of R2P and counter-terrorism.

3.2 *Old States*

Variations of sovereignty can be explained, at least in part, by the evolutionary process of a state. The United Nations is built upon the concept of the modern Western (Weberian) State modelled by the majority European states that founded the organisation.[50] This definition of the state emerged from a lengthy and violent process of state formation.[51] Rulers constructed internal order so that they might more effectively combat external threats. In the process they engaged in constant negotiation with their populations to exchange security

47 Stephen D. Krasner, 'Rethinking the Sovereign State Model', *Review of International Studies*, 27(5) 17–42 (2001).

48 Samuel M. Makinda, F. Wafula Okumu, and David Mickler, *The African Union: Addressing the Challenges of Peace, Security, and Governance*, 2nd ed. (London, [England]: Routledge, 2016), pp. 17–18.

49 Michael Barnett, 'The New United Nations Politics of Peace: From Juridical Sovereignty to Empirical Sovereignty', *Global Governance*, 1(1) 79–97 (1995), p. 80.

50 Anthony Giddens, *The Nation-State and Violence* (Cambridge: Polity Press, 1985), ProQuest, p. 17.

51 Charles Tilly, 'War Making and State Making as Organized Crime', *Politix*, 49, 97–124 (2000).

for resources.[52] Over time, the state honed its capacity to provide services to the population and established what became known as the 'social contract' between the rulers and the ruled.[53] This relationship eventually evolved to include unified social goals that fostered loyalty and patriotism towards the state, making it a 'legitimate', if self-interested, ruler.[54] In this model, states understand threats to be primarily military-based and external in nature. State security, therefore, is understood as the protection of state institutions and national interests through the domination or deterrence against 'others'.[55] Evolving over hundreds of years, this understanding of the nature of 'the state' was captured in treaties between European states and eventually codified the idea that the sovereign reigned supreme domestically and controlled the state's relations with the outside world.[56]

This model of the state is the one that shapes the contemporary theory and practice of statecraft and security.[57] States with this historical evolutionary model usually have both juridical and empirical sovereignty and often have popular sovereignty maintained through some form of democratic process. For these states, R2P and counter-terrorism are likely to be interpreted as aligned and complimentary norms that resonate with their understanding of sovereignty. Protecting their civilians from atrocity crimes or terrorism would be among the guarantees provided under the social contract and such states would have existing institutions which would be capable of implementing these norms without undue conflict.

3.3 *New States*

The number of states within the United Nations has almost quadrupled since its founding in 1945. Most of these states emerged as the result of decolonisation or, more recently, the fall of the Soviet Union. The UN now hosts diverse conceptions of sovereignty, with unique histories, political philosophies, and capacities. While the founding states of the United Nations often had centuries to coalesce into their modern political forms, states emerging in the 1940s,

52 Eboe Hutchful, 'From Military Security to Human Security' in John Akokpari, Angela Ndinga-Muvumba, and Tim Murithi (eds.), *African Union and Its Institutions* (Melville: Jacana Media, 2009), p. 67.

53 Jean-Jacques Rousseau, *The Social Contract*, ed. and trans. Maurice Cranston (London, UK: Penguin, 1968).

54 Cord Schmelzle and Eric Stollenwerk, 'Virtuous or Vicious Circle? Governance Effectiveness and Legitimacy in Areas of Limited Statehood', *Journal of Intervention and Statebuilding*, 12(4) 449–467 (2018), p. 450.

55 Hutchful, 'From Military Security to Human Security', pp. 67–68.

56 Deng, 'From "Sovereignty as Responsibility" to the "Responsibility to Protect"', p. 355.

57 Hutchful, 'From Military Security to Human Security', p. 68.

1950s, and 1960s were birthed swiftly, into forms foreign to them, and carrying legacies of colonial trauma and coercive infrastructure.[58]

Many post-colonial states never evolved to protect civilians.[59] In the rush to decolonise, these new states were recognised under what Robert Jackson calls 'negative-sovereignty', or 'juridical sovereignty' given by the formal legal recognition of the state by the international community.[60] This entitled states to non-intervention but did not require them to have full control over their territory or legitimacy with their people.[61] In many instances, sovereignty in former colonial states was, at best, a 'legal fiction' that was not matched by governance and administrative capacity.[62] New states emerged burdened not only with a foreign idea of sovereignty but also with the vestiges, experience, and memory of colonial oppression.[63] Post-colonial and post-Soviet states structures were built on an anti-democratic foundation of colonial or soviet authoritarianism.[64] Many, but not all, of these states understood sovereignty as control over the populations and these structures did not change with decolonisation or the collapse of the Soviet Union, resulting in native, but often weak and authoritarian, governments relying on the military to keep domestic order. These states – with a few notable exceptions – struggle to deliver the necessary services to be considered to have empirical sovereignty. Most also have some level of democratic process as a nod towards popular sovereignty but these processes have varied levels of transparency. For these states, R2P and

58 Schmelzle and Stollenwerk, 'Virtuous or Vicious Circle?', p. 450; Tilly, 'War Making and State Making as Organized Crime'.

59 Peter Ekeh, 'Individuals' Basic Needs and the Limits of Democracy in Africa' in Bruce Berman, Dickson Eyoh, and William Kymlicka (eds.), *Ethnicity and Democracy in Africa* (Oxford: James Currey; Athens: Ohio University Press, 2004), p. 23.

60 Robert H. Jackson, *Quasi-States: Sovereignty, International Relations and the Third World* (Cambridge: Cambridge University Press, 1990). pp. 27, 77–78. See also Robert H. Jackson, 'Sovereignty in World Politics: A Glance at the Conceptual and Historical Landscape', *Political Studies*, 47(3) 431–456 (1999), p. 446; Benedict Kingsbury, 'Sovereignty and Inequality', *European Journal of International Law*, 9(4) 599–625 (1998), pp. 607–608.

61 The 1960 General Assembly Declaration on the Granting of Independence to Colonial Countries and Peoples (UNGA Res. 1514 (XV), 14 December 1960) does not make the exercise of sovereign authority a condition for the recognition of statehood but instead reduced the criteria for statehood to a defined territory and a permanent population. See Zaum, *The Sovereignty Paradox*, p. 33.

62 Jakkie Cilliers and Kathryn Sturman, 'The Right of Intervention: Enforcement Challenges for the African Union', *African Security Review*, 11(3) 28–39 (2002), p. 31.

63 Basil Davidson, *The Black Man's Burden: Africa and the Curse of the Nation State* (London: James Currey, 1992).

64 Cilliers and Sturman, 'The Right of Intervention', p. 3.

counter-terrorism are likely to diverge as sovereignty continues to be about control of the population through a basic monopoly of force.

4 Sovereignties Collide

Within the limited constraints of the Cold War, diverse sovereignties were able to coexist. The end of the Cold War then reignited discussions on the rights and responsibilities of the state and the international community. Then UN Secretary-General Boutros Boutros-Ghali declared that it was time to rethink what was meant by sovereignty:

> A major intellectual requirement of our time is to rethink the question of sovereignty—not to weaken its essence, which is crucial to international security and co-operation, but to recognise that it may take more than one form and perform more than one function. This perception could help solve problems both within and among states. And underlying the rights of the individual and the rights of peoples is a dimension of universal sovereignty that resides in all humanity and provides all peoples with legitimate involvement in issues affecting the world as a whole. It is a sense that increasingly finds expression in the gradual expansion of international law.[65]

The atrocities in Bosnia, Rwanda, and Somalia shortly thereafter only reaffirmed Boutros-Ghali's call, and the idea of humanitarian intervention emerged as an 'advance guard' to limit the excesses of sovereignty.[66] In advocating for sovereignty based on responsibility, a new standard for sovereignty emerged that states were increasingly pushed to uphold.[67] However, high-level discussions on sovereignty and civilian protection ground to a halt as counter-terrorism emerged as a normative force. The war on terror upended status quo sovereignty and challenged efforts to expand sovereign responsibilities with pure power politics.[68] This state of flux and the presence of dual, potentially

65 Boutros Boutros-Ghali, 'Empowering the United Nations', *Foreign Affairs*, 71(5) 89–102 (1992/1993), p. 99.

66 Tom J. Farer, 'Humanitarian Intervention before and after 9/11: Legality and Legitimacy', in, J. L. Holzgrefe and Robert O. Keohane (eds.), *Humanitarian Intervention: Ethical, Legal and Political Dilemmas* (Cambridge: Cambridge University Press, 2003), p. 55.

67 Zaum, *The Sovereignty Paradox*, p. 227.

68 Alastair Finlan, 'International Security' in Mary Buckley and Robert Singh (eds.), *The Bush Doctrine and the War on Terrorism: Global Responses, Global Consequences* (London: Routledge, 2006), p. 159.

contradictory, norm regimes allowed states to prioritise the norm or norm regime aspects that aligned with their national self-interests. While new states may not have been fully in a normative 'revolt against the west' as Bull might have argued,[69] they actively engaged in norm localisation and subsidiary to 'redefine the meaning and scope of the pre-existing European-derived global norms to reflect Third World conditions'.[70] States began to interpret and modify R2P and counter-terrorism norm regimes to align with sovereignty in new and unexpected ways. The next section provides two case studies which illustrate how states align the R2P and counter-terrorism norm regimes with their unique conceptions of sovereignty. In the case of both China and Sri Lanka, the state has prioritised counter-terrorism over R2P and has been able to reframe R2P in such a way that the norm supports, or at least does not conflict with, the state's counter-terrorism efforts.

4.1 *China: The 'People's' War on Terrorism*

China is a prime example of a state that has pursued particular interpretations of R2P and counter-terrorism based on priorities driven by its unique conception of sovereignty. The Chinese have a pluralist view of the international system which is built on the centrality of the state and emphasises non-intervention, territoriality, minimalist international law, and – most importantly – state centrism.[71] In China, the idea of the 'state' as a domestic entity is a complex mixture of its old semi-colonial identity and that of a former Third World socialist state.[72] Chinese sovereignty has evolved to revolve around the preservation and perpetuation of the Chinese Communist Party (CCP) as noted by former Chinese State Councillor Dai Bingguo, who defined China's 'core interests' as 'China's form of government and political system and stability, namely the leadership of the Communist Party of China, the socialist system and socialism with Chinese characteristics'.[73] This conception of sovereignty results in a hierarchy of strategic priorities that aim to find the 'right

69 Hedley Bull, *Intervention in World Politics* (Oxford: Clarendon, 1984).

70 Acharya, 'Norm Subsidiarity and Regional Orders', p. 100.

71 Robert H. Jackson, *The Global Covenant: Human Conduct in a World of States* (New York: Oxford University Press, 2003); Barry Buzan, *From International to World Society?: English School Theory and the Social Structure of Globalisation*, Cambridge Studies in International Relations, vol. 95 (Cambridge: Cambridge University Press, 2004).

72 Rosemary Foot, 'Chinese Power and the Idea of a Responsible State', *The China Journal* (Canberra, ACT), 45, 1–19 (2001); Rosemary Foot, 'Chinese Power and the Idea of a Responsible State' in Yongjin Zhang and Greg Austin (eds.), *Power and Responsibility in Chinese Foreign Policy* (Canberra: ANU E Press, 2013), p. 41.

73 Dai Bingguo, 'Adhere to the Path of Peaceful Development', news release, 6 December 2010, http://www.gov.cn/ldhd/2010-12/06/content_1760381.htm, accessed 1 February 2022.

balance between justice and interest' and influence how state responsibility and international norms like R2P and counter-terrorism are understood.[74]

As a veto-wielding permanent member of the UN Security Council, China has successfully pushed the supremacy of more traditional conceptions of sovereignty to curtail the interventionist tendencies of R2P. Initially cautious of R2P, China shifted to endorsing a conservative interpretation of the concept in an effort to limit the norm's impact while fostering its desired image of a responsible power.[75] The Chinese government began to actively engage in 'rhetorical adaptation'[76] of R2P to shape 'the discursive and behavioural environment of the concepts' application to make it more compatible with its own preferences'.[77] In particular, China was clear that R2P should not 'contravene the principle of state sovereignty and the principle of non-interference of internal affairs'.[78] Instead, Beijing emphasised Pillar One, the state capacity-building functions of the R2P norm, as a way of supporting the state in protecting its citizens as a broader group.[79] From there, China continued a 'norm containment' strategy where it slowed down the emergence of the norm, minimised its use, and protected traditional sovereignty by curtailing any expansion of the concept.[80] After the R2P facilitated regime change in Libya in 2011, China developed the concept of 'responsible protection' which used the costs of intervention in economic, political, and social terms as a way to further limit

---

74 Vitaly Kozyrev, 'Harmonizing "Responsibility to Protect": China's Vision of a Post-Sovereign World', *International Relations*, 30(3) 328–345 (2016), p. 329.

75 Zheng Chen, 'China and the Responsibility to Protect', *The Journal of Contemporary China*, 25(101) 686–700 (2016), p. 687; Adrian Gallagher, 'To Name and Shame or Not, and If So, How? A Pragmatic Analysis of Naming and Shaming the Chinese Government over Mass Atrocity Crimes against the Uyghurs and Other Muslim Minorities in Xinjiang', *Journal of Global Security Studies*, 6(4) 1–16 (2021), p. 7.

76 Courtney J. Fung, 'Rhetorical Adaptation, Normative Resistance and International Order-Making: China's Advancement of the Responsibility to Protect', *Cooperation and Conflict*, 55(2) 193–215 (2020), p. 196.

77 Rosemary Foot, 'The Responsibility to Protect (R2P) and Its Evolution: Beijing's Influence on Norm Creation in Humanitarian Areas', *St. Antony's International Review*, 6(2) 47–66 (2011), p. 57.

78 Liu Zhenmin, 'Statement by Ambassador Liu Zhenmin at the Plenary Session of the General Assembly on the Question of "Responsibility to Protect," 27 July' in *Permanent Mission of the People's Republic of China to the United Nations* (New York: United Nations, 2009).

79 Foot, 'The Responsibility to Protect (R2P) and Its Evolution', p. 47.

80 Sarah Teitt, 'The Responsibility to Protect and China's Peacekeeping Policy', *International Peacekeeping*, 18(3) 297–312 (2011), p. 306; Andrew Garwood-Gowers, 'China and the "Responsibility to Protect": The Implications of the Libyan Intervention', *Asian Journal of International Law*, 2(2) 375–393 (2012), p. 381; Courtney J. Fung, 'Just Not in the Neighbourhood: China's Views on the Application of the Responsibility to Protect in the DPRK', *The China Quarterly* (London), 246, 565–585 (2021).

military intervention and avoid regime change.[81] This was China's justification for its multiple vetoes against intervention in Syria at the Security Council.

At the same time China was shaping R2P to bolster the sanctity of the state, it was engaging counter-terrorism as a mechanism for protecting its own brand of sovereignty. Chinese sovereignty is understood to include support of the Chinese Communist Party and its associated 'socialism with Chinese characteristics'. This means that threats to the CCP could be considered as synonymous with threats to the Chinese State and can justify 'all necessary measures' including subordination of individual's human rights to protect the collective human rights of the nation.[82] This interaction between the CCP, traditional sovereignty, and human rights has allowed China to use the global war on terror narrative to justify the systematic oppression of Uyghur's in Xinjiang to its domestic populations while using its sovereign rights – along with a focused disinformation campaign – to deflect international condemnation.[83]

The ethnic conflict in Xinjiang has been a challenge for the CCP since it claimed power in 1949.[84] Before 9/11, the Chinese government under the leadership of Xi Jinping had begun to tighten social controls to foster the 'great revival or rejuvenation of the Chinese nation'.[85] This included framing unrest in Xinjiang as a 'zero-sum political struggle of life or death' against the 'three evils' of 'separatism, terrorism and extremism'.[86] Leveraging the conductive post-9/11 environment, the Chinese government released several documents about alleged Uyghur terrorist networks. The CCP was able to convince the UN Security Council that at least one Uyghur group, the Eastern Turkistan Islamic Movement, was a terrorist organisation and therefore a global threat and a legitimate enemy in the global war on terror.[87] Labelling the Uyghurs as terrorists rather than separatists 'substantively altered the relationship between the state and Uyghurs' in that, while separatists may be engaged with

81 Fung, 'Rhetorical Adaptation, Normative Resistance and International Order-Making', pp. 204–205.

82 Vitaly Kozyrev, 'Harmonizing "Responsibility to Protect": China's Vision of a Post-Sovereign World', *International Relations* 30 (3) 328–345 (2016), p. 332.

83 Albert Zhang, Jacob Wallis, and Zoe Meers, 'Strange Bedfellows on Xinjiang: The CCP, Fringe Media and US Social Media Platforms', Australian Strategic Policy Institute, 2021.

84 Michael Clarke, 'The Impact of Ethnic Minorities on China's Foreign Policy: The Case of Xinjiang and the Uyghur', *China Report*, 53(1) 1–25 (2017), p. 9.

85 Elizabeth C. Economy, *The Third Revolution: Xi Jinping and the New Chinese State* (Oxford: Oxford University Press, 2018), p. 3.

86 David Tobin, 'A "Struggle of Life or Death": Han and Uyghur Insecurities on China's North-West Frontier', *The China Quarterly*, 242, 301–323 (2020).

87 Sean R. Roberts, 'The Biopolitics of China's "War on Terror" and the Exclusion of the Uyghurs', *Critical Asian Studies*, 50(2) 232–258 (2018), p. 233.

to better understand their grievances, terrorists are an unchangeable threat to all society and humanity, and 'must be suppressed, eliminated, [and/]or quarantined'.[88] China incorporated discourse from the war on terror to imbue the Uyghur issue with fear of the 'other', justify increasingly forceful actions, and portray Han violence against Uyghur's as a rational response to terrorism.[89] From there, China was able to reframe its actions in Xinjiang as a response to religious extremism which threatened China's territorial integrity to align with the counter-terrorism norm.[90]

For the Chinese government to successfully justify its actions through interpretations of counter-terrorism and R2P, it has made active efforts to hide evidence of the worst state abuses or obscure their actions through strategic disinformation.[91] Domestically, the CCP has framed its actions as a massive deradicalisation effort, portraying mass surveillance and oppression as 'preventative policing' and internment camps as 'reform schools' and any acts to resist these efforts as 'terror'.[92] When questioned by the international community, Chinese authorities have denied their actions in Xinjiang[93] and refused to conduct their own investigations or allow international monitors to do so. They have also used their position on the Security Council to block accountability initiatives at the United Nations, effectively sidelining R2P as an option.[94]

China's concern stems from the fact that actions undertaken by the CCP could amount to state terrorism.[95] Beginning in earnest in 2009, Uyghur's were

88 *ibid.*, p. 234.

89 Michael Clarke, *Terrorism and Counter-Terrorism in China: Domestic and Foreign Policy Dimensions* (Oxford: Oxford University Press, 2018), p. 32; Joanne Smith Finley, 'Securitization, Insecurity and Conflict in Contemporary Xinjiang: Has PRC Counter-Terrorism Evolved into State Terror?', *Central Asian Survey*, 38(1) 1–26 (2019); Tobin, 'A "Struggle of Life or Death"'.

90 Rosemary Foot, 'R2P Sidelined: The International Response to China's Repression of Muslim Minorities in Xinjiang', *Global Responsibility to Protect*, 13(1) 29–32 (2021), p. 30; Pablo A. Rodríguez-Merino, 'Old "Counter-Revolution", New "Terrorism": Historicizing the Framing of Violence in Xinjiang by the Chinese State', *Central Asian Survey*, 38(1) 27–45 (2019), pp. 27–28.

91 Zhang, Wallis, and Meers, 'Strange Bedfellows on Xinjiang'.

92 Henryk Szadziewski and Anonymous, 'Meet the "New" Uyghurs: CGTN's Role in Mediawashing Genocide', Uyghur Human Rights Project, 2021; Sean R. Roberts, 'Cultural Genocide, 2017–2020' in *The War on the Uyghurs: China's Internal Campaign against a Muslim Minority* (Princeton: Princeton University Press, 2020), 202; Adrian Zenz, '"Thoroughly Reforming Them Towards a Healthy Heart Attitude": China's Political Re-Education Campaign in Xinjiang', *Central Asian Survey*, 38(1) 102–108 (2019); Adrian Zenz, '"End the Dominance of the Uyghur Ethnic Group": An Analysis of Beijing's Population Optimization Strategy in Southern Xinjiang', *Central Asian Survey*, 40(3) 291–312 (2021), p. 292.

93 Zenz, '"Thoroughly Reforming Them Towards a Healthy Heart Attitude"'.

94 Foot, 'R2P Sidelined'.

95 Smith Finley, 'Securitization, Insecurity and Conflict in Contemporary Xinjiang'.

systemically excluded from Chinese society, seen as either potential terrorists or their sympathisers. The 'People's War on Terror' was launched in 2014 and called for terrorists to be 'chased down the street like rats'.[96] Rhetoric used to justify countering the terrorist 'threat' of the Uyghurs began to increasingly resemble rhetoric used to justify atrocity crimes. Mass surveillance and incarceration, forced abortions and sterilisation, and the curtailment of religious freedom all constitute crimes which fall within the parameters of R2P and there is credible evidence that the Chinese government has engaged in crimes against humanity and genocide against the Uyghurs.[97]

In China the counter-terrorism norm regime has been aligned with Chinese conceptions of sovereignty by identifying Uyghur cultural differences as 'terrorist' in nature and therefore an existential threat to the Chinese nation and justifying the internment of people based on these characteristics.[98] This is supported by China's interpretation of human rights as collective, the protection of which takes precedence over those of the individual.[99] This then aligns with China's framing of a 'thin' R2P which has given it primacy to determine how protection can best be guaranteed and placed the 'state at the centre and in a role as the provider or curtailer of the rights of individuals'.[100]

4.2 *Sri Lanka*

Much like China, Sri Lanka was able to successfully combine R2P and counter-terrorism to portray civilian deaths as necessary in an effort to beat the existential terrorist threat posed to the state by the Liberation Tigers of Tamil Eelam (LTTE). Under the rule of the current president Mahinda Rajapaksa, Sri Lanka has come to embody a 'Schmittian' concept of sovereignty based on centralised power. The executive has the monopoly on decision-making while

---

96 Ondřej Klimes, 'Advancing "Ethnic Unity" and "De-Extremization": Ideational Governance in Xinjiang under "New Circumstances" (2012–2017)', *Chinese Journal of Political Science*, 23(3) 413–436 (2018), p. 417.

97 Cecilia Jacob, Adrian Gallagher, and Charles T. Hunt, 'Pursuing Accountability and Protection for the Uighur and Muslim Minorities in China', *Global Responsibility to Protect*, 13(1) 5–8 (2021), p. 6; Simon-Skjodt Center for the Prevention of Genocide, *To Make Us Slowly Disappear: The Chinese Government's Assault on the Uyghurs* (Washington DC: United States Holocaust Memorial Museum, November 2021), pp. 38–45; Joanne Smith Finley, 'Why Scholars and Activists Increasingly Fear a Uyghur Genocide in Xinjiang', *Journal of Genocide Research*, 23(3) 348–370 (2021), pp. 348–370.

98 Smith Finley, 'Securitization, Insecurity and Conflict in Contemporary Xinjiang', p. 2.

99 Mikelli Marzzini, L. A. Ribeiro, Marcelo de Almeida Medeiros, and Alexandre Cesar Cunha Leite, 'China's Engagement with R2P: Pluralist Shaper?', *Global Responsibility to Protect*, 12(3) 271–298 (2020), p. 280.

100 Foot, 'R2P Sidelined', p. 311.

the influence of international and foreign actors, domestic state institutions, and even the courts and justice system are curtailed.[101] Its anti-pluralist order is defined by one unified political community and emphasised by distinctions between 'us' and 'them'; in particular, the presence of an existential 'enemy' in the form of the LTTE.[102]

The conflict between the LTTE and the Sri Lankan government dates from the 1970s, with the LTTE wishing to establish a separate state of Tamil Eelam in the north and east of the country. After the failure of the 2002–2004 peace process and the 2005 election of Mahinda Rajapaksa, the Sri Lankan government shifted towards a military strategy to defeat the LTTE. The Rajapaksa government began to reject claims by the Tamils of collective grievances and ethnic enmity and instead identified the LTTE as a terrorist group with no claim to represent any community.[103] This allowed the Sri Lankan government to cast the people of Sri Lanka collectively as victims of a terrorist group.

The conflict between the Sri Lankan government and the LTTE culminated in 2008–2009. Engaging the rhetoric of the global war on terror and leveraging support from states strongly supportive of the global war on terror, the Sri Lankan government was able to wage a brutal conventional ground war against the LTTE.[104] By March of 2009, the UN Office of the High-Commission on Human Rights (OHCHR) cautioned that government and LTTE actions 'may constitute international crimes, entailing individual responsibility, including for war crimes and crimes against humanity'.[105] In the final stages of the war hundreds of thousands of civilians became trapped between the forces of the Sri Lankan government and the LTTE, and an estimated 40,000 were killed.[106]

Both the government and the LTTE failed to protect civilians during this time; however, the LTTE's clear structure and longstanding status as a terrorist organisation made it easier for the Sri Lankan government to evade most of the blame for atrocities.[107] This was due in part to intentional efforts by

101 David G. Lewis, 'Sri Lanka's Schmittian Peace: Sovereignty, Enmity and Illiberal Order', *Conflict, Security & Development*, 20(1) 15–37 (2020), pp. 18–19.

102 *ibid.*, pp. 21–22.

103 *ibid.*

104 Damien Kingsbury, *Sri Lanka and the Responsibility to Protect: Politics, Ethnicity and Genocide* (Florence SC: Taylor & Francis Group, 2011), pp. 133–134.

105 OHCHR, 'Navi Pillay: Serious Violations of International Law Committed in Sri Lanka Conflict', Office of the High-Commission on Human Rights, News and Press Release, 13 March 2009.

106 Secretary-General's Internal Review Panel on United Nations Action in Sri Lanka, *Report of the Secretary-General's Internal Review Panel on United Nations Action in Sri Lanka*, 2012.

107 United Nations Security Council, 'Security Council Press Statement on Sri Lanka', news release, 13 May 2009.

the Sri Lankan government to deny or obscure its involvement in any crimes, including obscuring its actions, intimidating whistle-blowers, and systematically hiding or destroying evidence.[108] International condemnation of the government's actions was also limited as the UN wanted to keep humanitarian lines open and it knew that the government had wide support among key UN member states while the LTTE had none.[109] The Sri Lankan government effectively obscured the plight of Tamil civilians and used the rhetorical power of the global war on terror to mute criticism.[110]

At the same time, the government reiterated its right as the sovereign to be the primary responder to both protecting civilian and countering terrorism. Sri Lanka's representative to the UN pointed out that

> ... the role of Governments in civilian protection should be respected as it is their primary responsibility to protect their own citizens. The United Nations and humanitarian agencies must support and assist Governments, and in doing so be sensitive to ground realities, including by respecting the sovereignty of States.[111]

This position was subsequently supported by an ICISS commissioner who argued that the government had the right to determine what is needed to defeat the LTTE as part of its responsibility to protect.[112] In the end, the Sri Lankan government was successful in crafting a narrative that engaged R2P to justify the right to address the terrorist threat of the LTTE while simultaneously arguing that the heavy-handed actions taken by the state in the process of combating this threat were justifiable due to its existential nature.

---

108 Megan Price, 'The End Days of the Fourth Eelam War: Sri Lanka's Denialist Challenge to the Laws of War', *Ethics & International Affairs*, online, 1–25 (2022); Glenn Porter and Steven Freeland, 'Island of Impunity? Investigation into International Crimes in the Final Stages of the Sri Lankan Civil War', Public Interest Advocacy Centre, Sydney, NSW, 2014.

109 Gareth J. Evans, 'Remembering Sri Lanka's Killing Fields', *Project Syndicate*, 26 October 2012, https://www.project-syndicate.org/commentary/accountability-for-sri-lanka-s-official-killers-by-gareth-evans.

110 Kim Nackers, 'Sri Lanka' in Alex J. Bellamy and Tim Dunne (eds.), *The Oxford Handbook of the Responsibility to Protect* (United Kingdom: Oxford University Press, 2016), pp. 885–886.

111 Mr Kohona, Sri Lankan representative to the UN, S/PV.6531, 10 May 2011, p. 30.

112 Jennifer M. Welsh, 'Norm Contestation and the Responsibility to Protect', *Global Responsibility to Protect*, 5(4) 365–396 (2013), p. 386.

5 Conclusion

This chapter has argued that R2P and counter-terrorism are norm regimes which encompass a number of proscriptive and prescriptive norms. They share similarities through their core proscriptive norms forbidding atrocity crimes and terrorist attacks (which often constitute atrocity crimes such as crimes against humanity). Their difference lies in their less defined prescriptive norms, which are used by states to manipulate these norm regimes in such a way that they align with local conceptions of sovereignty. Extreme interpretations of prescriptive norms can result in modifications to the norm regime that essentially contradict the norm's intended purpose.

As the China and Sri Lanka case studies show, norms that are primarily implemented by states are subject to norm localisation and subsidiary. When interpreting norms for domestic implementation states will interpret, and even reconstruct, norms to build necessary congruence between the norm's content and local beliefs and practices.[113] As states will always prioritise their survival, norms will be modified to align with and support their local understandings of sovereignty. This includes subsuming and reinterpreting one norm over another that suits their domestic interests more.

At the same time, actions stemming from norms must also be justified to the international community. When state actions go beyond what can be justified by norm manipulation, they are often hidden from international scrutiny. In the case of China, the government was able stretch the counter-terrorism norm regime to the extent that it was used to identify an entire group of people as terrorists. This was sold to domestic audiences as a form of deradicalisation. At the same time, to avoid international condemnation, China focused on disinformation about what was occurring in Xinjiang to maintain claims of counter-terrorism and relied on claims to traditional sovereignty to avoid enacting R2P. Alternatively, Sri Lanka focused on international narratives around R2P's first pillar, which places primacy for action with the state, to push back against calls for external interventions and maintain their autonomy. This was successful, even as Sri Lanka's counter-terrorism efforts amounted to human rights violations.

The nature of R2P and counter-terrorism as norm regimes allows them to address some of the most vexing challenges of the twenty-first century. As the same time, their combination of proscriptive and prescriptive norms makes them vulnerable to reinterpretation by states who will strive to align them to

113 Acharya, 'How Ideas Spread', p. 241.

support local conceptions of sovereignty. The diverse and sometimes problematic outcomes of these interpretations of R2P and counter-terrorism do not imply that the norms themselves are at fault but rather that the international community needs to consider the nuanced and varied nature of states and state sovereignty when calling for their application and place clearer parameters on their rhetorical use.

CHAPTER 2

The Responsibility to Protect from Terror: The Ethics of Foreign Counter-terrorist Interventions

Isaac Taylor
Associate Senior Lecturer, Department of Philosophy, Stockholm University, Stockholm, Sweden
isaac.taylor@philosophy.su.se

Abstract

The use of military force abroad is a significant part of some states' counter-terrorist efforts. Can these operations be ethically justified? This chapter considers whether the underlying principles that philosophers have put forward to justify humanitarian interventions (which may underlie the international norm of the responsibility to protect (R2P)) can also give support for foreign counter-terrorist interventions of this sort. While it finds that the limits to international action that are imposed by the need to respect state sovereignty do not rule out counter-terrorist interventions, it urges caution in supporting an international norm permitting them. Because such a norm would be open to manipulation and abuse, it may be preferable to discourage appealing to it in order to justify military counter-terrorism.

Keywords

basic rights – counter-terrorism – humanitarian intervention – just war theory – responsibility to protect sovereignty

 | DOI:10.1163/9789004548114_004

1 Introduction[1]

Despite conscious efforts by the international community to steer towards more preventative measures,[2] the use of military force remained a significant part of some states' counter-terrorist efforts in the decades following the attacks of 11 September 2001. This was certainly true of US policy, where the use of drone strikes has been a much-discussed tool in counter-terrorism abroad. These sorts of operations, because they involve action within the borders of foreign sovereign states, can be termed 'counter-terrorist interventions'. The fact that they are sometimes done without the consent of the state in which they are conducted makes this a controversial strategy.[3] Whether it is one that will ultimately be permitted or shunned according to the emerging and fluid international norm regime surrounding counter-terrorism remains an open question.

Of course, at least since the responsibility to protect (R2P) emerged as an international norm in the 1990s and 2000s, state sovereignty has no longer been thought of as an absolute barrier to the use of force across borders. The United Nations General Assembly's 2005 World Summit Outcome Document, which is perhaps the first authoritative statement of this, places the responsibility to prevent the atrocity crimes of genocide, war crimes, ethnic cleansing, and crimes against humanity on the international community.[4] Subsequent developments of the idea have seen three pillars specified: the (initial) responsibility of states to prevent the four atrocity crimes occurring within their borders (the first pillar), the responsibility of states to assist each other in their protection responsibilities (the second pillar); and the responsibility of the international community to take collective action to remedy cases of failure (the third pillar).[5] Because the third pillar permits external interference in some circumstances (for example, through humanitarian interventions) it has had the effect of limiting the claims that states can make to be left alone on the

---

1 I am very grateful to Shannon Zimmerman and two anonymous reviewers for comments on earlier drafts of this chapter.

2 'Plan of Action to Prevent Violent Extremism: Report of the Secretary-General', UNGA A/70/674, 29 May 2015.

3 The former Prime Minister of Pakistan Nawaz Sharif called the counter-terrorist drone strikes conducted by the United States in Pakistan 'a violation of our territorial integrity'. See BBC, 'Pakistan PM Sharif Discusses Drones with Barack Obama', *BBC News*, 23 October 2013, https://www.bbc.com/news/world-asia-24636444.

4 '2005 World Summit Outcome', UNGA Res. 60/1, 16 September 2005.

5 United Nations General Assembly, 'Implementing the Responsibility to Protect: Report of the Secretary General', A63/677, 12 January 2009, https://www.un.org/ruleoflaw/blog/document/report-of-the-secretary-general-implementing-the-responsibility-to-protect/.

basis of sovereignty. It might be thought that foreign counter-terrorist interventions will come to be viewed as another instance of permissible interference on the basis of similar considerations.[6]

My concern in this chapter, however, is not whether norms permitting counter-terrorist interventions will come to be accepted by the international community, but rather whether they *should* be. In particular, I will assess whether this line of thought – the idea that the considerations behind allowing humanitarian interventions should lead us to also permit counter-terrorist interventions – can be justified. This is not the only possible justification of counter-terrorist interventions but, as I will show in due course, it is a particularly important one to consider.

After providing some background on existing international law surrounding the use of military force, as well as the just war literature that is thought to underlie its rationale (section two), I move on to examine more closely two explanations about why at least some humanitarian interventions do not violate state sovereignty. While a collectivist explanation put forward by Michael Walzer does not extend easily to counter-terrorist interventions (section three), a more individualist account provided by David Luban might suggest that counter-terrorist interventions may be consistent with a proper respect for sovereignty (section four). Nonetheless, I argue, we should not necessarily welcome permissions to engage in these operations being institutionalised as international laws or norms. The potential for abuse and manipulation of such norms – another important factor to consider – may be too great a cost to pay (section five).

I have thus far spoken unproblematically about counter-terrorism, but the barrier between counter-terrorist actions and other sorts of policy is not always clearly made in discussions. Before proceeding, then, terrorism needs to be defined. For the purposes of this chapter, I will understand terrorism to be the use of violence against civilian targets with the aim of spreading fear among a wider population. This is a purely stipulative definition. I make no claim that this definition, either in whole or in part, can explain the unique wrongness of terrorism, which has been the task of philosophers putting forward their own accounts.[7] We often define political concepts with particular purposes in mind and, as we will see below, my definition of terrorism picks out a form

6 For an account of the complex interplay between R2P and the counter-terrorism norm regime more generally, see Shannon Zimmerman, 'Strange Bedfellows: Terrorism/Counter-Terrorism and the Responsibility to Protect' in Charles T. Hunt and Phil Orchard (eds.), *Constructing the Responsibility to Protect* (London: Routledge, 2020).

7 See, for example, Robert E. Goodin, *What's Wrong with Terrorism?* (Cambridge: Polity, 2006); Tamar Meisels, *The Trouble with Terror: Liberty, Security, and the Response to Terrorism*

of violence which cannot neatly be addressed with existing principles from mainstream theories in the ethics of war. It thus represents a category of action that warrants further investigation to determine whether forceful responses to it can be justified and, if so, what form these can permissibly take.[8]

2 From Humanitarian Intervention to Counter-terrorist Intervention

State sovereignty has long been thought of as a strong normative barrier to international action. Existing frameworks governing the ethics of war and peace are built around a prohibition on aggression, which the UN General Assembly defined in 1974 as 'the use of armed force by a State against the sovereignty, territorial integrity or political independence of another State, or in any other manner inconsistent with the Charter of the United Nations'.[9] Later developments – most notably in the Rome Statute of the International Criminal Court and subsequent amendments to it[10] – have seen more detail be filled out with respect to what sorts of actions can constitute aggression: primarily the use of military force across borders and blockades. In addition, a distinction is made between an *act* of aggression and a *crime* of aggression. The latter differs from the former in meeting a standard of sufficient 'gravity'. Such a standard, which is to be applied by the UN Security Council in determining whether an act of aggression also amounts to a crime, can be understood in a 'common-sense' manner where crimes of aggression are characterised as constituting a threat to international peace and security.[11] All in all, existing normative frameworks in this area are 'aggression-centered'.[12] They place restrictions on the use of military force against foreign states, and the most significant legitimating reason for going to war is thought to be responses to (certain forms of) aggression.

As previously mentioned, this picture began to change in the 1990s with the emergence of R2P, which weakened the taboo on military border crossing by states. Far from being out of step with the aggression-centred underpinning of

(Cambridge: Cambridge University Press, 2008), pp. 7–29; Samuel Scheffler, 'Is Terrorism Morally Distinctive?', *Journal of Political Philosophy* 14(1) 1–17 (2006).

8 Also note that my definition does not require that terrorists only be non-state actors (as some legal definitions do); states can commit acts of terrorism on this view.

9 'Definition of Aggression', UNGA Res. 3314 (XXIX), 14 December 1974.

10 International Criminal Court, *Rome Statute of the International Criminal Court* (International Criminal Court: The Hague, 2011), article 8 *bis*.

11 David Scheffer, 'The Complex Crime of Aggression under the Rome Statute', *Leiden Journal of International Law* 23(4) 897–904 (2010), p. 899.

12 In the terms of Laura Valentini, 'Just War and Global Justice' in David Held and Pietro Maffettone (eds.), *Global Political Theory* (Cambridge: Polity Press, 2016), p. 145.

international law, though, R2P might in fact be thought to be derivable from the normative basis of that law. Just war theory is a tradition in philosophy, developed over the course of centuries, that specifies the moral principles which states (and other actors) must meet in order to engage in warfare permissibly. One such principle is that of just cause – the requirement that a war may only be pursued for certain sorts of reasons, which was taken up by the framers of international law in the twentieth century. A response to aggression is held to be one such cause by many just war theorists. But, more recently, many have held that humanitarian intervention to prevent serious violations of human rights is another just cause.[13]

A successful defence of humanitarian interventions, as these just war theorists seek to provide, must accomplish (at least) two tasks. First, it must be shown that such interventions do not undermine state sovereignty. Since sovereignty is taken to be an important barrier to action in just war theory, just as it is in international law, no action that violates it will be permitted on this framework. In the following two sections, I will consider two attempts at doing this found within the literature. Second, it must also be shown that there are no significant negative effects of institutionalising a norm that permits humanitarian intervention. When we permit a particular action in the international sphere, the effects may not be limited to that one event. We may in fact change the normative landscape, altering what is and what is not allowed, and the sorts of justifications for action that states and others can offer. We should thus ensure that these wider effects on the international community are acceptable. This is thus an important task, yet one that has often been neglected by philosophers.[14] Nonetheless, just war theorists sometimes do attempt to show that alleged problems with their theories being deployed in practice are not sufficient to warrant abandoning them. In responding to worries about the co-option of just war theory by military practitioners, for example, Walzer has argued that the theory can still restrain unjust violence through a process of immanent critique.[15]

---

13 See, for example, David Luban, 'Just War and Human Rights', *Philosophy & Public Affairs* 9(2) 160–181 (1980); David Rodin, 'Rethinking Responsibility to Protect: The Case for Human Sovereignty' in Don E. Scheid (ed.), *The Ethics of Armed Humanitarian Intervention* (Cambridge: Cambridge University Press, 2014); Michael Walzer, *Just and Unjust Wars: A Moral Argument with Historical Illustrations*, 4th ed. (New York: Basic Books, 2006 [1977]), pp. 86–108.

14 Allen Buchanan, *Institutionalizing the Just War* (Oxford: Oxford University Press, 2018), pp. 7–8.

15 Michael Walzer, 'The Triumph of Just War Theory (and the Dangers of Success)', *Social Research* 69(4) 925–944 (2002), p. 942.

As previously mentioned, states are increasingly using force across borders in more limited counter-terrorist operations. The status of such acts in international law is disputed. On the one hand, they might be thought of as acts of aggression and thus ruled out, on the other, some claim that customary international law permits the targeted killing of terrorist suspects.[16] My focus here, however, is not what the law says, but what it *should* say. I will consider whether counter-terrorist interventions can be thought of as a more general instance of permissible interventions within just war theory, which so far have been thought to have been limited to humanitarian interventions. If this is the case, the practice of counter-terrorist intervention, like the practice of humanitarian intervention, must be shown to both not necessarily violate state sovereignty and to have no unacceptable effects of being institutionalised. I will ultimately argue that the proposed justification of counter-terrorist interventions can accomplish the first task (at least on some understandings of the nature and value of sovereignty) but will fail to accomplish the second.

Investigating whether counter-terrorist interventions are consistent with the commitments of just war theory – and, in particular, whether they can be understood as a type of permissible intervention – is not the only way in which one might try to justify these operations. Other theorists sought to characterise them as acts of policing,[17] acts of punishment,[18] or acts of self-defence,[19] for instance, and thus subject to different moral principles than the standard ones of just war theory (at least those which have been adopted by the international community). But I focus on what potential justifications can be offered from within just war theory for two reasons. First, it is a justificatory strategy that has received comparatively little attention in the literature. It is thus important in itself to consider whether this strategy can succeed (especially given objections to the other strategies on offer).[20] Second, given that the success

16 Philip Alston, *Report of the Special Rapporteur on Extrajudicial, Summary or Arbitrary Executions: Addendum*, A/HRC/14/24/Add.6, 28 May 2010, https://digitallibrary.un.org/record/685887?ln=en.

17 Stephen Coleman, 'Just War, Irregular War, and Terrorism' in Paolo Tripodi and Jessica Wolfendale (eds.), *New Wars and New Soldiers: Military Ethics in the Contemporary World* (Farnham: Ashgate, 2011).

18 Christian Nikolaus Braun, 'The Morality of Retributive Targeted Killing', *Journal of Military Ethics* 18(3) 170–188 (2019); Anh Lee, 'Targeted Killing for Retribution Only is Practically Impossible: A Rejoinder to Christian Braun', *Journal of Military Ethics* 20(2) 145–151 (2021).

19 Bradley Jay Strawser, *Killing bin Laden: A Moral Analysis* (New York: Palgrave MacMillan, 2014).

20 Jeff McMahan, 'War, Terrorism, and the "War on Terror"' in Chris Miller (ed.), *War on Terror: The Oxford Amnesty Lectures* (Manchester: Manchester University Press, 2009); Isaac Taylor, *The Ethics of Counterterrorism* (London: Routledge, 2018), p. 94.

of new international norms may depend on their being congruent with the wider normative environment,[21] it may be thought likely that any future norm permitting counter-terrorism will be built on the already established norm of R2P, and this will affect the permissions and limits that the norm will impose on international actors. Such a justification is likely to draw from the principles of just war theory. It is therefore vital to determine if this justification is sound.

Even if the suggested justification succeeds, however, this does not mean that any given counter-terrorist intervention will be morally permissible. There may be more particular objections to any given proposed intervention – maybe it will be a disproportionate response, for example. There may even be objections to various types of interventions more generally. Neil Renic, for instance, has argued that the asymmetry that drones bring about in warfare means that their use is problematic from the perspective of just war theory.[22] The justification for counter-terrorist interventions that I will consider, however, seeks to defend *all* forms of military intervention with this aim against potential objections that they will violate state sovereignty and lead to counterproductive effects when laws and norms are adjusted to allow them. The fact that I ultimately find it to be unable to answer both these sorts of objections calls into question a far greater range of potential permissions that we might grant to states.

3 Collectivist Just War Theory

Just war theory is a long and heterogeneous tradition in philosophy. It is consequently not possible in a chapter such as this to survey all the variations within it, and all the possible accounts of humanitarian intervention that correspond to these. I will instead limit myself to considering only a few strands within the tradition which warrant particular attention for current purposes. In this section, I consider what can be called 'collectivist just war theory', which ascribes rights and obligations primarily to political collectives (like states). I focus on the influential version of this theory put forward by Michael Walzer,[23] in

21 Martha Finnemore and Kathryn Sikkink, 'International Norm Dynamics and Political Change', *International Organization* 52(4) 887–917 (1998), p. 908.

22 Neil C. Renic, 'Justified Killing in an Age of Radically Asymmetric Warfare', *European Journal of International Relations* 25(2) 408–430 (2019). For another objection, see Daniel Brunstetter and Megan Braun, 'The Implications of Drones on the Just War Tradition', *Ethics & International Affairs* 25(3) 337–358 (2011).

23 On the place of Walzer's theory in the just war tradition more broadly, see Chris Brown, 'Michael Walzer (1935–present)' in Daniel R. Brunstetter and Cian O'Driscoll (eds.), *Just War Thinkers: From Cicero to the 21st Century* (London: Routledge, 2018).

part because his theory can be viewed as a critical reconstruction of existing international law. Since I want to consider possible justifications for counter-terrorist interventions that might be built on existing practice, this is the best place to begin. I do consider another thinker – John Stuart Mill – in the discussion that follows, but his ideas, too, appear to be in line with contemporary international law (particularly the prohibition on aggressive war), and so also warrant discussion in the present context.

Walzer explains the rationale behind his collectivist approach by appealing to what he calls the 'domestic analogy'. From this perspective, we are to think of states largely as we think of individuals within a society (with a few exceptions, one of which will be discussed below). Individuals within a well-functioning state have rights, such as the right against assault, the right against theft of their property, and so on. But, Walzer argues, so should states in international society: primarily the rights of territorial integrity and political sovereignty.[24] Of course, states have no independent value aside from the people who make them up. Consequently, says Walzer, we must explain the value of the rights of states in terms of the individual interests they serve if these rights are to be morally defensible. And Walzer thinks such an explanation is possible. It is the exercise of their individual rights as a collective which generates the collective rights of the state, and it is this that generates the presumption against aggressive war. 'When states are attacked,' says Walzer, 'it is their members who are challenged, not only in their lives, but also in the sum of things they value most, including the political association they have made'.[25] Walzer thus endorses international law's prohibition on aggressive war, which he thinks gives protection to the common life that people have formed, which in turn is inextricably linked with the political institutions that they have developed to govern this.

Before considering the question of how humanitarian interventions fit into Walzer's theory, we need to consider an initial possibility for justifying counter-terrorist interventions against the claims of state sovereignty on his theory. It may be thought that terrorist acts, when they have an international dimension, constitute acts of aggression. When a terrorist group in one country targets citizens of another country, for instance, this might be considered to be aggression that justifies a forceful response by those citizens' state. For two reasons, however, I view this possibility as a non-starter.

For one thing, many acts of terrorism are often perpetrated by groups who do not constitute sovereign states. While they may operate within the territories

24 Walzer, *Just and Unjust Wars*, p. 53.

25 *ibid.*, p. 53.

of states, crossing those states' borders without their consent may thus be more problematic than when the threat that justifies intervention comes the state itself. Of course, nothing in the definition of terrorism used here rules out the conceptual possibility of states carrying out acts of terrorism: in such cases, there may be a stronger case for intervening in that state in response. There may even be a case to be made that states which support, fund, or protect terrorist groups operating within their borders are the appropriate target of intervention in response to terrorism.[26] But, since terrorism is often carried out by non-state groups without the support of any state,[27] the proposed justification will be unsuccessful in many cases.

More significantly, though, many acts of terrorism – even terrorist attacks that states are complicit in – cannot be considered to be acts of aggression, even on the most permissive reading of the term as it is used in existing doctrine. Such terrorism does not threaten the integrity of national borders in the way that an invasion does. The attacks in New York and Washington DC on 11 September 2001 killed US citizens, but US territory was not threatened in the same way as an invasion would threaten it. Of course, acts of terrorism could also be committed in the course of an invasion (an invading army might target civilians as well as combatants, for example). In such a case, an act of aggression would have taken place, but it would be the unauthorised border crossing by military forces rather than the terrorism. Since we are primarily concerned with the question of whether terrorism itself might justify foreign interventions here, we can set these cases aside.

So, *if* the only just cause for war is a response to aggression, counter-terrorist interventions will not generally be justified as an act of war. However, Walzer accepts that the rights-based domestic framework should not be transferred to the international sphere (where states, and not individuals, are the holders of rights) without modification. Most relevant for our purposes, he thinks that, in certain cases, intervention to prevent severe government repression might be permissible. In such cases, it is not aggression that provides a just cause for war. Rather, it is the plight of people in foreign countries. It may be thought that this argument could be adopted to justify counter-terrorist interventions as well.

---

26 This rationale is suggested with respect to the 2001 invasion of Afghanistan in Nicholas Fotion, *War and Ethics: A New Just War Theory* (London: Continuum, 2007), p. 29.

27 The fact that non-state groups tend to lack the resources of sovereign states may mean that there are incentives for them to pursue their goals through terrorism. Cf. Nicholas Fotion, Joanne K. Lakea, and Boris Kashnokov, *Terrorism: The New World Disorder* (London: Continuum, 2007), p. 92.

In thinking about the permissibility of humanitarian interventions, Walzer begins by considering the views that John Stuart Mill put forward in his influential piece 'A Few Words on Non-Intervention'. Mill asks whether military force aimed at freeing a people from the rule of a dictator should be used. He arrives at a negative conclusion. For Mill, if a society is to effectively maintain freedom after getting rid of a dictatorial regime, its people must possess certain virtues, and '[t]he only test possessing any real value, of a people's having become fit for popular institutions, is that they, or a sufficient portion of them to prevail in the contest, are willing to brave labour and danger for their liberation'.[28] It is only through struggling for their own freedom, in other words, that they can become properly prepared for that freedom. Crucially, Mill thinks, even outside assistance in the fight for freedom can compromise the development of the necessary virtues: 'if they have not sufficient love of liberty to be able to wrest it from merely domestic oppressors, the liberty which is bestowed on them by other hands than their own, will have nothing real, nothing permanent'.[29]

If Mill is read as making the empirical point that foreign interventions will never create stable democracies, this might be disputed. More recent research suggests that humanitarian interventions can lead to just such a stable regime so long as they are carried out in certain ways.[30] On Walzer's reading, however, the point is at least partly conceptual. The very nature of freedom requires a form of self-determination as a nation which, in turn, involves overcoming one's own challenges without any help.[31] Outside intervention precludes this possibility.

Although Walzer shares Mill's scepticism about the desirability of attempting to 'export democracy' through force, he nonetheless allows that there might be cases in which humanitarian intervention could be justified. These are cases 'when the violation of human rights within a set of boundaries is so terrible that it makes talk of community or self-determination or "arduous struggle" seem cynical and irrelevant, that is, in cases of enslavement or massacre'.[32] In such cases, Walzer's reasons for thinking that states should be treated

28 John Stuart Mill, 'A Few Words on Non-Intervention' in John M. Robson (ed.), *The Collected Works of John Stuart Mill*, vol. 21, *Essays on Equality, Law, and Education* (Toronto: University of Toronto Press, 1984), p. 122.

29 *ibid.*

30 See, for example, Theodora-Ismene Gizelis and Kristin E. Kosek, 'Why Humanitarian Interventions Succeed or Fail: The Role of Local Participation', *Cooperation & Conflict* 40(4) 363–383 (2005).

31 Walzer, *Just and Unjust Wars*, pp. 87–88.

32 *ibid.*, p. 90.

as having rights against external intervention – namely, that the state represents the common life of the individuals, and attacking the state involves an attack on that common life – do not apply. This permission might come close to the principle contained in key R2P documents – in particular the permission to intervene in cases involving the four atrocity crimes, which seem to be paradigmatic cases of a denial of self-determination.

Could this permission generate a justification for counter-terrorist interventions as well, perhaps in countries where terrorists threaten the population? If it does, it will have limited application. Acts of terrorism that would be serious enough to trigger intervention, for Walzer, are unlikely to be perpetrated by sub-state groups, who would lack the resources to conduct them on a scale big enough to count. Some forms of state terrorism might be serious enough, but generally only if it is accompanied by the 'enslavement or massacre' that Walzer envisages undermining state sovereignty. Without reaching that level, the state in question may remain self-determining. Once again, responding to terrorism, by itself, will rarely be considered to be a just cause for war according to collectivist just war theory: few counter-terrorist interventions will be justified.

However, it may be thought that the theory at least has the tools with which we can come to grips with these sorts of conflicts. In the preface to the fourth edition of *Just and Unjust Wars*, Walzer argues that the standard principles of just war theory need to be supplemented with a new set of principles for dealing with cases like this. Because these measures fall short of a full-scale war (and are less destructive as a result), placing requirements meant only for wars would seem to be too stringent: 'We urgently need a theory of just and unjust uses of force. This shouldn't be an overly tolerant or permissive theory, but it will certainly be more permissive than the theory of just and unjust war'.[33] Could such a theory of '*jus ad vim*', as Walzer calls it, justify counter-terrorist interventions, which tend to look precisely like the uses of force short of war that he has in mind, against the claims of state sovereignty? Since, as we saw above, Walzer's account of a just war is unable to justify these because terrorism rarely rises to the level of either aggression or 'enslavement and massacre', this route may appear to be promising.

Such a theory, though, would take us far from the principles of just war theory as standardly understood. Recall that, on Walzer's account, the only two just causes for war are responses to aggression and the prevention of atrocities so serious that the national community suffering them is no longer self-determining. Note that both aggression and self-determination are all-or-nothing

33 *ibid.*, p. xv.

matters: they do not admit of degrees. An invasion constitutes aggression irrespective of the scale of it. Self-determination occurs when a people have a certain degree of control over their shared life; it does not require the maximum degree of control (for example, through democratic mechanisms). What this means is that Walzer cannot rely on a simple modification of the principle of just cause in order to arrive at a corresponding principle for *jus ad vim*. He cannot, that is, simply formulate the principle to say that force short of war would be permissible whenever there is aggression which does not reach the level that would justify warfare, or lack of self-determination which does not reach the level that would justify humanitarian intervention. He would need to identify different sorts of problems that would be appropriately responded to via the force short of war.[34] I conclude that Walzer's collectivist approach will not justify counter-terrorist interventions as acts of war: the value of sovereignty tells against these. This is not to say that they could be justified using another framework, but it goes beyond the scope of this chapter to consider this.

4 Individualist Just War Theory

The collectivist approach has come in for much criticism more generally, especially with respect to its apparent inability to justify many humanitarian interventions. Walzer's qualifications aside, the approach appears to require the international community to stand by even when governments are engaged in heinous acts against their own people. The success of R2P suggests that this is a view that most are not willing to endorse on reflection. An alternative approach, which may be gaining traction in international opinion, would treat individuals as the primary holders of rights. The value of sovereignty on this view, is understood in more individualistic terms. In this section, I consider whether one influential treatment of humanitarian intervention of this sort – put forward by David Luban[35] – will provide more promising resources for defending counter-terrorist interventions against claims of state sovereignty.

---

34 Walzer seems to be aware of this point as he suggests that the prevention, as opposed to the preemption, of aggression might be permitted under *jus ad vim*. See *ibid*. Preventative war is ruled impermissible by Walzer's theory.

35 Luban, 'Just War and Human Rights'. For other individualistic approaches to the just cause for war, see, for example, Cécile Fabre, *Cosmopolitan War* (Oxford: Oxford University Press, 2012); Jeff McMahan, 'Unjust War and the Crime of Aggression' in Claus Kreß and Stefan Barriga (eds.), *The Crime of Aggression: A Commentary*, vol. 2 (Cambridge: Cambridge University Press, 2017).

For Luban, the domestic analogy, by granting rights to states liberally, places value in them too uncritically. Of course, states can be valuable and so we might think that in some circumstances they should be granted rights against non-interference, but this value must ultimately depend on it serving the interests of its citizens. Not all states will do this, but only ones that are legitimate:

> one should distinguish mere de facto exercise of sovereign power from legitimate exercise of it. The natural argument would then be that the duty of non-intervention exists only toward states which are legitimate (in the sense of the term employed in normative political theory).[36]

Individuals, and not states, are the primary possessors of moral rights in this view. If states are properly protected by sovereignty, this is because they are in some sense the collective exercise of individual rights of their citizens. And this is only going to be the case in what Luban terms 'legitimate' states. Something like this idea may underlie the recognition of sovereignty as involving responsibility, which may be viewed as a precursor to the emergence of R2P.[37]

But what conditions need to be in place for a state to be legitimate? Here Luban turns to social contract theory for an answer. According to this view, 'a political community is made legitimate by the consent (tacit or explicit) of its members; it thereby acquires rights which derive from the rights of its members'.[38] But this in turn raises a further question, namely: how can we know whether consent is given? There may of course be rare cases where a political community rises up together in an authentic expression of opposition to a government.[39] But more commonly the question of whether a population has in some sense consented to their state, and even what consent would look like, is more difficult to discern.

Instead of trying to specify the various ways in which a people could express their consent, or lack thereof, Luban turns instead to a framework that makes state sovereignty dependent on human rights. A just cause for war, says Luban, is one in defence of (certain) human rights.[40] Crucially for our purposes, this suggestion looks much more likely to justify humanitarian intervention than

---

36 Luban, 'Just War and Human Rights', p. 164. Note that legitimacy here refers to normative legitimacy, meaning a moral right to rule, and not sociological legitimacy, which refers to being recognised as an agent with a right to rule by others.

37 Francis M. Deng, 'From "Sovereignty as Responsibility" to the "Responsibility to Protect"', *Global Responsibility to Protect* 2, 353–370 (2010).

38 Luban, 'Just War and Human Rights', p. 167.

39 Luban considers a case of this sort in *ibid.*, pp. 170–171.

40 *ibid*, p. 175.

Walzer's collectivist approach. When states are violating the rights of their own citizens, a just cause for war is would be present here even if they are not at the level of seriousness that Walzer requires for intervention to be permissible. Two questions need to be adequately answered if this approach can be sustained, though. First, which rights should be the ones whose violation generates a just cause for war? Second, why should violations of these rights, and only violations of these rights, be considered a just cause for war?

While one possible human rights approach to warfare would hold that *any* violation of human rights would constitute a just cause for war, such a position seems difficult to motivate. Suppose that we think there is a human right to the highest attainable standard of health, and that existing healthcare policies in the United States violated this right. Would a country like Canada be justified in military intervention to ensure the right is met?[41] Most would say not, and not merely because such an intervention would be disproportionate or had undesirable effects on the broader international system, for example. It looks like there are certain rights whose violation does not justify intervention, even in principle.

Luban avoids the implausible implication that such interventions would be potentially justified by restricting just causes for war as a defence of what are called 'basic rights'.[42] In an influential treatment of this concept, Henry Shue writes that a basic right is a right whose enjoyment is a necessary condition of enjoying any other right.[43] The most obvious example of a basic right is a right to security: if individuals lack security – if there is a high risk that they will face physical harm – then they will be unable to enjoy a right to protest, for example. The point is not simply that the right to protest contingently requires a degree of security. The link is more conceptual: the right to protest is normally understood to involve a right to protest *in conditions of security*.[44] (Shue argues that there is also a basic right to subsistence,[45] but we need not concern ourselves with this idea here.)

This explains why basic rights are particularly important and thus also, I think, why there is a presumptive case that violations of basic rights constitute a just cause for intervention in a state. Given that war is an inevitably risky

41 The example is set out in Christopher Kutz, 'Democracy, Defence, and the Threat of Intervention' in Cécile Fabre and Seth Lazar (eds.), *The Morality of Defensive War* (Oxford: Oxford University Press, 2014), pp. 234–235.

42 Luban, 'Just War and Human Rights', p. 175.

43 Henry Shue, *Basic Rights: Subsistence, Affluence, and US Foreign Policy* (Princeton: Princeton University Press, 1980), p. 19.

44 *ibid.*, pp. 21–22.

45 *ibid.*, pp. 22–29.

and damaging activity, it seems likely that we should only pursue it if we think we can achieve something particularly valuable. But why should the failure to meet basic rights be the point at which the prohibition on intervention disappears? Why should it not also be permissible, for example, to intervene to protect other important rights, even if they are not basic? While Luban gives no explicit answer to this question, I think that a rationale for this can be constructed from what he says.

Recall that Luban views political authority to be based on a social contract. The same is true of Walzer, who explains that '"[c]ontract" is a metaphor for a process of association and mutuality, the ongoing character of which the state claims to protect against external encroachment'.[46] The sort of consent that this contract is made valid by is not supposed to be the actual, explicit consent of the governed: few people have actually promised to obey their state. Rather, it is simply by being part of the formation of a common life. Insofar as a state protects that common life, it can be viewed as having a right to rule and a right against external intervention (which derives from the rights of individuals). When a state fails to protect this, it loses these rights, and can no longer claim the protections that go along with sovereignty.

Luban might agree that, through participation within a common life, individuals in some sense consent to a government that protects that life. Nonetheless, he would want to place additional limits on state sovereignty. Walzer's view appears to suggest that any participation is sufficient: short of rule by sheer force, any interaction between a government and a people would constitute a form of consent. For Luban, however, it seems that a more meaningful form of participation is required. On my reading, this is where basic rights come in. If individuals' basic rights are met, they will at least have the necessary preconditions for shaping their society and changing aspects of it that they disagree with. Although it may be difficult to push for change in a society where the full list of democratic freedoms is not respected, one can at least do so in the knowledge that one can be sure of a basic standard of security. This is why I think Luban limits a just cause for humanitarian intervention as the defence of basic rights: when they are met, it looks like there is some participation from society.

Luban's human rights approach is potentially capable of justifying a number of humanitarian interventions. Certainly, a state perpetrating one of the four atrocity crimes of R2P would qualify, but Luban's proposal would probably mean that there is a just cause in other cases too. This is because all violations of basic rights create a presumptive case for intervention, and not just those

46 Walzer, *Just and Unjust Wars*, p. 54.

violations that are widespread enough to collectively qualify as genocide, war crimes, ethnic cleansing, or crimes against humanity. Nonetheless, we might think that relying on something like R2P's more limited permissions is an appropriate way to combine Luban's principled position with more pragmatic factors that need to be considered when formulating an international norm.

Could the approach be used to justify any counter-terrorist interventions? Could the prevention of terrorism be understood as a just cause for war? A potential problem here is that the way in which terrorism tends to undermine rights does not appear to constitute a just cause for war on this approach. Security, of course, is taken to be a basic right by both Luban and Shue, and certain people's security is certainly undermined by acts of terrorism (namely: those who are killed and maimed in terrorist incidents). But this does not show that the presence of terrorism in a country means that basic rights are not met there, and thus that intervention is permissible.

The reason is the following. If governments are to meet the obligations that basic rights place on them, they only need to prevent 'standard threats' to those rights materialising.[47] Just because someone is murdered within a country, this does not mean that the government fails to meet the right to security. For there will always be cases, no matter what the government does, where these sorts of incidents will happen. What governments *are* required to guarantee, however, is to ensure that attacks on the person that arise from *widespread, predictable* and *remediable* causes. It is by protecting their citizens against these sorts of threats that a government most plausibly gains its right to rule. This requirement is most obviously violated when a government turns its power against its own citizens and uses violence to repress any opposition to their rule. But it might also be violated if the state was simply unable to prevent widespread violations of basic rights by sub-state groups operating within its territory. In such cases, citizens owe no obedience to their state as a matter of right (although it may be in their interest to continue to support the failing state if this provides them with the best chances of escaping poverty and insecurity in the long run).

Does terrorism constitute a standard threat to security? Whether this is the case may depend on whether we are talking about state terrorism or non-state terrorism (my definition encompasses both). When a state or state-like entity rules with the use of terrorism, there are certainly standard threats to individuals' security. Those who intervene to rescue the terrorised plausibly have a just cause for war, according to the human rights view. The state terrorism would most likely violate basic rights to security, as understood by Shue, and

47 Shue, *Basic Rights*, pp. 32–33.

might even involve one of the four atrocity crimes of R2P. But terrorist groups, particularly non-state groups, do not always commit violence on such a scale. Their actions tend to be one-off acts of violence that kill or maim a more limited number of targets. On the face of it, this would not be systemic enough to constitute a just cause for war on the approach considered here.

I want to suggest, however, that such an approach might, despite appearances, be fruitfully appealed to in such cases.[48] This will require us to rethink how security as a basic right should be defined, though. Security in this context is normally understood in terms of physical integrity: a condition of security is one in which there is a low probability of being physically harmed. But, on reflection, we might want to expand our conception beyond these concerns. To see this, consider someone who lives in a totalitarian state. She knows that, if she steps out of line, she will be the victim of the repressive state apparatus. Knowing this, she decides to refrain from opposing or even criticising the government. As a result, it may be very unlikely that she will be the victim of physical harm. Nonetheless, many would be reluctant to describe her situation as one of security.

Intuitions aside, I think that there are good reasons to expand our conception of security to cover cases like this. Recall that security is taken to be a basic right because it is necessary for all other rights to be enjoyed. Some forms of physical safety are of course necessary, but one must also be sufficiently free from fear if other rights are to be effectively exercised. This is not to say that all forms of fear are like this: those of us who live in any state may obey laws in part because of a fear of criminal punishment, but it would be implausible to say, on the basis of this, that we are deprived of our basic rights (and this is true even if the laws are not fully just). Rather, I want to suggest, only a certain form of fear undermines our ability to enjoy other rights.

I mean that form of fear that the political theorist Hannah Arendt identifies as the *modus operandi* of totalitarian regimes. In her work *The Origins of Totalitarianism*, she describes 'the bestial, desperate terror which, when confronted by real, present horror, inexorably paralyzes everything that is not a mere reaction'.[49] What Arendt has in mind here, I think, is a form of fear that, unlike ordinary state coercion, which leaves our autonomy intact, undermines any autonomous functioning in those who feel it. They become conditioned to

48 Another strategy, not considered here, is to develop a theory of *jus ad vim* by adjusting the principles of individualistic *jus ad bellum*. See Daniel Brunstetter and Megan Braun, 'From *Jus ad Bellum* to *Jus ad Vim*: Recalibrating Our Understanding of the Moral Use of Force', *Ethics & International Affairs* 27(1) 87–106 (2013).

49 Hannah Arendt, *The Origins of Totalitarianism* (New York: Harcourt, 1968), p. 441.

follow proscribed manners of behaviour which are unthreatening to the ruling elite, perhaps without even realising that they are doing so.

Jeremy Waldron has suggested that it is by appealing to this sort of fear – he refers to it as 'Arendtian terror' – which might be useful in distinguishing terrorism from other forms of coercion.[50] The strategy of some terrorists may not simply be to threaten a group with enough violence that they will rationally choose to make political concessions rather than suffer the promised threat. Rather, they seek to undermine the very capacity for rational deliberation in those who witness acts of violence. They seek to cause a knee-jerk reaction to their deliberately high-profile attacks.

Whatever the intentions of actual terrorists, the effect of their actions might be this form of Arendtian terror in a population. And, by bringing this about, they may undermine individuals' ability to exercise their rights effectively. What good are formal rights to free movement, to peaceful protest, and to vote, for example, if one adapts one's preferences not to engage in the actions that these rights permit as a result of being terrorised? What this shows is that freedom from terror, just as much as freedom from physical assault, should be understood as a precondition for all other rights. And this, in turn, may necessitate expanding the concept of the basic right to security to include freedom from terror as well.[51]

If I am right that freedom from terror should be included within the basic right of security, this suggests a way in which Luban's theory might be appealed to in order to justify counter-terrorist interventions as well as humanitarian interventions, against claims of state sovereignty. In both cases, the rationale is the same: disregarding the sovereignty of a foreign state can be justified in order to protect the basic right to security of those in the target state. Just because terrorist groups generally do not pose a standard threat to physical safety, this does not mean that they do not pose a standard threat to security. And responding to such a standard threat, just as much as responding to a standard threat to physical safety, might be considered to be a just cause for war.

---

50 Jeremy Waldron, *Torture, Terror, and Trade-Offs: Philosophy for the White House* (Oxford: Oxford University Press, 2010), pp. 48–79.

51 One might, alternatively, think that there is a basic right to freedom from terror that is distinct from the basic right to physical safety. Nothing in my argument here hinges on how concerns about terror are incorporated into a framework of basic rights.

5 Institutionalisation

I have suggested that state sovereignty – which is given significant weight in just war theory – need not pose a barrier to counter-terrorist interventions, so long as we adopt certain individualistic premises. But this does not tell us whether such operations should be permitted by international law and norms more generally. It has often been noted that the overall permissibility of an international practice regarding war must take into account the effects of institutionalisation of the practice. In some cases, having an institution in place may make otherwise problematic actions permissible.[52] In other cases, however, institutionalisation may result in unintended and undesirable side-effects,[53] or agents may lack the necessary knowledge to correctly apply principles specifying permissible action.[54] While these might be common problems for institutionalising frameworks surrounding war and peace, I will suggest in this section that there are particularly acute problems that would plague any prospect of permitting counter-terrorist interventions in international norms.

In a recent article, Elisabeth Forster and Isaac Taylor argue that various influential norms governing the use of force in the international sphere are problematic because they can be co-opted by international actors to justify particularistic actions that go against the intention of the norms' framers. Insofar as the actions that are made possible by appeal to these norms subvert the stated goal that the normative frameworks as a whole are supposed to serve – normally understood as peace – we might view their use in the international sphere as self-defeating.[55] Implementing these sorts of norms will take us further away from the goal that their institutionalisation was supposed to bring us closer to.

52 Allen Buchanan and Robert O. Keohane, 'The Preventative Use of Force: A Cosmopolitan Institutional Proposal', *Ethics & International Affairs* 18(1) 1–22 (2012). Relatedly, it might be thought, the move to different types of war that existing institutions do not neatly cover is problematic because it makes going to war easier. See Michael Ignatieff, *Virtual War: Kosovo and Beyond* (London: Picador, 2001).

53 Ken Booth, 'Ten Flaws of Just Wars', *The International Journal of Human Rights* 4(3–4) 314–324 (2007), pp. 316–317. Relatedly, it has been thought that actors can often pursue illegitimate goals by using law that they would otherwise pursue with more conventional military operations. See Charles J. Dunlap, Jr, 'Lawfare Today…and Tomorrow', *International Law Studies* 87, 315–325 (2011).

54 Janina Dill, 'Should International Law Ensure the Moral Acceptability of War', *Leiden Journal of International Law* 26(2) 253–270 (2013).

55 Elisabeth Forster and Isaac Taylor, 'Asking the Fox to Guard the Chicken Coop: In Defense of Minimalism in the Ethics of War and Peace', *Journal of International Political Theory* 18(1) 91–109 (2022).

What is the problem with these norms? Forster and Taylor argue that they involve 'essentially contested concepts', that is concepts whose internally complex nature means that there is no universally recognised way of adjudicating between rival interpretations of them.[56] Because a number of different, and incompatible, definitions of the concepts in question can be put forward, self-serving international actors are free to deploy whatever specification of them best suits their purposes. For example, as we saw above, many existing frameworks governing warfare state that a just cause for war will normally be a response to aggression, where aggression is understood as a threat to the territorial integrity of a state. But issues arise once we begin to try to draw the line between aggression and non-aggression. Where do borders really lie? What if two states disagree about the legitimacy of a claimed border? Since both sides in such a case could claim that the other has engaged in an unlawful border crossing, the norm against aggression would lack any of the constraining effect that the framers of international law intended. This, Forster and Taylor maintain, is precisely what happened in the Korean War of 1950–1953.[57]

We are now in a position to see a problem with developing any norms justifying counter-terrorist interventions. Such norms would permit military action across borders in response to terrorism. But terrorism itself might be considered to be an essentially contested concept. The platitude 'one man's terrorist is another man's freedom fighter' is at least correct if it is understood as making a sociological claim about the way in which the label of terrorism is used. Many groups have been called terrorists, but these accusations are often controversial and made without clear criteria. Since the concept of terrorism is elastic in this way, it looks dangerous to grant a permission to engage in warfare dependent on one's opponents being plausibly portrayed as terrorists. It would be too easy for unscrupulous actors to co-opt such a framework and launch unjustified wars on the basis of a mere accusation of terrorism. Although Forster and Taylor do not mention the concept of terrorism, it looks like an essentially contested concept in much the same way as aggression is. And, if worries about the use of essentially contested concepts in international norms governing armed conflict are well-founded, this is a problem for the sort of norm under consideration.

It may be objected here that there is a quick fix to this. So long as we set out a clear definition of terrorism – maybe along the lines of the one I sketched in

---

56 *ibid.*, pp. 98–99. The idea of an essentially contested concept originates in W. B. Gallie, 'Essentially Contested Concepts', *Proceedings of the Aristotelian Society* 56, 167–198 (1955–56).

57 Forster and Taylor, 'Asking the Fox to Guard the Chicken Coop', pp. 101–102.

the introduction – there would be no possibility of manipulation. We could then welcome a norm that permitted (and even encouraged) counter-terrorist interventions without worrying too much about it being abused. Just because terrorism lacks a universally acknowledged definition now, we can imagine one being specified in the future.[58]

However, I am not sure that this strategy would solve the problem entirely. There are, in fact, two reasons why institutionalising a definition of terrorism may not allay the worries discussed here. The first is that, given the sort of actors who tend to use terrorism, it may often be difficult to prove that a certain group has committed acts of terrorism and, more importantly, it may also be difficult to prove that they have not. Terrorist groups, especially groups that emerged in the last few decades, are often highly decentralised. The individuals who commit acts of terrorism often have only a very loose connection with the overall group. The extreme case of this, of course, is the so-called 'lone wolf' terrorist who merely relies on leaders to provide inspiration and guidance. But other cases in which resources are provided to the 'franchises' of a fragmented terrorist organisation have also been seen: this was the way in which Al-Qaeda operated under Osama bin Laden, for example.[59] It may well be difficult to conclusively prove the link between a group and an individual terrorist in such circumstances, and it might thus be difficult to justify military action against the group as an act of terrorism. But some political actors may well play on the inevitable uncertainty that is involved in such assessments to argue that a tight connection need not be proven in order for a counter-terrorist intervention to be warranted.

The second reason is that the concept of terrorism has an emotive content. It is not merely a label that one attaches to an individual or group for the purposes of conceptual clarity. Rather, when we make the case that an organisation are terrorists, we mean to condemn them on the basis of this. What this means is that the plausibility of an accusation of terrorism may depend just as much on how the target of the accusation is viewed by a constituency as its meeting certain objective standards. Thus, even if an international body were to set out a precise definition of terrorism, it would still be possible for unscrupulous actors to depart from it. Just because a particular concept ceases

58 Coming to authoritative definitions of terms is suggested as a solution to the more general problem of the co-option of normative frameworks in Lonneke Peperkamp, 'Restraining the Fox: Minimalism in the Ethics of War and Peace', *Journal of International Political Theory* 18(1) 110–122 (2022), pp. 112–113.

59 Peter L. Bergen, *Holy War, Inc.: Inside the Secret World of Osama bin Laden* (New York: Touchstone, 2002).

being essentially contested, this does not mean that it would not continue to be *contestable* by those acting in bad faith.

The potential for international norms to be co-opted in this way, of course, is not unique to those norms surrounding counter-terrorism. Indeed, R2P itself might be similarly vulnerable. This is what some commentators think happened, for example, when the Sri Lankan government appealed to R2P in order to justify military action against the Liberation Tigers of Tamil Eelam in 2009, where between 150,000 and 300,000 civilians were caught up in the conflict – on some readings this might in fact count as an atrocity crime itself.[60] Nonetheless, it might be thought that counter-terrorist norms might be even more vulnerable, given certain limiting tendencies of R2P.[61] Even if we think that misapplications of R2P can be reined in, and thus that the problems of institutionalising it are minimal, then, it may still be the case that any counter-terrorist norm regime built on similar principles would be problematic.

Is there any alternative to using essentially contested concepts (or concepts that are contestable)? Forster and Taylor argue for a principle of 'minimalism' to guide the development of international norms surrounding armed conflict. This would require these norms to be formulated without essentially contested concepts, in such a way that would reduce the possibilities for manipulation. While working in an international environment while constrained by minimalist norms may well form a barrier to some justified uses of armed conflict, the overall benefits in reining in illegitimate forms of violence may be worth the cost. When applied to counter-terrorism, this principle suggests that the optimal normative framework would not encourage or allow foreign interventions to fight terrorists, since this would invite abuse. It may be better to limit (legal) just causes for wars and other uses of force to simpler, less contestable, evils, such as the four atrocity crimes of R2P.

While an individualistic version of just war theory – such as the human rights approach of Luban – appears capable of justifying counter-terrorist interventions in isolation, then, an international norm based on this permission might be undesirable. Of course, the problems that Forster and Taylor identify may plague a wide variety of international norms governing the use of force, these problems might be particularly acute in the case at hand, considering the emotive nature of the concept of terrorism, as well as the sociological

60 Zimmerman, 'Strange Bedfellows', pp. 136–138.

61 Ned Dobos, 'On the Uses and "Abuses" of Responsibility to Protect', in C. A. J. Coady, Ned Dobos, and Sagar Sanyal (eds.), *Challenges for Humanitarian Intervention: Ethical Demand and Political Reality* (Oxford: Oxford University Press, 2018).

factors that make proving (or disproving) that a certain group is engaged in terrorism difficult.

6 Conclusion

This chapter has urged caution in welcoming a norm that would legitimate foreign interventions as part of a counter-terrorist strategy. While the importance of respecting state sovereignty may not pose a moral barrier to such operations, the question of institutionalisation of norms permitting them raises further issues that should limit our enthusiasm. Nonetheless, we should remember that counter-terrorism can and should be a multifaceted phenomenon. The other aspects of the emerging counter-terrorism norm regime – especially those that support building states' capacity to prevent and combat terrorism – may look less susceptible to manipulation that norms governing the use of force.[62] For this reason, any support that this aspect of the norm regime can receive from the corresponding second pillar of R2P might be viewed as more desirable.

62 Forster and Taylor argue that it is norms surrounding the use of military force that are the most problematic in this regard. See Forster and Taylor, 'Asking the Fox to Guard the Chicken Coop', p. 105.

CHAPTER 3

'Are All Humans Human? Or Are Some More Human than Others?' R2P, Terrorism, and the Protection of Civilians

Sascha Nanlohy
Sessional Academic, School of Social and Political Sciences, University of Sydney, Sydney, Australia
sascha.nanlohy@sydney.edu.au

Abstract

Terrorism is often cited in the justifications of state perpetrators of mass atrocities. The reality behind these claims runs the gamut from thin pretext to genuine security threats. Irrespective of this reality, the discursive abuse of counter-terrorism to perpetrate atrocities is a key challenge to the Responsibility to Protect. Perpetrators employing the language of counter-terrorism to justify their actions, in an attempt to pre-empt objections or interventions, disincentivises external action by actors unwilling to incur the risk that they may inadvertently protect terrorists. This risks limiting the application and successful operationalisation of the Responsibility to Protect to relatively simple or ideal cases. This chapter provides a comparative analysis of two crises often described as successes or failures for R2P, Kenya (2007–08) and Sri Lanka (2009) respectively, to demonstrate this challenge for the operationalisation of R2P even in cases with complex conflict dynamics.

Keywords

terrorism – Sri Lanka – Kenya – operationalisation – R2P

 | DOI:10.1163/9789004548114_005

1 Introduction

The Responsibility to Protect (R2P) and counter-terrorism are thematic norms that have emerged concurrently in the early years of the twenty-first century.[1] R2P sets out a normative framework to prevent mass atrocities, emphasising sovereign responsibility. It established the international community's responsibility to prevent, react, and rebuild – interventions scaling in severity with the use of force as a last resort.[2] Counter-terrorism came to dominate the lives of much of the world following the 9/11 attacks on the United States and subsequent War on Terror. Counter-terrorism prioritises the degrading and destruction of terrorist groups and networks to prevent future attacks, sometimes at the expense of civil liberties. These two norms share a focus on state responsibility with transnational coordination and cooperation. While both effectively focus on protection of civilians, counter-terrorism has complicated the operationalisation of R2P. This chapter examines the challenge that has, and will likely continue to, hamper the operationalisation of R2P. That is, how does the international community respond to situations, such as those in Sri Lanka, Syria, China, Myanmar or Ethiopia, where civilians are at risk of mass atrocities, but perpetrators employ the language of counter-terrorism to justify their actions and pre-empt objections or interventions? While in some cases this language is employed to create a securitised fig leaf of legitimacy for repression, the more bedevilling problem is when there *are* terrorist groups embedded within vulnerable civilian populations.

Perpetrators are too often able to justify atrocities under the guise of counter-terrorism. This in turn disincentivises external action by actors unwilling to incur the risk that they may inadvertently protect terrorists. The mixing of mass atrocities with legitimate counter-terrorism also adds complexity as to whether and how R2P applies. Debates over legitimacy, sovereignty, and proportionality can slow or stall the authorisation and operationalisation of external interventions. In effect, employing the terrorism card has become a licence to commit atrocities. This research does not seek to discredit or undermine the value and importance of R2P in advancing the prevention of mass atrocities; however, this problem speaks to the limits of R2P's universality and is reflective of Romeo Dallaire's question: 'are all humans human? Or are some more human than others?'[3] I argue that the oversimplification of conflict dynamics

1 I want to thank Shannon Zimmerman, Rhiannon Neilsen, and the two anonymous reviewers for their assistance and feedback in the development of this chapter.

2 Gareth Evans, *The Responsibility to Protect: Ending Mass Atrocity Crimes Once and for All* (Washington DC: Brookings Institution Press, 2008).

3 Romeo Dallaire, *Shake Hands with the Devil: The Failure of Humanity in Rwanda* (Toronto: Random House Canada, 2003), p. 522.

in mass atrocity cases, and the framing that is often necessary to mobilise sufficient political will, inhibits the application and operationalisation of R2P in cases where bad actors are embedded within populations. The inability to parse the legitimate use of force in counter-terror or counter-insurgency operations and deliberate campaigns of atrocities allows international actors to obfuscate and delay action, or simply do nothing. In retrospect, these failures then manifest in claims of partiality or weakness.

It is imperative to interrogate the potential weaknesses and failures to protect for two reasons. First, these failures often hold vital lessons for future attempts. Second, they drive discussion and debate that is critical to the normative power of R2P. This much is made abundantly clear by the overt focus on the failures of the Libyan intervention. Yet the intervention in Ivory Coast was contemporaneous to Libya, and although not perfect, was far more successful. Often, the debate over R2P is driven far more by discussions of Libya, Syria, and Myanmar than it is Kenya, Guinea, or Kyrgyzstan. Advancing human protection via the R2P requires engaging with critiques from actors of both good and bad faith, with the latter eager to hobble progress where their self-interest is threatened.

This chapter offers a comparative case analysis to demonstrate the problem of how narratives of counter-terrorism affect the operationalisation of R2P across temporally comparable cases of international responses to mass atrocities. I compare the case of Kenya following the 2007 presidential election with Sri Lanka in 2009 during the final months of the civil war. Both (otherwise significantly different) cases have been discussed as successes or failures of R2P. I argue that the issue of terrorism wrapped in geopolitical imperatives in both cases augmented the international incentives that likely had an effect on the response to each respective crisis. This analysis expands our understanding of the variation of outcomes in these cases, comparing the rapid and relatively effective response to Kenya's post-election violence with the manifest failure to protect Tamil civilians in areas under the control of the Liberation Tigers of Tamil Eelam (LTTE). While there are many dissimilarities between these cases, their temporal similarity allows some control for the international community's attitude to R2P.

2 The Terrorist Card: A Licence to Commit Atrocities

Countering terrorism is often at the core of justification of states' use of force. Liberation movements during decolonisation and beyond were often labelled terrorist organisations. In some cases, this was relatively accurate but was nevertheless used to justify disproportionate repression.[4] Most prominent among external justifications for intervention is the US 'War on Terror', waged predominantly under the second Bush administration and to varying degrees thereafter. The United States and state actors often used the label of terrorism as an instrument to legitimise overt and covert intervention. US support for the Contras in Nicaragua was premised on their fight against 'terrorist' Sandinistas – the act of labelling a critical element of the broader strategy.[5] Before and after the onset of the war on terror, Russia used the language of terrorism to describe the actions of Chechen rebels, sometimes with justification, implicitly justifying the atrocities of their counter-insurgency wars.[6] Terrorism has also been shown to reduce the likelihood of external intervention in favour of those actors who use terror attacks as a strategy.[7] Whether the likelihood of intervention influences the use or framing of opposition actors as terrorists is uncertain; it does, however, fit a logic that would seek to dissuade support for opposition groups. There is no accepted definition of terrorism, for the purposes of this chapter I adopt that of the Report of the High-Level Panel on Threats, Challenges and Change:

> any action, in addition to actions already specified by the existing conventions on aspects of terrorism, the Geneva Conventions and Security Council resolution 1566 (2004), that is intended to cause death or serious bodily harm to civilians or non-combatants, when the purpose of such an act, by its nature or context, is to intimidate a population, or to compel a Government or an international organization to do or to abstain from doing any act.[8]

How terrorism is used and abused as a label clearly affects the likelihood and nature of R2P being applied. For the most part, this is often extremely challenging in cases where some truth exists around the use of terrorism. Real and

4 David Anderson, *Histories of the Hanged: The Dirty War in Kenya and the End of Empire* (New York: W. W. Norton, 2005).

5 Michael J. Schroeder, 'Bandits and Blanket Thieves, Communists and Terrorists: The Politics of Naming Sandinistas in Nicaragua, 1927–36 and 1979–90', *Third World Quarterly*, 26(1) 67–86 (2005).

6 John Russell, 'Terrorists, Bandits, Spooks and Thieves: Russian Demonization of the Chechens before and since 9/11', *Third World Quarterly*, 26(1) 101–116 (2005).

7 Charity Butcher, 'Terrorism and External Audiences: Influencing Foreign Intervention into Civil Wars', *Terrorism and Political Violence*, 28(4) 774–794 (2016).

8 United Nations, *Report of the Secretary-General's High-Level Panel on Threats, Challenges and Change: A More Secure World: Our Shared Responsibility*, A/59/565, 2 December 2004, para. 164.

significant terror threats do exist in particular cases and states hold the legitimate authority to address those threats. The problem arises where the methods and strategies of counter-terrorism are instead applied across an entire group, as is common in counter-insurgency. The process in which counter-terrorism campaigns can morph into mass atrocities is similar, and at times indistinguishable, from the process Ernesto Verdeja describes of counter-insurgency,

> Counterinsurgency campaigns … may become genocidal if state forces move from combating rebel forces to targeting for destruction the civilian groups that ostensibly support the rebellion. These campaigns may begin by killing individual political opponents, forced relocations, and widespread and indiscriminate killings of their supporters; and eventually coalesce into policies of systematic and deliberate destruction of the group.[9]

There are cases where minor threats are magnified as part of an effort to justify atrocities against a larger ethnic group. In 2017, the Tatmadaw campaign that killed at least 10,000 Rohingya civilians and expelled 700,000 into Bangladesh was framed and justified as a response to attacks by the Arakan Rakhine Salvation Army (ARSA).[10] While ARSA committed terror attacks, they were a relatively weak and small group whose violence was a thin justification for a disproportionate military campaign that deliberately killed and targeted civilians on the basis of their ethnicity and religion.[11] Terrorism has been invoked in justifications of repression and systematic destruction of Uyghur culture by Chinese authorities in Xinxiang.[12] In Ethiopia in 2020 and 2021, descriptions of Tigrayans as terrorists were commonly used in justifications of atrocities committed by Ethiopian and Eritrean forces.[13]

Terrorism framing and strategies that can be justified as counter-terrorism easily meld into the toxification of target groups as security necessitates

---

9 Ernesto Verdeja, 'Debating Definitions' in Adam Lupel and Ernesto Verdeja (eds.), *Responding to Genocide: The Politics of International Action* (Boulder CO: Lynne Rienner Publishers, 2013), p. 40.

10 Ronan Lee, *Myanmar's Rohingya Genocide: Identity, History and Hate Speech* (London, I.B. Tauris, 2021).

11 *ibid.*

12 Sheena Chestnut Greitens, Myunghee Lee, and Emir Yazici, 'Counterterrorism and Preventive Repression: China's Changing Strategy in Xinjiang', *International Security*, 44(3) 9–47 (2020).

13 Australian Broadcasting Corporation, 'Ethiopia Conflict in Tigray Region Sparks War Crime Fears as some 14,500 Flee to Sudan, UN says', 14 November 2020.

action, under what Jonathan Leader Maynard describes as 'atrocity-justifying ideologies'.[14] Such justifications are often thin, yet the responsibility to protect civilians remains even in cases where terrorism is ongoing and atrocities occur amidst legitimate military or policing operations. Yet there is insufficient discussion of how to sufficiently manage this tension. Alan Kuperman has clearly demonstrated the vexing issue of terrorism and intervention where an Islamic terrorist uprising coincided with other moderate demonstrations in Libya.[15] His argument illustrates why there are risks in intervening where conflict dynamics are complex and there are risks of adverse consequences. Indeed, it is only in the Libyan case where such concerns were largely put aside by intervening NATO forces. However, as Alex Bellamy and Stephen McLoughlin describe it, the confluence of international dynamics that allowed the use of force in Libya was extremely rare and is unlikely to manifest on regular occasions.[16] The post-intervention fall-out in Libya has been at the core of much of the criticism by those sceptical of R2P.

3 R2P's Dilemma: Political Will vs. Conflict Complexity

The problem of the protection of civilians in cases involving bad actors, terrorists in particular, is perhaps driven by the original narratives that informed efforts to protect them. The adoption of the responsibility to protect was a monumental achievement for its proponents. The 2005 United Nations World Summit adopted the R2P with the following tenets: states have the responsibility to protect their people; the international community must engage to empower states in their responsibility; and should a state 'manifestly fail' in its responsibility, the international community has the responsibility to protect civilians.[17] While both sovereign and international responsibility has a

14 Rhiannon S. Neilsen, '"Toxification" as a More Precise Early Warning Sign for Genocide than Dehumanization? An Emerging Research Agenda', *Genocide Studies and Prevention: An International Journal*, 9(1) 83–95 (2015); Jonathan Leader Maynard, 'Combatting Atrocity-Justifying Ideologies' in Serena K. Sharma and Jennifer M. Welsh (eds.), *The Responsibility to Prevent: Overcoming the Challenges of Atrocity Prevention* (Oxford: Oxford University Press, 2015).

15 Alan J. Kuperman, 'Did the R2P Foster Violence in Libya?', *Genocide Studies and Prevention: An International Journal*, 13(2) 37–57 (2019).

16 Alex J. Bellamy and Stephen McLoughlin, 'Human Protection and the Politics of Armed Intervention: With Responsibility Comes Accountability', *Global Responsibility to Protect*, 11(3) 333–361 (2019).

17 '2005 World Summit Outcome', UNGA Res. 60/1, 16 September 2005, p. 30.

long history, this was a major development.[18] Yet the need for R2P was overwhelmingly framed in light of two major examples of genocide and mass atrocities that necessitated such a radical shift in the international system, the genocides in Rwanda and Bosnia. In both cases there were clear, unambiguous examples of genocide that required an immediate response, yet that response was inadequate or not forthcoming. The failure to respond was key to the debates regarding sovereignty and intervention in the galvanising of the international community to support the concept at the UN World Summit. The framing was arguably essential to drive the political will required for R2P, emphasising the innocence of victims as a better case for action – especially where that action is as significant as the last resort mechanism of the use of force. This framing extends to domestic justifications for interventions. But what little support may be generated for supporting an intervention will certainly be hampered by recognising any inherent complexity and difficulty in application. A Manichean framing is needed, and in some cases does come closer to reflecting a reality. This framing, however, creates challenges for cases where ambiguity exists. Where bad actors are embedded within, or form part of a target group, it becomes simpler to do nothing to avoid the risk of being seen to or actually providing material support to terror groups or insurgencies in the name of humanitarian action. Rather, the framing for conflict and response falls into counter-insurgency or counter-terrorism; where multiple frames could coexist there is confusion and space for obfuscation, disincentivising effective action. The stakes are high for intervention, as Bellamy and McLoughlin contend, and the cost of inaction relatively meagre. Few votes are clearly to be won intervening in foreign humanitarian crises – and even where successful, the political costs of failure or casualties are far clearer.[19] In such a context the incidental support of terror groups would present a serious political risk, at least for democratic interveners. As such the framing of events as terrorism and counter-terrorism, rather than some other form of political violence, is perhaps more important than the violence itself. An honest cogent assessment of the complex conflict dynamics and the real potential cost and actual consequences are often missing. Where ambiguity exists, the likelihood of inaction, late or insufficient action increases. We are too often left with perfect or ideal cases for R2P – that is, clear cases of mass atrocities with simple or

18 Luke Glanville, *Sharing Responsibility: The History and Future of Protection from Atrocities* (Princeton: Princeton University Press, 2021).

19 Bellamy and McLoughlin, 'Human Protection and the Politics of Armed Intervention', p. 345.

simplified conflict dynamics or narratives, where external interests incentivise action, and the risks of adverse consequences are low.

This is a fundamental problem for the progress of the R2P given cases involving a high risk of mass atrocities that include ambiguity and bad actors on both sides of a conflict. Casting groups only as perpetrator and target, evil and innocent, may suit short-term appeals to mobilise political will but are often thin narratives, easily deconstructed. Conflicts are generally complex, and the existence of bad actors within a target population should not reduce the expectations of protection afforded to vulnerable civilians.

To illustrate this issue I draw upon two case studies, a year apart, roughly within the same international context: Kenya and the post-election crisis of 2007–2008 and the final stages of the Sri Lankan civil war between January and May of 2009. The starkly different responses – swift and effective in Kenya versus the manifest failure to protect vulnerable Tamil civilians in Sri Lanka – lay bare the problem presented in this chapter. Kenya was an ideal case for R2P in which compromise between the conflicting parties remained possible and the international community's interests clearly incentivised the forceful response. This compared to the broadly insufficient actions of the international community in Sri Lanka. In that case, the prospect of protecting civilians may have also entailed the possibility of incidentally supporting a terror group and acted against counter-terrorism. This, seemingly, dissuaded strong action from Western actors. Sri Lanka rejected attempts to intervene on the grounds that by fighting terrorism they were protecting civilians, invoking Pillar One of R2P, which enshrines responsibility to protect civilians with the sovereign state.[20] Responsibility was deferred to India, who in turn were hamstrung by geopolitical concerns, which combined with their hatred of the LTTE informed a permissive attitude to the slaughter of civilians. Ambiguity drove ambivalence, and even after the conflict ended, action to hold perpetrators accountable has been largely ineffective or absent. In the debates regarding R2P, Kenya is often held up as a success story; Sri Lanka, on the other hand, has been often neglected or forgotten for the ambiguity and multiple frames that applied to the case. The effect of terrorism and counter-terrorism does not provide a causal explanation for the variation of outcomes across these two cases. Nevertheless, I argue terrorism framing is an important factor that can aid explanation and demonstrates a broader problem with the operationalisation of R2P.

20 Shannon Zimmerman, 'Strange Bedfellows: Terrorism/Counter-terrorism and the Responsibility to Protect' in Charles T. Hunt, Phil Orchard (eds), *Constructing the Responsibility to Protect: Contestation and Consolidation*, (London: Routledge, 2020), p. 9.

4 Kenya

In the wake of disputed elections in December 2007, at least 1,133 people were killed, thousands wounded, and 350,000 displaced.[21] The violence, predicated on a conflict between ethno-nationalist political parties, was quelled by a mediation team of eminent African personalities who brokered a political solution for a power-sharing government.

Mass atrocities do not occur in a vacuum. The 2007 Kenyan presidential election results sparked a latent conflict with a significant risk of mass atrocities. Yet the broad support for peace from Kenyan society, the lack of involvement from Kenya's armed forces, and the absence of difficult actors, like terror groups, made it far easier to resolve than many other crises to which the R2P label is attached.[22] Resolution was also made easier by virtue of geopolitical interests that incentivised Kenyan stability.

Despite public commitments to peaceful campaigning, the 2007 election campaign affirmed divisive tribal politics. Fought between Raila Odinga's Orange Democratic Movement (ODM) and President Mwai Kibaki's People's National Union (PNU), both sought to generate fear of the other to provoke mass turnout. Elections 'heightened expectations of Kenyans by promising to redress these issues overnight', thereby raising the stakes of electoral victory.[23] The ODM framed the Kibaki administration and ethnic Kikuyus as one and the same, using decolonisation-era populism through its 'Kenya against the Kikuyu' rhetoric to invent a class from an ethnic group.[24] Their campaign targeted prominent Kikuyus 'in banking, government, trade, outmigration, education, and commercial farming'.[25] Hate speech was broadcast in which 'Kikuyus were identified … as *madoadoa* [a Kiswahili word for stains or spots] translated in this specific context as spotted hyenas to be violently expelled from the Rift Valley'.[26] Such language is a sign of toxification, a process using language to construct a group as a threat which is synonymous with impending

21 Truth, Justice, and Reconciliation Commission of Kenya, 'Commission of Inquiry into Post Election Violence, *Waki Report*, Nairobi, 2008, p. 305 (*Waki Report*).

22 Monica Kathina Juma, 'African Mediation of the Kenyan post-2007 Election Crisis', *Journal of Contemporary African Studies*, 27(3) 407–430 (2009).

23 Njoki S. Ndungu, 'Kenya: The December 2007 Election Crisis', *Mediterranean Quarterly*, 19(4) 111–121 (2008), p. 113.

24 Peter Kagwanja, 'Courting Genocide: Populism, Ethno-nationalism and the Informalisation of Violence in Kenya's 2008 Post-Election Crisis', *Journal of Contemporary African Studies*, 3(27) 365–387 (2009), p. 374.

25 *ibid.*

26 Kagwanja, 'Courting Genocide', p. 380.

mass atrocities.[27] For Kikuyus, the idea that survival was contingent on a PNU victory became prominent. So virulent was the nature of anti-Kikuyu propaganda, PNU strategists easily cultivated fear of an ODM win, as Peter Kagwanja noted:

> anti-Kikuyu leaflets were circulated in the Rift Valley ... it was alleged that if the ODM won the elections it planned to carry out genocide against no less than one million Kikuyu in order to change Kenya's electoral demography permanently to ensure that the ODM ruled in perpetuity.[28]

The intended effect of this propaganda was to strike fear in Kikuyu voters ahead of the vote. Scapegoating and fear-mongering on both sides built a self-perpetuating fear of the outcome of the election.

4.1 *The Election and Post-election Violence*

On 27 December 2007 Kenyans voted in parliamentary and presidential elections. The ODM dominated the early parliamentary election results; however, as the presidential result was delayed, suspicions of interference radiated.[29] Under a cloud of suspicion the Electoral Commission of Kenya announced the presidential results on 30 December, delivering victory to the PNU and Kibaki.[30] This set off a wave of violent activity, some spontaneous, while others, in areas of the Rift Valley, pointed towards long-term preparation. Minutes after the election results were announced in Eldoret the houses of Kikuyu elders were set alight.[31] Fighters, armed with machetes and petrol bombs, were transported to the area by lorries.[32] Witnesses reported that anti-Kikuyu militia identified each other by painting their faces with white ochre. Leaders of the gangs identified houses to be burned and those to be spared, demonstrating prior preparation.[33] The burning of the Kenyan Assemblies of God church in Kiambaa outside Eldoret crystallised the escalatory potential of the violence. Around 200 Kalenjin youths converged on the church, where over 100 Kikuyu women and children had sought sanctuary. The youths surrounded

27 Neilsen, 'Toxification'.

28 Kagwanja, 'Courting Genocide', p. 374.

29 *ibid.*, p. 368.

30 George Wachira, Thomas Arendshorst, and Simon Charles, *Citizens in Action: Making Peace in the Post-Election Crisis in Kenya – 2008* (Nairobi: NPI-Africa, 2010), p. 3.

31 Kimani Njogui (ed.), *Healing the Wound: Personal Narratives About the 2007 Post-Election Violence in Kenya* (Nairobi: Twaweza Communications, 2009), p. 18.

32 *ibid.*, p. 19.

33 *ibid.*, pp. 20–21.

the church, using mattresses to block escape, and set it alight killing 28 and injuring 54.[34] Kiambaa garnered significant media coverage both inside Kenya and internationally.

Kenyan police also bear responsibility – 405 deaths were attributed to police.[35] While some occurred amidst riots, Human Rights Watch found that 'the majority of people shot in Kisumu died in the residential slum areas far from the shops in the commercial center' where demonstrations took place.[36] Retaliatory violence began as displaced Kikuyus arrived in Central Province with Kikuyu militias attacking Luos in Nakuru and Naivasha.[37] In one incident, Kikuyu youths blocked the highway to Nakuru and demanded to see the identity cards of anyone stopped. While Kikuyus passed unharmed, Luo or Kalenjin were murdered.[38] Justifications for atrocity were also seemingly proffered at lower levels of Kikuyu leadership as Raila Odinga and Luos were branded as terrorists and devil worshippers planning a revolution.[39] While it may not be possible to know what would have occurred in Kenya without internal and external responses to de-escalate the crisis, there can be relative confidence that Kenya was at a significant risk of further, more extensive atrocities.

4.2 *Kenya's Strategic Importance*

As violence intensified, the international community responded with speed and coordination. This may have been due to the economic and strategic importance of Kenya in trade and counter-terrorism. The unified response of the international community was led by former UN Secretary-General Kofi Annan and was underpinned by an implicit commitment to the responsibility to protect. As Annan later reflected,

> I saw the crisis in the R2P prism with a Kenyan government unable to contain the situation or protect its people ... I knew if the international community did not intervene things would go hopelessly wrong ... Kenya is a successful example of R2P at work.[40]

34 *Waki Report*, p. 46.

35 *ibid.*, pp. 311, 342–343.

36 Human Rights Watch, *Ballots to Bullets: Organized Political Violence and Kenya's Crisis of Governance* (New York: Human Rights Watch, 2008), p. 28.

37 Office of the United Nations High Commissioner for Human Rights, *Report from OHCHR Fact-Finding Mission to Kenya 6–28 February 2008*, p. 10.

38 International Crisis Group, *Kenya in Crisis*, Crisis Group Africa Report no. 137, 21 February 2008, p. 13.

39 *Waki Report*, p. 216.

40 Roger Cohen, 'How Kofi Annan Rescued Kenya', *New York Review of Books*, 55(13) (14 August 2008), p. 52.

'We cannot let this happen to Kenya', said Annan arriving in Nairobi on 22 January.[41] The assumption that the international community could not afford to let Kenya fail, and that failure was considered a possibility, drove the response. Kenya, regardless of its internal issues, was perceived as a beacon of stability. The international hub for East Africa: host to the continental headquarters for media, non-governmental and international organisations.[42] In that period, Kenya played a critical role in the war on terror – this made its stability even more critical. Since the Al Qaeda bombing of the US embassy in Nairobi in 1998 the US understood the importance of Kenya as a partner in the war on terror, even before 9/11. The Bush administration saw Kenya as a bulwark against Islamic terror in the Horn of Africa and contributed over 200 million dollars to counter-terrorism funding in Kenya from 2003 to 2006, held regular joint exercises, and collaborated closely on operations.[43] US awareness of Kenya's significance would have been further informed by the emergence of Al Shabaab in Somalia and its designation as a terrorist group by the US in February 2008 amidst the electoral crisis.[44] In the face of new and growing threats the stability of an important regional partner was critical, this likely had some effect on the international response.

Within the first hours of the violence, an Africa-led international response began. African leaders and eminent personalities began work to restore calm with former President of Sierra Leone Ahmed Tejan Kabbah and Archbishop Desmond Tutu making attempts.[45] US Assistant Secretary of State Jendayi Fraser visited and made some attempts to bring the leaders together as the United States threatened travel bans on those suspected of masterminding the violence.[46] African Union chair John Kufour made the first significant breakthrough, convincing Kibaki and Odinga to engage in international mediation conducted by a panel of eminent African personalities.[47] The panel was chaired

41 Roger Cohen, 'African Genocide Averted', *New York Times*, 3 March 2008.

42 Meredith Preston McGhie and Serena Sharma, 'Kenya' in Irwin Cotler and Jared Genser (eds.), *The Responsibility to Protect: The Promise of Stopping Mass Atrocities in Our Time* (Oxford: Oxford University Press, 2012), p. 281.

43 Jeremy Prestholdt, 'Kenya, the United States and Counterterrorism', *Africa Today*, 57(4) 3–27 (2011), p. 11; Jodi Vittori, Kristin Bremer, and Pasquale Vittori, 'Islam in Tanzania and Kenya: Ally or Threat in the War on Terror', *Studies in Conflict and Terrorism*, 32(12) 1075–1099 (2009).

44 United States Department of State, *Designation of al Shabaab as a Terrorist Organization* (Washington DC: Office of the Coordinator for Counterterrorism, 26 February 2008).

45 Wachira et al., *Citizens in Action*, p. 20.

46 Daniel Branch, *Kenya: Between Hope and Despair, 1963–2011* (New Haven CT: Yale University Press, 2011), pp. 277–278.

47 Elisabeth Lindenmayer and Josie Lianna Kaye, *A Choice for Peace? The Story of Forty-One Days of Mediation in Kenya* (New York: International Peace Institute, 2009), p. 6.

by former UN Secretary-General Kofi Annan and included Graça Machel and Benjamin Mpaka. When it arrived in Kenya, they consulted with Kenyan civil society groups before initiating the mediation process. By 1 February, just days after the national dialogue had begun, an agreement on ending the violence had been reached and, aside from a small number of sporadic incidents, peace largely returned.[48]

The international community used its leverage wisely. Draft public statements on Kenya from US Secretary of State Condoleezza Rice were first submitted to Annan for approval.[49] The European Union warned that Kenya, without a peace agreement, faced financial sanctions and leaders would be subject to travel bans.[50] In his address to the African Union, UN Secretary-General Ban Ki-moon called for the leaders to show vision and come together, and pledged complete support for the Annan mediation mission.[51] During the crisis, few directly linked Kenya and R2P. However, then French Foreign Minister Bernard Kouchner noted:

> We are very concerned about the violence which is continuing to convulse Kenya ... We fear lest these excesses plunge Kenya into a deadly conflict of an ethnic character. In the name of the Responsibility to Protect, it is urgent to help the people of Kenya ... The United Nations Security Council must take up this question and act.[52]

By combining a multitude of pressures from Kenyan civil society and the international community, Annan presented the parties with no choice but to compromise or cease to enjoy the benefits of power. After nearly a month of intense mediation the parties signed the Agreement on the Principles of Partnership of the Coalition Government, establishing a power-sharing arrangement that brought the crisis to an end.

Kenya has, for R2P advocates, represented a prominent success story. The violence, as clearly outlined, was an R2P situation. Conscience-shocking acts and the clear potential for escalation focused the minds of the international community who 'did not simply defer to the shibboleth of national sovereignty,

48 *ibid.*, p. 8.

49 David Hamburg, *Preventing Genocide: Practical Steps Toward Early Detection and Effective Action* (London: Paradigm Publishers, 2010), p. 289.

50 Makumi Mwagiru, *The Water's Edge: Mediation of Violent Electoral Conflict in Kenya* (Nairobi: Institute for Diplomatic and International Studies, 2008), p. 79.

51 Ban Ki-moon, *Address to the African Union Summit in Addis Ababa on January 31, 2008.*

52 Bernard Kouchner, 'Violence in Kenya (January 31, 2008): Statement Made by Foreign and European Affairs Minister Bernard Kouchner', *France Diplomatie.*

but acted'.[53] The case of Kenya does not, in itself, present a complete success of R2P, however. The core tenet of R2P is *prevention*, and the failure to heed the warning signs of Kenya represents a failure to prevent.[54] Yet the geopolitical imperatives, paired with a crisis in its early stages, represented an ideal case for the R2P. There was broad support for peace from the grassroots through to the international community, no involvement of armed forces, no significant divisions at the international level, and political leaders willing to de-escalate and compromise.

5 Sri Lanka

The end of the Sri Lankan civil war in 2009 between the Sri Lankan Army and the Liberation Tigers of Tamil Eelam (LTTE) saw significant atrocities committed against Tamil civilians. The conflict began in 1983 involving multiple groups and phases with the LTTE emerging as the dominant Tamil group in the 1990s. The LTTE increasingly turned to terror tactics with suicide bombings and the assassinations of former Indian Prime Minister Rajiv Gandhi in 1991 and Sri Lankan President Ranasinghe Premadasa in 1993.[55] Through multiple phases of civil war Sri Lanka forces were unable to defeat the LTTE. A ceasefire in 2002 brought about a monitoring mission, led by Norway, that negotiated a precarious peace until 2005.[56] The period was replete with ceasefire violations. Yet in that time, the LTTE built a quasi-state, administering services to an area of north-eastern Sri Lanka.[57] The ceasefire effectively ended in 2005 when the LTTE assassinated Sri Lankan Foreign Minister Lakshman Kadirgamar, marking the resumption of violent confrontation.[58] The assassination and ceasefire violations lost what remained of the LTTE's international legitimacy. The European Union declared the group a terror organisation in October 2006, joining the US and India who had previously done so.[59] This coincided with the

53 Thomas G. Weiss, 'Halting Atrocities in Kenya, Acting Sooner rather than Later', *Great Decisions 2010* (New York: Foreign Policy Association, 2010), p. 17.

54 Noële Crossley, 'A Model Case of R2P Prevention? Mediation in the Aftermath of Kenya's 2007 Presidential Elections', *Global Responsibility to Protect*, 5(2) 192–214 (2013).

55 Sumit Ganguly, 'Ending the Sri Lankan Civil War', *Daedalus*, 147(1) 78–89 (2018).

56 International Crisis Group, 'Sri Lanka: Sinhala Nationalism and the Elusive Southern Consensus', Asia Report no. 141 (Brussels: International Crisis Group, 2007).

57 Damien Kingsbury, *Sri Lanka and the Responsibility to Protect: Politics, Ethnicity and Genocide* (New York: London: Routledge, 2012), p. 72.

58 Sandra Destradi, *Indian Foreign and Security Policy in South Asia: Regional Power Strategies* (New York: Routledge, 2012), p. 69.

59 International Crisis Group, 'War Crimes in Sri Lanka' (Brussels: International Crisis Group, 2010), p. 3.

2005 Sri Lankan election in which a hard-line Sinhalese coalition was elected, with Mahinda Rajapaksa becoming president. President Rajapaksa changed the conflict dynamics, giving carte blanche to his military to manage the war. Sri Lanka increased military spending from 2.8 per cent of GDP in 2006 to 3.3 per cent, in 2007.[60] As Ganguly notes, 'This increase in the military budget also enabled an expansion of the armed forces from 120,000 personnel in 2005 to 300,000 in 2009.'[61] The Eelam War IV began, and as Peter Layton wrote, 'the Sri Lankan government finally decided to change its strategic objective, from negotiating with the LTTE to annihilating it'.[62]

The Eelam War IV, fought between 2006 and May 2009, saw intense fighting with significant casualties, as the Sri Lankan Army (SLA) retook eastern and parts of north-eastern Sri Lanka. The conflict dynamics changed after the SLA took the LTTE's unofficial capital, Kilinochchi, in early January 2009 and the strategically significant Elephant Pass, capturing of the entire Jaffna peninsula on 15 January.[63] This major strategic victory propelled the rapid advance of the SLA as the LTTE, and hundreds of thousands of Tamil civilians compelled to follow them, retreated to their last stronghold of Mullaitivu. At this point the LTTE had been all but defeated, protecting itself by holding hostage up to 330,000 Tamil civilians that remained with them.

It must be recognised that the LTTE was a particularly egregious non-state actor. The LTTE's use of suicide bombers, chemical weapons attacks, civilian targeting, assassinations, and forced conscription of child soldiers place them in a company of truly repugnant groups.[64] In the final phase of the civil war, the LTTE turned civilians into human shields and shot many of those caught attempting to escape the rebel-held zone.[65] The crimes of the LTTE, however, do not justify the means used by the SLA to bring about their end. There is no justification for the deliberate slaughter of tens of thousands of civilians. There were multiple instances in the final phase of the conflict between January and May 2009 where options of negotiation provided viable alternatives for ending

60 Ganguly, 'Ending the Sri Lankan Civil War', pp. 84–85.

61 *ibid.*, p. 85.

62 Peter Layton, 'How Sri Lanka Won the War', *The Diplomat*, 9 April 2015.

63 Secretary-General's Internal Review Panel on United Nations Action in Sri Lanka, *Report of the Secretary-General's Internal Review Panel on United Nations Action in Sri Lanka* (New York: United Nations, November 2012).

64 S. D. Selvadurai and M. L. R. Smith, 'Black Tigers, Bronze Lotus: The Evolution and Dynamics of Sri Lanka's Strategies of Dirty War', *Studies in Conflict & Terrorism*, 36(7) 547–572 (2013).

65 UN Secretary-General, *Report of the Secretary-General's Panel of Experts on Accountability in Sri Lanka*, 31 March 2011, pp. 65–66.

the conflict. The Sri Lankan army persisted nevertheless, tasked with achieving their singular and deadly task: the complete and final destruction of the LTTE. The SLA designated areas in the Wanni as 'No Fire Zones' (NFZs), and directed civilians to gather there for protection. Hundreds of thousands of civilians moved into these zones, alongside humanitarian organisations and UN staff, under the assumption that they would be protected from the conflict. The SLA then proceeded to specifically target the NFZs with a bombardment of mortars and other heavy artillery. As the UN Panel of Experts report describes,

> From as early as 6 February 2009, the SLA continuously shelled within the area that became the second NFZ, from all directions, including land, air and sea. It is estimated that there were between 300,000 and 330,000 civilians in that small area. The SLA assault employed aerial bombardment, long-range artillery, howitzers and MBRLs [multi-barrel rocket launchers] as well as small mortars, RPGs [rocket-propelled grenades] and small arms fire, some of it fired from a close range. MBRLs are unguided missile systems designed to shell large areas, but if used in densely populated areas, are indiscriminate in their effect and likely to cause large numbers of casualties.[66]

The SLA were repeatedly informed, by UN agencies, that they were bombing civilians, including schools and hospitals. As Tameshnie Deane writes, 'In line with its military counterinsurgency strategy, the government forces continued to repeatedly bomb and shell the increasingly constricted populated areas, even during the periods of "safe-passage", and in most cases, with the knowledge that they were attacking civilians'.[67] These actions meet the criteria for targeted mass killing, as civilians of a specific ethnic and religious group were deliberately and disproportionately targeted in order to expel and affect the political activity of the group.[68] Between January and May 2009, the SLA slowly gained control over more territory, altering the location and size of NFZs multiple times and continuing to target civilians. The SLA also restricted humanitarian aid and bombed convoys to deliberately limit the capacity of the remaining

66 *ibid.*, p. 28.

67 Tameshnie Deane, 'Historical and Political Background to the Erosion of the Rule of Law and Human Rights During Sri Lanka's Civil War and the Way Forward', *Small Wars & Insurgencies*, 27(6) 971–995 (2016), p. 980.

68 Charles Butcher, Benjamin E. Goldsmith, Sascha Nanlohy, David Muchlinski, and Arcot Sowmya, 'Introducing the Targeted Mass Killing Dataset for the Study and Forecasting of Mass Atrocities', *Journal of Conflict Resolution*, 64(7–8) 1524–1547 (2020).

civilian population to survive.[69] The final days of the conflict between 13 and 18 May were the most violent. The UN estimated that 100,000 civilians remained in the area, unable to leave. As the Panel of Experts report describes,

> Due to a lack of space in the third NFZ, civilians had nowhere to hide from the shelling, which was coming in from all sides. Shells rained down everywhere and bullets whizzed through the air. Many died and were buried under their bunkers or shelters, without their deaths being recorded. Black smoke and the stench of dead bodies filled the air … The scene was described as reminiscent of hell.[70]

When the SLA had destroyed the last remnants of LTTE resistance around 17 May, they entered the area of around 400 square metres in total, on a small stretch of sand between the ocean and the lagoon. The SLA summarily executed many of those suspected to be LTTE fighters, as confirmed by footage shot by SLA soldiers themselves; these extrajudicial killings constituting additional war crimes.[71] The hundreds of thousands who surrendered were interrogated and many thousands detained for months in prison camps in dire conditions where many more perished.[72] Hundreds of suspected LTTE members were forcibly disappeared after being seen surrendering on 17 May.[73] Between 40,000 and 70,000 Tamil civilians were killed in the final months of the war, according to the UN Panel of Experts.[74] This strategy sought not just to annihilate the LTTE but to communicate resolve to future Tamil or minority groups that might seek to challenge the supremacy of the Sinhala nationalist state.

The Sri Lankan government ably utilised a war on terror discourse to justify their actions. The Rajapaksa government was elected on a platform of 'ending terrorism'.[75] Having labelled Tamil rebellion as 'terrorism' since the 1980s, the discursive narrative had long been established.[76] As such, it was easily

69 UN Secretary-General, *Report of the Secretary-General's Panel of Experts on Accountability in Sri Lanka*.

70 *ibid.*, pp. 35–36.

71 Callum Macrae (dir.), *No Fire Zone: The Killing Fields of Sri Lanka* (United Kingdom: Outsider Films, 2013).

72 Kingsbury, *Sri Lanka and the Responsibility to Protect*.

73 Frances Harrison and Patrick Ball, 'How Many People Disappeared on 17–19 May 2009 in Sri Lanka', International Truth and Justice Project, 2018.

74 UN Secretary-General, *Report of the Secretary-General's Panel of Experts on Accountability in Sri Lanka*.

75 Ajay Parasram, 'Erasing Tamil Eelam: De/Re Territorialisation in the Global War on Terror', *Geopolitics*, 17(4) 903–925 (2012), p. 918.

76 Suthaharan Nadarajah and Dhananjayan Sriskandarajah, 'Liberation Struggle or Terrorism? The Politics of Naming the LTTE', *Third World Quarterly*, 26(1) 87–100 (2005).

adapted to a post-9/11 world. As Shannon Zimmerman articulates, from the 9/11 attacks onwards, a consistent narrative (often supported by LTTE attacks) framed the eventual response as one of counter-terrorism.[77] Gerrit Kurtz and Madhan Mohan Jaganathan clearly illustrate the way in which Sri Lanka was able to successfully adopt a counter-terrorism narrative as a shield for its own crimes.[78] For at least the period prior to the final phase of the civil war they received support from the US and United Kingdom, including explicit approval of their resolve to militarily defeat the LTTE.[79] They further argue,

> The international debate was considerably biased in favour of the Sri Lankan government. The LTTE's track record of violence against civilians, forced recruitment of children, and suicide attacks seem to have legitimised the government's counterinsurgency operation in the eyes of most governments.[80]

The global war on terror augmented the narrative, and, in turn, the boundaries of acceptable conduct to include the deliberate killing of civilians in the name of combating terrorism. For this strategy to be successful, however, there needed to be sufficient support for its use internationally. It is true that China and Russia, along with others, stymied effective action in the UN Security Council. It was, however, the inaction of India, Sri Lanka's closest neighbour who has often dominated its politics, that best encapsulates the challenge of responding to a case like Sri Lanka.

Intervention without Indian support was unviable. The role of India, as the main regional power, in driving the insufficient, often ambivalent response to the crisis is perhaps best summed up by their opposition to US-led efforts to evacuate civilians from LTTE held areas. In March 2009, the proposal from the US to evacuate civilians using 'military assets from the US Pacific Command, based in Hawaii failed because of resistance from the LTTE and India's preference for a UN effort (the Indian opposition reportedly convinced the Sri Lankan government to reject the offer as well)'.[81] Eelam War IV coincided with increased geostrategic competition for influence in Sri Lanka between India and China. As Destradi contends, 'the competition between India and China

77 Zimmerman, 'Strange Bedfellows'.

78 Gerrit Kurtz and Madhan Mohan Jaganathan, 'Protection in Peril: Counterterrorism Discourse and International Engagement in Sri Lanka in 2009', *Global Society*, 30(1) 94–112 (2016).

79 *ibid.*, p. 105.

80 *ibid.*, p. 99.

81 Kurtz and Jaganathan, 'Protection in Peril', p. 100.

induced New Delhi to support Colombo's military efforts against the LTTE in order to avoid losing its influence on Sri Lanka to an extra-regional actor'.[82] While the SLA purchased arms from a variety of sources, the bulk during the period of interest came from China. Throughout the fourth Eelam War, Chinese assistance was believed to be worth US $1 billion annually.[83]

In March 2007, Sri Lanka and China signed eight agreements on closer economic cooperation, investment, and other issues.[84] The joint communique explicitly set the stage for Chinese support for Sri Lanka's counter-insurgency. It affirmed both states were 'resolved to fight tirelessly against the three evil forces of terrorism, separatism and extremism and will step up consultation and coordinating on regional and international counter-terrorism action'.[85] This signal of support for Sri Lanka's civil war strategy coincided with the significant increase in military support from China to Sri Lanka. During the previous three Eelam wars, India had either been on the side of the Tamil rebels or had taken a 'hands off' approach. It was only with its acquiescence that such an extreme military solution was seemingly attempted.[86] India's inability or unwillingness to intervene to prevent or stop the atrocities speaks to the problem of ambiguity. In the absence of a clear narrative around which political will can coalesce, geopolitical interests and realpolitik will fill the vacuum.

Final defeat of the LTTE occurred after the most significant Western powers had designated the LTTE as a terrorist organisation. While the end of the civil war came at a period where the 'war on terror' rhetoric of the Bush administration in the United States had been swept away by the incoming Obama administration, there was little sympathy for the LTTE in the West. Eelam War IV had begun in 2006 and was significantly tied to a counter-terrorism narrative. Many Western powers were otherwise preoccupied with the fallout from the global financial crisis and the war in Gaza. The Obama administration made a series of efforts from naming and shaming through to threats of prosecution and failed attempts to evacuate civilians. With China, India and Russia in their corner, however, the administration appeared unwilling to spend significant political capital where it held no real interests. As such, the Government of Sri Lanka could effectively ignore any appeals for restraint from the West.[87] At the

---

82 Sandra Destradi, 'India and Sri Lanka's Civil War: The Failure of Regional Conflict Management in South Asia', *Asian Survey*, 52(3) 595–616 (2012), pp. 597–98.

83 Sameer P. Lalwani, 'Size Still Matters: Explaining Sri Lanka's Counterinsurgency Victory over the Tamil Tigers', *Small Wars & Insurgencies*, 28(1) 119–165 (2017), p. 146.

84 'China, Sri Lanka Agree to Cooperate on Counter-Terrorism', *The Press Trust of India*, 4 March 2007.

85 *ibid.*

86 Destradi, 'India and Sri Lanka's Civil War'.

87 Kingsbury, *Sri Lanka and the Responsibility to Protect*, p. 79.

UN Security Council, the crisis in Sri Lanka never made it onto the agenda, as China and Russia both blocked resolutions on the crisis.[88] With the obvious political cost of being seen to be protecting a designated terrorist organisation, many Western powers were hesitant to use too much political capital. The failure to act is reflected in the statement made on 15 May 2009 by Francis Deng, then UN Special Adviser to the Secretary-General on the Prevention of Genocide, calling on both sides of the conflict to show respect for international humanitarian law and seek a peaceful solution.[89] Though an uncontentious statement, its relative ambiguity in relation to the Sri Lankan government's actions while specifically noting the LTTE's horrific use of human shields is revealing. It reflects a permissive attitude whereby the international community had decided to look the other way until it was all over. The framing of the conflict as a counter-terrorism war allowed the Sri Lankan Army to commit mass atrocities with impunity. Despite the atrocities of the Sri Lankan Army along with those of the LTTE being one of the first true tests of the R2P, the international community manifestly failed in their obligation. This can, at least in part, be explained by the ambiguity of the conflict dynamics that blended counter-insurgency, counter-terrorism, and mass atrocities into a mire that disincentivised the operationalisation of R2P to effectively protect civilians.

6 Discussion

These two cases illustrate the way terrorism and counter-terrorism narratives can augment and complicate the application and operationalisation of the R2P. Terrorism was an implicit factor that shaped external responses to imminent and ongoing mass atrocities in both cases. The effect was clear, *disincentivising* the effective operationalisation of R2P in Sri Lanka while *incentivising* its rapid and successful use in Kenya. In Sri Lanka, the government was able to co-opt the language of the R2P, wrapped in war on terror era counter-terrorism doctrine to implement their final solution to the Tamil Tiger problem and with it, send a message to any other groups that may seek to challenge the Sinhala nationalist regime. By using the language of counter-terrorism over many years, but especially post-9/11, there was a clear attempt to set the agenda, initially during peace negotiations and later in the conduct of Eelam War IV. In a global atmosphere that was still overwhelmingly willing to accept extreme

88 International Crisis Group, 'War Crimes in Sri Lanka', p. 7.

89 United Nations Office of the Special Advisor to the Secretary-General on the Prevention of Genocide, 'Statement on Sri Lanka', 15 May 2009.

means to justify particular ends, what was portrayed as strong counter-terrorism strategy was largely accepted. Indeed, the failure of peace process, which eventually led to the failure of R2P was in part significantly undermined by a lack of support from the United States for the Norwegian-led mediation. This, as Nissen argues, was partly due to the adopted framing of the LTTE as a terror group, and later the acceptance of the Rajapaksa regime's military solution to the conflict.[90] This co-option to their own ends appears to have been relatively easy, as Richmond and Tellidis argue, 'orthodox terrorism approaches undermined liberal peacebuilding and evacuated local alterity in conformity with the nationalist Sinhala strategy of the post-independence era'.[91] That the LTTE was a terrorist organisation does not justify the disproportionate targeting of civilians. The failure to effectively disentangle counter-terrorism from an ethno-nationalist campaign of targeted mass killing signals a genuine failure of the international community to operationalise the R2P when tested.

In Kenya, terrorism was a factor in the international response, albeit from the standpoint that Kenya played a critical role in the war on terror in Africa. A weaker or theoretically collapsed state could have proven dangerous for the US and other states involved in the war on terror. During the mediation talks, a congressional subcommittee on Africa noted that 'Kenya was too important in the region and the world to be allowed to go the way of Rwanda and Somalia'.[92] The level of international coordination on Kenya is exemplified by US collaboration on official statements with lead mediator Annan. US Secretary of State Rice's lockstep approach on Kenya was unusual for Bush administration efforts around multilateralism; as a member of the mediation team noted, 'this was unheard of! I would give the statements to Annan and he would approve them before they went out'.[93] This was not necessarily the only possible framing, but it was the prevailing one. As discussed, some Kikuyu politicians and political leaders had described Luos as terrorists in a deluge of hate speech during the post-election violence.[94] Indeed, attacks like that at the Kiambaa church in Eldoret reasonably fit under definitions of terrorism. The targeting of civilians designed to achieve a political objective is relatively clear in this case. Whether

---

90 Ada Nissen, 'Troublesome Peace Making: How American Views on Terrorism Affected Norwegian Mediation in Sri Lanka, 2000–2009', *Diplomacy and Statecraft*, 26(3) 522–542 (2018).

91 Oliver P. Richmond and Ioannis Tellidis, 'The Complex Relationship Between Peacebuilding and Terrorism Approaches: Towards Post-Terrorism and a Post-Liberal Peace', *Terrorism and Political Violence*, 24(1) 120–143 (2012), p. 127.

92 Mwagiru, *The Water's Edge*, p. 125.

93 Cohen, 'How Kofi Annan Rescued Kenya', p. 52.

94 *Waki Report*, p. 216.

the audience was the government or Kikuyu civilians is less certain. It would not, however, have been a significant stretch from parts of the international community or media to adopt a terrorism framing in siding with the government against the ODM had such a path been chosen. It was perhaps the competing predominance of the anti-Islamic fundamentalist war on terror and Kenya's role in fighting it in the Horn of Africa that determined such a framing would not be adopted, even where it conceivably could have been. The stark contrast with how the US support, or lack thereof, for peace processes was affected by terrorism framings and impacted subsequent outcomes in Kenya compared to Sri Lanka is clear. An unambiguous choice of framing as terrorism versus ethnic conflict drastically affected responses between the two crises. While we cannot be entirely certain of the extent to which strategic interests directly augmented the international response, it is not difficult to see why the confluence of direct interests made Kenya an ideal case for R2P. The conflict was at a much earlier stage. There was no mass militarisation and no involvement of armed forces. There was broad support for peace across Kenyan society. The level of external unity was commendable between Kenya's neighbours, the African Union, United Nations, and the broader international community. As such the odds of a positive outcome were good. Operationalising R2P in Kenya was easier than it would have been in Sri Lanka, but the general lack of *any* attempts to apply R2P in the latter case is rooted in the prioritisation of a counter-terrorism narrative and, from a civilian protection perspective, the ambiguity of its conflict narrative and the lack of a coherent, cohesive set of interests in preventing atrocities.

This comparative variation of framing does to an extent reflect the varied magnitude and level of difficulty in resolving the cases. It also, however, demonstrates the ability of the international community to distinguish genuine terrorism and counter-terror responses from illegitimate ones that act as part of the justificatory mechanism for atrocities. It also demonstrates that complex conflict dynamics will often be framed to fit overly simplistic narratives, and that the international community can choose which narrative they are willing to accept. It is often the interests of powerful states that underpin that choice. To paraphrase the oft-cited adage, it seems one state's R2P emergency is another's counter-terrorism operation. This dynamic is clear from observing other cases of intervention and non-intervention. NATO was willing and able to overlook the human rights abuses committed by the Kosovo Liberation Army in 1999 both before and following its intervention, due at least in part to a clear narrative that stemmed from the genocide in Bosnia four years earlier.[95]

95 Alan J. Kuperman, 'The Moral Hazard of Humanitarian Intervention: Lessons from the Balkans', *International Studies Quarterly*, 52(1) 49–80 (2008).

A similar willingness to overlook crimes committed by anti-Gaddafi rebels also prevailed in Libya following the 2011 intervention.[96] Meanwhile, perhaps emboldened by the success for impunity and non-interference in Sri Lanka, Asia's great powers China and India acted in unison with their descriptions of the 'Clearance Operations' against the Rohingya as counter-terrorism.[97] This is despite the clear evidence that the violence unleashed was grossly disproportionate compared to the threat ARSA legitimately represented. This is not to downplay the crimes of the LTTE or overstate Kenya as a simple and easy case of conflict resolution. Rather it is an illustration of how complexity breeds ambiguity, and from ambiguity, states, and at times the broader international community, can pick the narrative that suits, according to their own interests and priorities. In some cases, this will be grounded in a clear narrative of terrorism and counter-terrorism, at other times it will act merely as a fig leaf to justify atrocities. The framing of conflicts and events as terrorism and counter-terrorism or ethnic conflict, electoral violence, tribal conflict, intercommunal violence, etc has significant effects on how the international community responds. These forms of political violence may manifest in very similar forms, yet it is often how they are labelled that informs external responses. In this way, framing may be more important than the ground truth of events in how R2P can be operationalised. Ultimately, the international community must be more aware and better able to respond to the use of counter-terrorism as a cover for the disproportionate use of force that often results in mass atrocities.

This chapter prompts important questions about how the R2P is applied and operationalised. There is broad recognition of its imperfections, but it remains an important normative banner under which the international community can rally in an effort to prevent and mitigate mass atrocities. There are, however, clearly critical weaknesses that imperil its future success. In the case studies presented in this chapter, one state, whose stability was at risk, was a critical partner to international efforts in *combating* terrorism; in the other, the designated *target* of the violence was a terrorist organisation, a fact used to justify mass atrocities against the population within which the group operated. These characteristics were intertwined with a variety of other geopolitical dynamics; however, it augmented the international response to atrocities and demonstrates the gap between promise and practice for the R2P. The ability of states to carry out atrocities with relative impunity after labelling the targets 'terrorists' is one such challenge, and one likely to persist. There are cases where such a claim is clearly illegitimate, though even in these cases it remains

96 Kuperman, 'Did the R2P Foster Violence in Libya?'.

97 Matteo Fumagalli, 'Myanmar 2017: The Rohingya Crisis between Radicalisation and Ethnic Cleansing', *Asia Maior* XXVIII (2018), p. 240.

a useful rhetorical device for perpetrating states or their external supporters to hide behind or muddy the waters to stymie intervention. This problem is particularly challenging where there is some degree of truth in such a label and atrocities can be set aside as permissible collateral damage; in effect, where the ends justify the means. It is a matter of genuine difficulty but one that needs to be grappled with to make progress towards the promise of the R2P. Situations in which there is a significant risk of mass atrocities are rarely black and white, vulnerable civilian populations will often include bad actors who use them as cover – creating grey zones. This problem does not negate the value of R2P as an evolving norm. Indeed, expecting the perfect application of a norm that is designed to grapple with the one of humanity's most intractable issues is akin to building a strawman for a bonfire.

Seeking to manage this issue, to disaggregate vulnerable populations from bad actors that operate amongst them is a critical issue for the future of civilian protection. Challenging the cloak-and-dagger justifications for operational strategies technically designed to counter terrorist activities but often used as cover for wholescale repression or atrocities is a first step. In practice, this could involve states, organisations, and advocates directly challenging the narrative of counter-terrorism, an approach akin to naming and shaming. Another key measure is challenging those states that support perpetrators and provide legitimacy at the international level by blocking discussions or resolutions at the UN Security Council. Assuming bad faith from states that protect or enable perpetrators only guarantees such behaviour will continue to manifest. It is exceedingly difficult to create costs for external actors that are permissive of atrocities. Seeking, however, to raise any cost for that permissiveness is urgent. Raising costs for permissiveness begins simply from not assuming that states who protect perpetrators don't care for their international reputation. To do so is to let them off the hook. Tighter controls or sanctions on military assistance for these operations are other urgent and necessary steps. The Arms Trade Treaty and mechanisms like the Global Magnitsky Act are potentially significant measures but are relatively recent initiatives, the full effects of which are difficult to measure.

There are a number of potential avenues for future research that stem from this chapter. I focus on the desire to avoid the appearance of supporting terrorist actors that is important to explaining the success of the terrorism card in some cases but this is just one possible mechanism and further research should consider in what other ways might terrorism affect international responses? From the very small sample of cases it appears that the potency of terrorism framing is very much case and context dependent. It would, however, be an important step to interrogate whether such framing is more or less likely to be adopted across a broader range of cases.

7 Conclusion

This chapter has argued that the use of counter-terrorism narratives can be co-opted to justify and implement mass atrocity campaigns with impunity. This presents a unique challenge to the operationalisation of the R2P. The ability of perpetrating states, and their external supporters, to craft and reinforce a message of legitimate use of force, shielding gross abuses of human rights, obviates the application of R2P. I have demonstrated how the cases of Kenya and Sri Lanka are a temporally comparative example of how the international community struggles to operationalise R2P in cases where bad actors such as terror groups are operating amid large civilian populations. There are large dissimilarities between the cases presented in this research and there are many confounding factors besides those presented that make Sri Lanka a difficult R2P case and Kenya an ideal one. Yet the fact that both are cited in discussions of R2P is reflective of the wide gamut of conflicts the norm is expected to be able to address. The efforts to address the failure to prevent atrocities has incidentally created problems where success in Kenya or Ivory Coast should by some natural process of momentum lead to success in Syria or Myanmar despite wholly differing conflict dynamics and geopolitical contexts.

The answer to Romeo Dallaire's question that forms the title to this chapter remains uncertain. There have been tremendous advances in efforts to prevent mass atrocities that continue a long tradition of humanitarianism. While still catastrophic, the severity of mass atrocities has waned significantly from the twentieth century's worst calamities.[98] These successes are, however, always relative so long as atrocities persist. An appreciation of the complexity and challenges of conflict dynamics where atrocities are likely or ongoing is essential to grappling with efforts to undo the progress made to date. I argue that one key challenge is managing the use of counter-terrorism discourses that build justifications for mass atrocities. Citing terrorism cannot continue to be a licence to commit atrocity crimes. At present R2P is shown to be effective in managing cases at an early stage of escalation to atrocities. As in Kenya, while the conflict roots were deep the dynamics were not such that the parties, with the help of the international community could not step back from the cliff. In

98 Butcher et al., 'Introducing the Targeted Mass Killing Dataset'.

Sri Lanka, however, a long established conflict that had developed into a dirty war lacked a clear or simple narrative around which a cohesive protection effort could coalesce. The starkness of outcomes is plain to see. Atrocity prevention, like war, is messy; embracing complexity is a necessary step to more effective prevention. Without such efforts history is bound to repeat and some humans will remain less human than others.

CHAPTER 4

Counter-terrorism, the Responsibility to Protect, and the Protection of Civilians: Exploring Norm Clusters in the Case of Mali

Adrian Gallagher
Professor of Global Security and Mass Atrocity Prevention, School of Politics and International Studies, University of Leeds, Leeds, UK
a.gallagher@leeds.ac.uk

Blake Lawrinson
School of Politics and International Studies, University of Leeds, Leeds, UK
b.w.lawrinson@leeds.ac.uk

Charles T. Hunt
Associate Professor of International Security, School of Global, Urban and Social Studies, RMIT University, Melbourne, VIC, Australia
charles.hunt@rmit.edu.au

Abstract

The United Nations Security Council passes resolutions that invoke multiple norms including the protection of civilians (PoC), the responsibility to protect (R2P), and counter-terrorism. The fact that these norms are invoked alongside one another raises questions about how they interact. While there have been studies on the relationship between PoC and R2P, as well as R2P and counter-terrorism, as far as the authors are aware, this is the first study that analyses the interplay between all three norms. To do this, the chapter utilises the concept of 'norm clusters' to discuss the internal structure of PoC, R2P, and counter-terrorism prior to analysing the linkages between them. The chapter proposes that PoC, R2P, and counter-terrorism can be viewed as a 'human protection norm cluster' but also highlights areas of tension and overlap between the three norms. At the empirical level, the chapter explores these dynamics in the United Nations Multidimensional Integrated Stabilization Mission in Mali (MINUSMA). Although all three norms embody the value of human protection, our findings evidence, first, these norms are not given equal weight, second, they are not mutually

 | DOI:10.1163/9789004548114_006

reinforcing, and third, even though counter-terrorism plays a more peripheral role, it has a detrimental impact upon PoC.

Keywords

counter-terrorism – norm clusters – protection of civilians – responsibility to protect – MINUSMA – Mali

The United Nations Security Council (UNSC) passes peacekeeping resolutions that invoke multiple norms including the protection of civilians (PoC), the responsibility to protect (R2P), and counter-terrorism. Historically, academics have predominantly analysed the evolution, robustness, and resilience of norms separately. This has changed in recent years precisely because norms are invoked alongside one another. Studies have emerged on the relationship between PoC and R2P,[1] as well as R2P and counter-terrorism,[2] but as far as the authors are aware, there has been no academic research on the relationship between all three norms. Addressing this lacuna, this chapter focuses on the relationship between PoC, R2P, and counter-terrorism through a case study of the UN Multidimensional Integrated Stabilization Mission in Mali (MINUSMA).

The crisis in Mali – triggered by a Tuareg rebellion in the north in 2012[3] – has deteriorated and in recent years, evolved, and spread to the point that one retired French general described it as a 'descent into hell'.[4] Amidst the

1 Paul D. Williams, 'The R2P, Protection of Civilians, and UN Peacekeeping Operations' in Alex Bellamy and Tim Dunne (eds.), *The Oxford Handbook of the Responsibility to Protect* (Oxford: Oxford University Press, 2016), pp. 524–544; Charles T. Hunt, 'Analyzing the Co-evolution of the Responsibility to Protect and the Protection of Civilians in UN Peace Operations', *International Peacekeeping*, 26(5) 630–659 (2019); Emily P. Rhoads and Jennifer Welsh, 'Close Cousins in Protection: The Evolution of Two Norms', *International Affairs*, 95(3) 597–617 (2019).

2 Jennifer Welsh, 'R2P's Next Ten Years, Deepening and Extending the Consensus' in Alex Bellamy and Tim Dunne (eds.), *The Oxford Handbook of the Responsibility to Protect* (Oxford: Oxford University Press, 2016), pp. 984–1000; Shannon Zimmerman, 'Strange Bedfellows: Terrorism/Counter-terrorism and the Responsibility to Protect' in Charles T. Hunt and Phil Orchard (eds.), *Constructing the Responsibility to Protect: Contestation and Consolidation* (Abingdon: Routledge, 2020), pp. 129–148.

3 For more detail, see Baz Lecocq, Gregory Mann, Bruce Whitehouse, Dida Badi, Lotte Pelckmans, Nadia Belalimat, Bruce Hall, and Wolfram Lacher, 'One Hippopotamus and Eight Blind Analysts: A Multivocal Analysis of the 2012 Political Crisis in the Divided Republic of Mali', *Review of African Political Economy*, 40(137) 343–357 (2013).

4 Signe M. Cold-Ravnkilde and Christine Nissen, 'Schizophrenic Agendas in the EU's External Actions in Mali', *International Affairs*, 96(4) 935–953 (2020), p. 935.

chaos, the question, 'what does this have to do with norms?' naturally arises. To illustrate this, it is helpful to consider the March 2019 massacre of over 100 civilians in Mali's central Mopti region.[5] Notably, this led to calls for 'the need to better prioritize protection of civilians in MINUSMA's mandate' and high-profile warnings of 'ethnic cleansing', 'atrocity crimes', and 'crimes against humanity'.[6] These statements highlight the role of different norms at play as we see calls to prioritise PoC alongside warnings of the four crimes covered by R2P, which raises questions about the relationship between R2P and PoC.[7] But within Mali, there is an additional level of complexity as MINUSMA operates alongside a number of counter-terrorism forces, including the regional G5-Sahel Joint Force[8] and the French-led Operation Barkhane who conduct offensive operations against jihadist groups which also pose a threat to civilians. France – the 'pen-holder' for the Security Council on MINUSMA – views this as a mutually reinforcing relationship even though this is widely disputed.[9] Indeed, the MINUSMA mandate refers

5 'More Than 100 Killed Amid Escalating Violence in Mali', *New York Times*, 23 March 2019, https://www.nytimes.com/2019/03/23/world/africa/mali-dozens-killed.html.

6 Jean-Herve Jezequel, 'Central Mali: Putting a Stop to Ethnic Cleansing', International Crisis Group, 25 March 2019, https://www.crisisgroup.org/africa/sahel/mali/centre-du-mali-enrayer-le-nettoyage-ethnique, accessed 11 May 2020; Namie Di Razza, 'Massacre in Mali Demonstrates Need to Prioritize Protection of Civilians in MINUSMA's Mandate', 15 April 2019, https://theglobalobservatory.org/2019/04/massacre-mali-demonstrates-need-prioritize-protection-civilians-minusma/, accessed 15 August 2020. See also Sean Smith and Alison Giffen, 'What Does MINUSMA's Revised Mandate Mean for the Protection of Civilians in Mali? Part 1: Prioritizing Protection Centre for Civilians in Conflict', 26 July 2019, https://civiliansinconflict.org/blog/minusma-revised-mandate-poc-mali/, accessed 28 August 2020.

7 Catherine Jones, 'The Responsibility to Protect or the Protection of Civilians: Which Policy Brand is more "Successful"?' in Aiden Hehir and Robert W. Murray (eds.), *Protecting Human Rights in the 21st Century* (Abingdon: Routledge, 2017), pp. 71–88; Rhoads and Welsh, 'Close Cousins in Protection'.

8 Comprised of troops from Mali, Chad, Niger, Burkina Faso, and Mauritania.

9 Bruno Charbonneau, 'Intervention in Mali: Building Peace between Peacekeeping and Counterterrorism', *Journal of Contemporary African Studies*, 35(4) 415–431 (2017); Bruno Charbonneau, 'The Military Intervention in Mali and Beyond: An Interview', 29 March, 2019, https://www.oxfordresearchgroup.org.uk/blog/the-french-intervention-in-mali-an-interview-with-bruno-charbonneau, accessed 2 September 2019; John Karlsrud, 'Towards UN Counter-terrorism Operations?', *Third World Quarterly*, 38(6) 1215–1231 (2017); John Karlsrud, 'From Liberal Peacebuilding to Stabilization and Counterterrorism', *International Peacekeeping*, 26(1) 1–21 (2019); John Karlsrud, 'UN Peace Operations, Terrorism, and Violent Extremism' in Cedric de Coning and Mateja Peter (eds.), *United Nations Peace Operations in a Changing Global Orde* (Palgrave Macmillan, 2019), pp. 153–168.

to coordination not cooperation and the mission does not conduct joint operations with these parallel forces. They do, however, have formal information sharing mechanisms[10] and have been at times co-located – in locations such as Tessalit in the far north of Mali, Barkhane units have been 'housed' inside the MINUSMA camp.[11] This empirical reality asks us to consider the norm dynamics at play as these three norms interact.

The chapter is structured in four sections. The first section uses the concept of 'norm clusters' to explain the tripartite 'problem-value-behavior' *structure* of PoC, R2P, and counter-terrorism.[12] In so doing, it highlights commonalities and differences between the norms while demonstrating that all three can be viewed as embodying a 'human protection' value which could lead one to conclude that they are naturally reinforcing.[13] Second, it examines the *linkages* between the three norms to highlight issues of complementarity and tension. Utilising Lantis and Wunderlich's understanding of 'norm clusters' as 'collections of aligned, but distinct, norms or principles that relate to a common, overarching issue area; they address different aspects and contain specific normative obligations', we propose that PoC, R2P and counter-terrorism can be viewed as a human protection norm cluster.[14] In other words, the three norms are norm clusters in and of themselves but also form part of a broader human protection norm cluster. With the conceptual foundations laid, the chapter then turns its attention to the case study of Mali.

Section three highlights that although the three norms are invoked alongside one another, they do not carry equal weight in their implementation. Simply speaking, PoC is at the core of MINUSMA, while counter-terrorism and R2P are peripheral. Fourth, it analyses the interaction between the three norms to reveal a complex dynamic that embodies elements of complementarity and tension. Despite the three norms embodying a human protection

---

10 Karlsrud, 'Towards UN Counter-terrorism Operations?', p. 1224.

11 Lisa Sharland and Alexandra Novosseloff, 'Partners and Competitors: Forces Operating in Parallel to UN Peace Operations', (New York: International Peace Institute, 2019). See also Shannon Zimmerman, *Global Governance*, forthcoming.

12 Carla Winston, 'Norm Structure, Diffusion and Evolution: A Conceptual Approach', *European Journal of International Relations*, 24(3) 638–661 (2018), p. 640.

13 Jean-Yves Le Drian, 'Mali: Statement by Mr. Jean-Yves Le Drian, Minister for Europe and Foreign Affairs Security Council', 29 March 2019, https://onu.delegfrance.org/Mali-the-peace-process-has-accelerated-over-the-past-six-months, accessed 16 August 2020.

14 Jeffrey S. Lantis and Carmen Wunderlich, 'Resiliency Dynamics of Norm Clusters: Norm Contestation and International Cooperation', *Review of International Studies*, 44(3) 570–593 (2018), p. 571.

value, we find that the peripheral norm of counter-terrorism has a detrimental impact on the core PoC norm and thus the human protection norm cluster more broadly.

1 Norm Clusters

In what is now commonly known as first wave norm scholarship, academics define norms as 'shared ideas, expectations, and beliefs about appropriate behaviour'.[15] Since this time, second and third wave norm scholarship has arisen as academics debate the stability of norms and their normativity as all norms are open to contestation.[16] Yet first wave definitions remain integral to contemporary norm research.[17] As norm research has developed, researchers have moved beyond studying individual norms to analyse ideas such 'norm clashes',[18] 'norm clusters',[19] 'norm complexity',[20] and 'norm collisions'.[21] We utilise the work on 'norm clusters' to first, explain the internal structure of the three norms prior to second, examining the links between them. In so doing, we utilise two studies on 'norm clusters'. The first is Winston's inward-looking focus on norm clusters in seeking to analyse the internal structure of norms, which is achieved by investigating the 'problem', 'value', and 'behaviour' within different norms.[22] In contrast, Lantis and Wunderlich analyse the interplay between different norms within a 'norm cluster' where the norms are aligned

15 Martha Finnemore and Kathryn Sikkink, 'International Norm Dynamics and Political Change', *International Organization*, 52(4) 887–917 (1998), p. 894.

16 Antje Wiener, *Contestation and Constitution of Norms in Global International Relations* (Cambridge: Cambridge University Press, 2018).

17 See Adrian Gallagher and Benedict Docherty, 'What Role[s] do Expectations Play in Norm Dynamics?' *International Politics*, (2021) https://doi.org/10.1057/s41311-021-00297-1.

18 Sonia Cardenas, 'Norm Collision: Explaining the Effects of International Human Rights Pressure on State Behaviour', *International Studies Review* 6(2) 213–231 (2004); Andrew P. Cortell and James J. Davis, 'When Norms Clash: International Norms, Domestic Practices, and Japan's Internalisation of the GATT/WTO', *Review of International Studies*, 31(1) 3–25 (2005).

19 Lantis and Wunderlich, 'Resiliency Dynamics of Norm Clusters'; Winston, 'Norm Structure, Diffusion and Evolution'.

20 Caroline Fehl, 'Bombs, Trials, and Rights: Norm Complexity and the Evolution of Liberal Intervention Practices', *Human Rights Quarterly*, 41(40) 893–915 (2019); Rhoads and Welsh, 'Close Cousins in Protection'.

21 Sassan Gholiagha, Anna Holzscheiter and Andrea Liese, 'Activating Norm Collisions: Interface Conflicts in International Drug Control', *Global Constitutionalism*, 9(2) 290–317 (2020).

22 Winston, 'Norm Structure, Diffusion and Evolution'.

or coupled and may or may not create obligations that coincide.[23] Accordingly, it is important to clarify that while both studies use the same term 'norm cluster', they are in fact very different which begs the question, can these studies be used together?

The two studies on norm clusters do not engage with each other – meaning that two understandings of norm clusters exist with nothing published, as of yet, on how they relate. At times it seems that the two understandings are used interchangeably in the literature.[24] The hope here is that we can add value by beginning to consider how different theorising of norm clusters can in fact be linked and used together in ways that have not previously been attempted. We are of the view that both studies are examples of third wave norm research in that they accept i) the centrality of norms, ii) view norms as embodying a dual quality and, iii) believe that there are linkages between the norms in question. Bearing in mind the only thing that norm scholars tend to agree on is just how complex norm dynamics are, could it not be the case that we have two sets of linkages: a) between the problem-value-behaviour elements in Winston's structure of a norm and b) between the norms which have a 'common, overarching issue area'.[25] In other words, norms can share a common normative grounding which we see as open to ongoing contestation as neither the structure of norms nor the relationship between them are fixed. The contention of this chapter is that in order to understand how the three norms interact,[26] one must recognise that the three norms in question all embody a commitment to solving 'the problem' of threats to civilians and 'the value' of human protection.[27] To put this another way, the internal structure of the norms in question helps us understand how they interact.

1.1 *The Tripartite Structure of PoC, R2P, and Counter-terrorism*

Winston explains that a norm's core embodies a tripartite structure consisting of a 'problem, a value, and a behavior'.[28] Building on this, Winston proposes the idea of a 'norm cluster' to capture 'multiple combinations of conceptually interlinked but distinct values and behaviors offering multiple

23 Lantis and Wunderlich, 'Resiliency Dynamics of Norm Clusters'.

24 Eglantine Staunton and Jason Ralph, 'The Responsibility to Protect Norm Cluster and the Challenge of Atrocity Prevention: An Analysis of the European Union's Strategy in Myanmar', *European Journal of International Relations*, 26(3) 660–686 (2020).

25 Lantis and Wunderlich, 'Resiliency Dynamics of Norm Clusters', p. 571. We discuss this further below.

26 *ibid.*

27 Winston, 'Norm Structure, Diffusion and Evolution'.

28 *ibid.*, p. 638.

acceptable solutions to similar and interlocking problems'.[29] Putting this into practice, Winston offers visual representations of three different norms clusters: nuclear proliferation treaty, anti-plastic bag, and transitional justice to illustrate that these can have a single and/or multiple problems, values, and behaviours within them. Some norm clusters are simple while others are far more complex. The nuclear proliferation treaty has one problem ('nuclear weapons exist'), one value ('nuclear war is undesirable'), and four behaviours ('no weapon transfer, no weapons development, no acceptance of transferred weapons, and reporting and verification'). Conversely, the transitional justice norm cluster is more complex with four problems ('oppression by democracy, authoritarianism, civil conflict, and grave breaches of international humanitarian law'), six values ('reconciliation, peace, transition/democracy, truth, rule of law, human rights, and accountability'), and five behaviours ('amnesty, commission, lustration, repatriation, and trial').[30]

In a similar vein, we present the 'problem-value-behavior' that form the internal structure of the PoC, R2P, and counter-terrorism norms. Table 1 illustrates the 'problem-value-behavior' internal structure of the PoC norm.

PoC is a complex concept which, in the words of Ralph Mamiya, has 'consistently confounded attempts at concrete definition'.[31] Although protection has a long history within humanitarianism, its relationship with military doctrines came to prominence in 1999 as the Security Council authorised peacekeepers

TABLE 1 Protection of civilians norm

Problem	Value	Behaviour
Violence against civilians	International humanitarian law International human rights law International refugee law Human protection Human security Human dignity	Protection through dialogue and engagement Provision of physical protection Establish a protective environment

29 *ibid.*

30 *ibid.*, pp. 650–653.

31 Ralph Mamiya, 'History and Conceptual Development of Protection of Civilians' in Haidi Willmot, Ralph Mamiya, Scott Sheeran, and Marc Weller (eds.), *Protection of Civilians* (Oxford: Oxford University Press, 2016), p. 64.

to protect civilians in Sierra Leone. The *problem* therefore is simple in that PoC addresses violence against civilians, whereas the *value* underpinning the norm is complicated. On one hand, we see appeals to international law embodied in its relationship with 'International Humanitarian Law', 'International Human Rights Law', and 'International Refugee Law'.[32] Yet, as Gordon rightly points out, the evolution of PoC has also seen it grounded on appeals to human security, human dignity, and human protection.[33] From a norm studies perspective, this reinforces critical reassessments which challenge the idea that norms are fixed.[34] We view PoC as having multifaceted and evolving normative underpinnings. Regarding *behaviour*, we draw on the operational parameters set out in the 2020 UN Peacekeeping Handbook on PoC which identifies three tiers, 'tier I: protection through dialogue and engagement', 'tier II: provision of physical protection', and 'tier III: establishment of protective environment'.[35] Despite such guidelines, norm contestation continues as scholars discuss the relationship between PoC and R2P. Table 2 sets out the structure of R2P, with its linkages to PoC being examined in the next section.

The R2P is regarded as a 'complex norm' which is 'particularly susceptible to contestation given its inherently indeterminate nature'.[36] It has also been labelled as a 'complex norm cluster' because of its links with other norms such as democracy, human rights, the rule of law, and conflict prevention to name a few.[37] We are of the view that the R2P is a norm cluster with an internal structure (Winston's understanding of norm clusters) and can still have links with other

32 Andrew Clapham, 'Protection of Civilians Under International Human Rights Law' in Haidi Willmot, Ralph Mamiya, Scott Sheeran, and Marc Weller (eds.), *Protection of Civilians* (Oxford: Oxford University Press, 2016), pp. 141–159; Erin Mooney, 'Displacement and the Protection of Civilians Under International Law' in Haidi Willmot, Ralph Mamiya, Scott Sheeran, and Marc Weller (eds.), *Protection of Civilians* (Oxford: Oxford University Press, 2016), pp. 177–204. Jamie A. Williamson, 'Protection of Civilians Under International Humanitarian Law' in Haidi Willmot, Ralph Mamiya, Scott Sheeran, and Marc Weller (eds.), *Protection of Civilians* (Oxford: Oxford University Press, 2016), pp. 160–176.

33 Stuart Gordon, 'The Protection of Civilians: An Evolving Paradigm?', *Stability: International Journal of Security and Development*, 2(2) 1–16 (2013).

34 Antje Wiener, 'Enacting Meaning-in-Use: Qualitative Research on Norms and International Relations', *Review of International Studies*, 35(1) 175–193 (2009).

35 UN Department of Peace Operations, *The Protection of Civilians in United Nations Peacekeeping Handbook* (New York: United Nations, 2020), p. 12. Also, UN, 'The Protection of Civilians in United Nations Peacekeeping Policy', Ref. 2019.17, United Nations Department of Peace Operations, New York, 2019.

36 Noha Shawki, 'The Responsibility to Protect: The Evolution of an International Norm', *Global Responsibility to Protect*, 3(2) 172–196 (2011); Jennifer Welsh, 'Norm Contestation and the Responsibility to Protect', *Global Responsibility to Protect*, 5(4) 365–396 (2013), p. 365.

37 Staunton and Ralph, 'The Responsibility to Protect Norm Cluster', pp. 663–666.

TABLE 2 Responsibility to protect norm

Problem	Value	Behaviour
Genocide War crimes Crimes against humanity Ethnic cleansing	Customary international law International humanitarian law 1948 genocide convention 1998 Rome statute Human protection Human rights Universal moral minimalism	Prevent the four crimes (including their incitement) Establish early warning systems Encourage and assist states to fulfil their R2P Use all coercive and non-coercive measures under Chapters VI, VII, and VIII of the UN Charter

norms (Lantis and Wunderlich's understanding of norm clusters) as a 'complex norm cluster' (to use Staunton and Ralph's terminology). Regarding its internal structure, it embodies both domestic and international responsibilities which were captured in the three pillar formulation: Pillar One refers to the domestic responsibility of states to protect their population from the four crimes, Pillar Two refers to the international responsibility to encourage and assist states to fulfil Pillar One, and Pillar Three refers to cases where a state is 'manifestly failing' to fulfil its R2P which permits the Security Council to consider 'timely and decisive response' measures under Chapters VI, VII, and VIII of the UN Charter on a case-by-case basis.[38] Because the R2P covers 'just' four crimes, identifying the *problem* is straightforward as it addresses the threat posed by genocide, war crimes, crimes against humanity, and ethnic cleansing, which are commonly known as 'atrocity crimes'.[39] Grounding R2P's *value* is more challenging. From a legal perspective, it is commonly accepted that R2P did not create any new laws but that the primary responsibility of states (Pillar One) to protect their population from the four crimes is grounded in Customary International Law, while International Humanitarian Law and the 1948 Genocide Convention place a

38 UN General Assembly (UNGA), *Report of the Secretary-General: Implementing the Responsibility to Protect*, A/63/677, 12 January 2009.

39 David Scheffer, 'Atrocity Crimes Framing the Responsibility to Protect' in Richard H. Cooper and Juliette V. Kohler (eds.), *Responsibility to Protect: The Global Moral Compact for the 21st Century* (Basingstoke: Palgrave Macmillan, 2009).

'number of obligations' on states to fulfil their responsibilities of 'encouragement' and 'assistance' under R2P's Pillar Two.[40] Finally, legal frameworks such as the Genocide Convention and the Rome Statute provide the legal grounding for considering more coercive measures. In addition, scholars appeal to the idea that these crimes violate a 'universal moral and legal minimalism' with R2P representing a 'newly legitimate moral minimum of global order'.[41] In so doing, they invoke values of universal moral and legal foundations. While some criticise R2P for adopting an 'atrocity lens' over a 'human rights lens', it is difficult to envisage how one can ground a commitment to preventing mass atrocities without ultimately invoking human rights.[42] At the behavioural level, R2P is broad in scope and we draw here on paragraphs 138 and 139 of the 2005 World Summit Outcome Document.[43]

As will be discussed below, the relationship between PoC and R2P is complex but the reality is that these norms are also increasingly invoked alongside counter-terrorism. Table 3 presents the tripartite structure of the counter-terrorism norm.

TABLE 3 Counter-terrorism norm

Problem	Value	Behaviour
Threat to government Threat to civilians	Sovereign authority Human protection Human rights	Intelligence and risk management State-led counter-terrorism operations International assistance to help governments address the threat posed by terrorism Global coalitions that act with or without consent of the host state

40 Ruben Reike and Alex J. Bellamy, 'The Responsibility to Protect and International Law', *Global Responsibility to Protect* 2(3) 276–280 (2010); Alex J. Bellamy, 'A Chronic Protection Problem: The DPRK and the Responsibility to Protect', *International Affairs*, 91(2) 225–244 (2015), p. 227.

41 Adrian Gallagher, *Genocide and Its Threat to Contemporary International Order* (Basingstoke: Palgrave, 2013); Michael W. Doyle, 'The Politics of Global Humanitarianism: The Responsibility to Protect before and after Libya', *International Politics*, 53(1) 14–31 (2016), p. 15.

42 Kirsten Ainley, 'From Atrocity Crimes to Human Rights: Expanding the Focus of the Responsibility to Protect', *Global Responsibility to Protect*, 9(3) 243–266 (2017).

43 A/RES/60/1, 24 October 2005, p. 30.

The counter-terrorism norm is built on vague foundations since there is no specific document and/or agreement to draw upon. Zimmerman highlights 19 different legal instruments associated with the prevention of terrorism.[44] Terrorism itself is not fixed and has historically been characterised by four 'waves' – 'Anarchist', 'Nationalist', 'Marxist', 'Religious'; or 'strains' – 'Socialist', 'Nationalist', 'Religious', and 'Exclusionist'.[45] Alongside this, there have been debates over whether terrorism can be 'just', which reflects the underlying ethical considerations that stem from the identification of a terrorist group and the response under the name of counter-terrorism.[46] Returning to Winston's tripartite framework, the *problem* that counter-terrorism seeks to address is terrorism. This is based on a commitment to the moral *value* of sovereign authority served by a wide range of associated national and international *behaviours* with the latter becoming more effective and formalised in the 1980s.[47] However, as Roberts points out, terrorist groups perpetrate human rights violations, and at times, foreign invasions have been justified as a 'means of restoring order or protecting a particular group'.[48] A critical aspect to bear in mind, therefore, is that counter-terrorism also embodies a human protection value and because of this, blurred boundaries arise between all three norm clusters. It is with this in mind that we shift our focus to understanding the linkages and tensions between these three norms at the conceptual level.

2 A Human Protection Norm Cluster

Having established the internal structure of the three norms in question, we turn our attention to Lantis and Wunderlich's understanding of 'norm clusters' as 'collections of aligned, but distinct, norms or principles that relate to a common, overarching issue area; they address different aspects and contain specific normative obligations'.[49] Against this backdrop, we view the overarching

44 Zimmerman, 'Strange Bedfellows', p. 2.

45 David C. Rapoport, 'The Fourth Wave: September 11 in the History of Terrorism', *Current History*, 100(650) 419–424 (2001); Tom Parker and Nick Sitter, 'The Four Horsemen of Terrorism. It's Not Waves, It's Strains', *Terrorism and Political Violence*, 28(2) 197–216 (2016).

46 Adam Roberts, 'Ethics, Terrorism and Counter-terrorism', *Terrorism and Political Violence*, 1(1) 48–69 (1989); Michael Walzer, *Arguing About War* (London: Yale University Press, [1987] 2004).

47 Rapoport, 'The Fourth Wave', p. 421.

48 Roberts, 'Ethics, Terrorism and Counter-terrorism', p. 58.

49 Lantis and Wunderlich, 'Resiliency Dynamics of Norm Clusters', p. 571.

'issue area' to be that of human protection within a broader 'international human protection regime'.[50]

At this point the reader may ask: why not keep PoC, R2P, and counter-terrorism as individual norms rather than viewing them as a norm cluster? We use an analogy here to illustrate our position further. In the 1950s, Martin Wight put forward the 'three traditions' of 'realism', 'rationalism', and 'revolutionism' in an attempt to capture the history of Western political thought. As Wight went on to explain, 'the three traditions are not like three railroad tracks running parallel into infinity ... the three traditions are streams, with eddies and cross-currents, sometimes interlacing and never for long confined to their own river bed'.[51] Drawing on this logic, we offer three interrelated points to defend our view that the PoC and R2P should be understood as a human protection norm cluster rather than individual norm clusters. The first refers to interwoven emergence. It is striking that when one reads the post-Cold War history of PoC and R2P they are driven by the very same crises: Bosnia, Rwanda, and Kosovo. The norms, therefore, are underpinned by a shared normative history in that they set out logics of appropriate behaviour in response to the same crises. In a slightly different way, R2P and counter-terrorism have also been on similar trajectory since 2001 – the year that the International Commission on Intervention and State Sovereignty (ICISS) report coining the phrase R2P was published and the 9/11 attacks on the United States which gave rise to a whole new counter-terrorism regime at the UN. Second, and linked to this, the conceptual foundations upon which all three norms are built are interrelated as shown by the internal structure of the three norms in question in that they embody 'the value' of human protection as they address 'the problem' of threats to civilians. Third, in upholding a 'third wave' view of norms as processes of contestation it is important to consider that these change over time, and in so doing, will take on different and perhaps increasingly blurred boundaries.[52] Bringing these three points together, it would be naive to suggest that we can separate these norms off from one another as parallel railroad tracks, and instead, we need to better understand the 'eddies and cross-currents' as they sometimes interlace (to use Wight's words).

Let us start with the linkages between R2P and PoC. As Rhoads and Welsh explain, the two norms were initially debated and implemented separately yet

50 Alex J. Bellamy, 'The Humanisation of Security? Towards an International Human Protection Regime', *European Journal of International Security*, 1(1) 112–133 (2016).

51 Martin Wight, *International Theory: The Three Traditions* (New York: Holmes and Meier, 1992), p. 260.

52 Wiener, *Contestation and Constitution of Norms in Global International Relations*.

have come together in recent years.[53] This is most evident through the UN's peacekeeping operations. Following the broadening of mission mandates in the 1990s, peacekeeping and PoC have increasingly intertwined.[54] As a result, PoC developed from an 'implied goal to a fundamental pillar of mission mandates', appearing in 95 per cent of mandates 1999–2017.[55] Peacekeeping is an important mechanism for implementing PoC since 'no other goal more clearly captures the ethos of what UN peacekeeping should be about than Protection of Civilians'.[56] However, academics have also argued that peacekeeping and R2P are interlinked for a similar reason.[57] The former UN Secretary-General Ban Ki-moon recognised the role of peacekeeping as a tool under R2P's Pillar Two.[58] What we see is a coming together of PoC and R2P in discursive practices[59] as, for example, they are invoked alongside one another in UNSC resolutions. Yet despite ideational interplay between the two norms, questions over whether these norms are on an equal footing remain unanswered and here tensions come to the fore.

To illustrate the tension between PoC and R2P, we draw on two types of norm contestation identified by Lantis and Wunderlich. First, 'conflicts that result from differing understandings of a norm's meaning'.[60] The broad scope of both PoC and R2P creates vague definitional parameters thus fuelling multiple interpretations and points of tension. At times, PoC and R2P are presented as 'sibling norms',[61] 'cousins in protection',[62] or as 'distinct but closely linked'[63]

53 Rhoads and Welsh, 'Close Cousins in Protection'.

54 Paul D. Williams, 'The Security Council's Peacekeeping Trilemma', *International Affairs*, 96(2) 479–499 (2020), p. 485.

55 David Curran, 'Muddling on Through? Cosmopolitan Peacekeeping and the Protection of Civilians', *International Peacekeeping*, 24(1) 63–85 (2017), p. 68.

56 Cedric de Coning, 'Protection of Civilians: From Generic to Context-Specific' in Mateja Peter (ed.), *United Nations Peace Operations: Aligning Principles and Practice* (Oslo: Norwegian Institute of International Affairs, 2015), p. 25.

57 Charles T. Hunt and Alex J. Bellamy, 'Mainstreaming the Responsibility to Protect in Peace Operations', *Civil Wars*, 13(1) 1–20 (2011), p. 1.

58 UNGA, *Responsibility to Protect: Timely and Decisive Response. Report of the Secretary-General*, A/66/874–S/2012/578, 25 July 2012, p. 5; UNGA, *A Vital and Enduring Commitment: Implementing the Responsibility to Protect. Report of the Secretary-General*, A/69/981–S/2015/500, 13 July 2015, p. 11.

59 Rhoads and Welsh, 'Close Cousins in Protection', p. 598.

60 Lantis and Wunderlich, 'Resiliency Dynamics of Norm Clusters', pp. 573–574.

61 Ramesh Thakur, 'The Responsibility to Protect at 15', *International Affairs*, 92(2) 415–434 (2016), p. 422.

62 Rhoads and Welsh, 'Close Cousins in Protection', p. 597.

63 Hunt, 'Analyzing the Co-evolution of the Responsibility to Protect and the Protection of Civilians in UN Peace Operations', p. 631.

in that they share a common commitment to human protection,[64] but display key differences.[65] The R2P sets out to protect people from four atrocity crimes whereas PoC is broader in scope.[66] While some have been keen to stress the common ground, others have rejected the idea that these are complementary norms. Tardy argues that 'issue-linkage between them is likely to be counter-productive' as there are differences in the coverage of crimes, methods of protection, and that R2P (particularly Pillar Three) is deemed more controversial than PoC.[67] However, R2P's Pillar Two is less controversial than Pillar Three and embodies operational parameters that facilitate interaction between R2P and PoC through peacekeeping operations,[68] which includes the use of force with the consent of the host state which has relevance for Mali.[69]

Second, we consider 'disputes about the relative weight of a norm'.[70] As UNSC resolutions increasingly invoke PoC and R2P, analysts try to understand what 'work' each norm is doing. If we compare and contrast PoC and R2P, the former holds more accumulative weight having been cited in most UNSC resolutions mandating peacekeeping missions since 1999. Furthermore, PoC is seen as less controversial and more widely accepted at the UN member state level. According to Sheeran and Kent, PoC has been more successful than the R2P in real terms because it has kept a 'low-profile'.[71] Within the R2P literature,

64 Alex J. Bellamy and Paul D. Williams, 'The New Politics of Protection? Côte d'Ivoire, Libya and the Responsibility to Protect', *International Affairs*, 87(4) 825–850 (2011), p. 827; Charles Sampford, 'A Tale of Two Norms', in Angus Francis, Vesselin Popovski, and Charles Sampford (eds.), *Norms of Protection: Responsibility to Protect, Protection of Civilians and Their Interaction* (New York: United Nations University Press), p. 105.

65 Vesselin Popovski, 'Siblings, but Not Twins: POC and R2P', 1 November 2011, https://unu.edu/publications/articles/siblings-but-not-twins-poc-and-r2p.html, accessed 27 June 2017.

66 Hugh Breakey, 'The Responsibility to Protect and the Protection of Civilians in Armed Conflict' in Angus Francis, Vesselin Popovski, and Charles Sampford (eds.), *Norms of Protection: Responsibility to Protect, Protection of Civilians and Their Interaction* (New York: United Nations University Press), p. 67; Williams, 'The R2P, Protection of Civilians, and UN Peacekeeping Operations', p. 528.

67 Thierry Tardy, 'The Dangerous Liaisons of the Responsibility to Protect and the Protection of Civilians in Peacekeeping Operations', *Global Responsibility to Protect*, 4(4) 424–448 (2012), p. 424.

68 Charles T. Hunt and Lisa Sharland, 'Implementing the Responsibility to Protect through United Nations Peacekeeping Operations: Opportunities and Challenges', in Cecilia Jacob and Martin Mennecke (eds.), *Implementing the Responsibility to Protect: A Future Agenda* (Abingdon: Routledge, 2019), pp. 215–235.

69 Adrian Gallagher, 'The Promise of Pillar II', *International Affairs*, 91 (6) 1259–1275 (2015), p. 1264.

70 Lantis and Wunderlich, 'Resiliency Dynamics of Norm Clusters', p. 574.

71 Scott Sheeran and Catherine Kent, 'Protection of Civilians, Responsibility to Protect, and Humanitarian Intervention: Conceptual and Normative Interactions' in Haidi Willmot,

the fact that it has been cited in over 80 UNSC resolutions is often viewed as evidence that the norm has gained traction. According to the Global Centre for the Responsibility to Protect, the norm was cited four times between 2005 and 2011 and 79 times since (including 43 times since January 2016).[72] Indeed, it is widely accepted that R2P 'language has become a broadly accepted practice for UNSC members'.[73] Yet critics have questioned whether these references to R2P represent meaningful engagement.[74] Putting this into context, Harrison found little evidence that R2P made a difference in any of the cases they studied: Darfur, Central African Republic, Kenya, Côte d'Ivoire, and Democratic Republic of Congo (DRC).[75] Pushing beyond these studies, the focus here on Mali offers a new empirical case but also situates R2P within the broader context of three norms.

Moving to counter-terrorism, placing this norm within the human protection norm cluster is controversial. Academics have stressed that as UN Peacekeeping operations have increasingly engaged in war and counter-terrorism they have lost their perception of impartiality, and in so doing, have undermined the objective of human protection.[76] This is not to suggest impartiality is fixed and it is here that our commitment to third wave norm research which views norms as processes comes back to the fore. As Rhoads explains, first wave studies on norms are limited because they fail to understand the changing nature of norms such as 'impartiality' which is shaped by the context in which it operates.[77] Within the context of the DRC, Rhoads argues that the UN has become 'one warring party among many' and it is precisely

---

Ralph Mamiya, Scott Sheeran, and Marc Weller (eds.), *Protection of Civilians* (Oxford: Oxford University Press, 2016), p. 61.

72 This was updated on 18 October 2021, see Global Centre for the Responsibility to Protect, UN Security Council Statements Referencing the R2P, https://www.globalr2p.org/resources/un-security-council-resolutions-and-presidential-statements-referencing-r2p/.

73 Jess Gifkins, 'R2P in the UN Security Council: Darfur, Libya and Beyond', *Cooperation and Conflict*, 51(2) 148–165 (2015), p. 159.

74 Aidan Hehir, *Hollow Norms and the Responsibility to Protect* (New York: Palgrave Macmillan; 2019).

75 Graham Harrison, 'Onwards and Sidewards? The Curious Case of the Responsibility to Protect and Mass Violence in Africa' *Journal of Intervention and State Building* 10 (2) 143–161 (2015).

76 Karlsrud, 'Towards UN Counter-terrorism Operations?'; Charbonneau, 'The Military Intervention in Mali and Beyond'; Alex J. Bellamy and Charles T. Hunt, 'Twenty-First Century UN Peace Operations: Protection, Force and the Changing Security Environment', *International Affairs* 91(6) 1277–1298 (2015).

77 Emily P. Rhoads, *Taking Sides in Peacekeeping: Impartiality and the Future of the United Nations* (Oxford: Oxford University Press, 2016).

this move which critics claim is undermining aspirations of peace.[78] The former UN Special Adviser to the UN Secretary-General on R2P Jennifer Welsh warned that R2P advocates are 'uncomfortable' with its 'close association' with counter-terrorism for fear that a 'security logic' will compromise a 'humanitarian logic'.[79] From an R2P perspective, a textbook case is Sri Lanka in 2009 as 40,000 people were killed while the government framed it as a War on Terror operation.[80] Despite such concerns, Welsh highlights that the 'connection is likely to endure' between R2P and counter-terrorism.[81]

The analysis above helps shed light on this enduring connection because the internal structure of the norms shows that they all embody a commitment to the value of human protection. As a result, and for reasons discussed, they can be viewed as a human protection norm cluster. We accept, however, that this is complicated because PoC and R2P are *primarily* driven by this value whereas counter-terrorism is not. This is why norms such as R2P and counter-terrorism have been described as 'strange bedfellows' which nonetheless have an evolving relationship.[82] As Zimmerman goes on to explain, 'what remains to be seen is how that relationship will play out and whether or not the protection of civilians is given the same effort and attention as initiatives to stop terrorism'.[83] Against this backdrop there is an urgent need to better understand the relationship between PoC, R2P, and counter-terrorism, which is why we now turn our attention to how this has played out in the case of Mali.

3 Evidencing the PoC, R2P, and Counter-Terrorism in Mali

To evidence and analyse the interaction between PoC, R2P, and counter-terrorism in Mali, we first collected each UN resolution on Mali, and reports from the Secretary-General on Mali, and then conducted keyword searches for

78 *ibid.*, p. 6. See also Charles T. Hunt, 'All Necessary Means to What Ends? The Unintended Consequences of the "Robust Turn" in UN Peace Operations', *International Peacekeeping* 24(1) 108–131 (2017).

79 Welsh, 'R2P's Next Ten Years, Deepening and Extending the Consensus', p. 993.

80 Welsh, 'Norm Contestation and the Responsibility to Protect', p. 386; Kimberly Nackers, 'Sri Lanka' in Alex Bellamy and Tim Dunne (eds.), *The Oxford Handbook of the Responsibility to Protect* (Oxford: Oxford University Press, 2016).

81 Welsh, 'R2P's Next Ten Years, Deepening and Extending the Consensus', p. 993.

82 Zimmerman, 'Strange Bedfellows'.

83 *ibid.*, p. 1.

each norm.[84] From here we examined MINUSMA's mandate in successive UN resolutions from 2013 to 2020 and Secretary-General reports on Mali to identify and analyse the interaction between PoC, R2P, and counter-terrorism. The following sections reveal the results of this analysis with the PoC and R2P being invoked together alongside the importance of countering terrorism in Mali, and in particular, its impact on the pursuit of PoC.

Finding evidence of the PoC norm in Mali is straightforward as the Security Council explicitly mandated MINUSMA 'to protect ... civilians under imminent threat of physical violence'.[85] The early mandating resolutions included references to several PoC values and behaviours.[86] Resolution 2164 (2014), for example, outlined the need for justice for violations of international humanitarian law – a core *value* of the PoC norm cluster.[87] The resolution equally mandated MINUSMA to provide physical civilian protection, which includes 'to deter threats', establishing a protective environment by conducting area patrols, and encouraging protection through dialogue and engagement such as supporting 'the implementation of the ceasefire and confidence-building measures on the ground'.[88] Though it has evolved over time to address shifting threats to civilians, PoC language has been a constant in seven subsequent iterations of MINUSMA's mandate from 2013 to 2020. These PoC values and behaviours have also featured regularly in reports of the UN Secretary-General on Mali.[89] MINUSMA for instance helped 'develop an integrated strategy on the protection of civilians', which is action consistent with all three of the behaviours in the PoC norm cluster.[90] In relation to the PoC behaviour of providing physical protection, it is also important to note how since 2016 the Security Council has mandated MINUSMA 'to take robust and active steps to protect civilians',

84 Keyword searches included 'responsibility to protect', 'terrorism', and the 'protection of civilians' and its variations of 'protect civilians', 'civilian protection', and 'protecting civilians'.

85 UNSC Res. 2100, 25 April 2013, p. 8.

86 UNSC Res. 2164, 25 June 2014, p. 6; UNSC Res. 2227, 29 June 2015, p. 7; UNSC Res. 2295, 29 June 2016, p. 8; UNSC Res. 2364, 29 June 2017, p. 9; UNSC Res. 2423, 28 June 2018, p. 11; UNSC Res. 2480, 28 June 2019, p. 8; UNSC Res. 2351, 29 June 2020, p. 9.

87 UNSC Res. 2164, 25 June 2014, p. 7.

88 *ibid.*, p. 6.

89 S/2013/338, 10 June 2013; S/2013/582, 1 October 2013; S/2014/229, 28 March 2014; S/2014/403, 9 June 2014; S/2014/692, 22 September 2014; S/2014/943, 23 December 2014; S/2015/219, 27 March 2015; S/2016/281, 28 March 2016; S/2016/498, 31 May 2016; S/2016/819, 29 September 2016; S/2017/271, 30 March 2017; S/2017/811, 28 September 2017; S/2018/273, 29 March 2018; S/2018/541, 6 June 2018; S/2019/262, 26 March 2019; S/2019/454, 31 May 2019; S/2020/223, 20 March 2020.

90 UNSC, *Report of the Secretary-General on the Situation in Mali*, S/2014/943, 23 December 2014, p. 8.

which appears to imply greater encouragement of the mission to use force to fulfil the PoC.[91] As the next section argues, this is an important change in the language of MINUSMA's mandate because it provides more latitude for peacekeepers to use force proactively in defence of the mandate, rather than just for their own protection. This in turn places the mission in a position where it may logically be expected to deter threats from terrorist groups and other non-state armed actors.

Grounding R2P in Mali is more complicated than the PoC. Returning to the tripartite structure embodied in the R2P, it is important to consider, first the problem (the four crimes), second the values (international law and human protection), and third the behaviours (international assistance) in the R2P norm cluster. Regarding the crimes, the issue is that R2P embodies a threshold that PoC does not. The High Commissioner for Human Rights Navi Pillay condemned armed groups for 'committing serious human rights violations and *possibly* war crimes'.[92] The statement gives a sense that the violence in Mali was thought to potentially equate to atrocity crimes, but this was still not clear. As Karlsrud explains, in January 2013, the International Criminal Court launched a formal investigation into the situation in Mali, yet on the very same day acknowledged that '[a]t this stage, the information available does not provide a reasonable basis to conclude that crimes against humanity under Article 7 have been committed'.[93] But of course, a crucial element of R2P is the prevention of atrocity crimes and so as the situation deteriorated there seemed to be a general acceptance that the violence amounted to war crimes and/or crimes against humanity. This was explicit in UN Resolution 2227 in 2015 as it strongly condemned the human rights violations, which could be associated with PoC, but went further as it claimed these acts 'may amount to crimes under the Rome Statute'.[94] R2P values were present through the emphasis on the pursuit of justice for 'war crimes and crimes against humanity',[95] in addition to the consistent importance of human protection from mass violence

91 UNSC Res. 2295, 29 June 2016, p. 8; UNSC Res. 2364, 29 June 2017, p. 9; UNSC Res. 2423, 28 June 2018, p. 9; UNSC Res. 2480, 28 June 2019, p. 8; UNSC Res. 2351, 29 June 2020, p. 9.

92 UN News, 'Top UN Official Condemns Amputations, Human Rights Violations in Northern Mali', 17 September 2012, https://news.un.org/en/story/2012/09/419792, accessed 1 September 2020, emphasis added.

93 John Karlsrud, 'Mali' in Alex J. Bellamy and Tim Dunne (eds), The Oxford Handbook of the Responsibility to Protect (Oxford: Oxford University Press, 2016), p.798.

94 UNSC Res. 2227, 29 June 2015. See also, UNSC Res. 2295, 29 June 2016; UNSC Res. 2374, 5 September 2017; UNSC Res. 2423, 28 June 2018; UNSC Res. 2480, 28 June 2019; UNSC Res. 2531, 29 June 2020.

95 UNSC Res. 2480, 28 June 2019, p. 9.

and atrocity crimes in UN resolutions between 2013 and 2020.[96] This appeals not only to potential violations of the Rome Statute, but also broader international humanitarian law, human protection, and human rights, all of which we define as core R2P values but of course, there is overlap with PoC.

In terms of behaviours, we see common references to both the domestic responsibility of the Malian government as well as the international responsibility to assist them. The African-led International Support Mission to Mali (AFISMA) was deployed to 'support the Malian authorities in their primary responsibility to protect the population'.[97] Similarly, part of Resolution 2100 that launched MINUSMA was assisting the Malian government which has a 'primary responsibility to protect'.[98] Although one could argue that governments have many responsibilities and the statements here do not reference the R2P explicitly, to return to the threat of mass atrocities raised by prominent actors above, it is evident that these references to domestic and international responsibilities were, in part, driven by fears of mass atrocities. From this perspective, the R2P did some of the work in authorising AFISMA and Operation Serval and thus the spirit of the R2P was evident even though there was no explicit R2P mandate underpinning MINUSMA despite alleged atrocity crimes and evolving protection threats from inter-communal violence in the centre of Mali from 2016 onwards.[99] Between 2015 and 2017, UN resolutions reiterated the 'primary responsibility of the Malian authorities to protect the population' but this was not made with reference to the R2P.[100] Between 2018 to 2020, UN resolutions on Mali were ambiguous in the use of R2P language, particularly in restating 'that the Malian authorities have primary responsibility to protect civilians in Mali'.[101] Accordingly, there were no clear attempts to explicitly invoke R2P with reference to MINUSMA despite there appearing to be perfectly

96 UNSC Res. 2100, 25 April 2013, p. 8; UNSC Res. 2164; 25 June 2014, p. 7; UNSC Res. 2227, 29 June 2015, p. 7; UNSC Res. 2295, 29 June 2016, p. 9; UNSC Res. 2364, 29 June 2017, p. 9; UNSC Res. 2423, 28 June 2018, p. 12; UNSC Res. 2480, 28 June 2019, p. 9; UNSC Res. 2351, 29 June 2020, p. 10.

97 UNSC Res. 2085, 20 December 2012, p. 4.

98 UNSC Res. 2100, 25 April 2013, pp. 8–9.

99 Resolutions between 2015 and 2017 reiterated the 'primary responsibility of the Malian authorities to protect the population' but this was not made with reference to the R2P, see UNSC Res. 2227, 29 June 2015, p. 2; UNSC Res. 2295, 29 June 2016, p. 4; UNSC Res. 2364, 29 June 2017, p. 5; UNSC Res. 2374, 29 June 2017, p. 5.

100 Between 2018 and 2020, UN resolutions on Mali were ambiguous in the use of R2P language, particularly in restating 'that the Malian authorities have primary responsibility to protect civilians in Mali', which implies a combination of language on the R2P and PoC.

101 UNSC Res. 2423, 28 June 2018, p. 11; UNSC Res. 2480, 28 June 2019, p. 8; UNSC Res. 2351, 29 June 2020, p. 9.

logical grounds to do so, which as to be discussed in the next section, highlights the peripheral role that the norm played.

Moving to counter-terrorism, the emergence and consolidation of non-state armed terrorist groups in Mali has generated the problems, values, and behaviours associated with counter-terrorism. Early in the crisis, the rise of jihadist groups in Mali linked to global terrorist networks such as Al Qaeda and Islamic State received notable attention from influential Security Council members such as China and France.[102] In authorising international responses, these powers have placed emphasis on terrorist threats to the government and population (the problem), the need to uphold the sovereign authority of the government (value), and the deployment of a constellation of interventions including MINUSMA and counter-terrorism forces such as Operation Barkhane and the G5-Sahel Joint Force (behaviour).

Despite early successes in pushing back the jihadist fighters, the Malian government with support from international forces has struggled to gain a monopoly of legitimate force over its territory. Jihadist governance including the imposition of strict interpretations of Sharia has returned and prevailed in many parts of the north as the years have passed, marked by an increase in asymmetric attacks since 2018.[103] In addition, terrorist groups have also extended their reach into the central regions of Mali, instrumentalising long-standing herder-farmer disputes over access to land and fuelling increasingly deadly

---

102 Li Baodong, 'Statement by Ambassador Li Baodong at the Security Council Ministerial Meeting on the Sahel Region Situation', 12 October 2012, http://chnun.chinamission.org.cn/eng/hyyfy/t997728.htm, accessed 16 August 2020; Liu Jieyi, 'Statement by Ambassador Liu Jieyi at the Security Council Briefing on Situation in the Sahel', 12 December 2013, https://www.fmprc.gov.cn/ce/ceun/eng/chinaandun/securitycouncil/thematicissues/other_thematicissues/t1109431.htm, accessed 16 August 2020; Gérard Araud, 'The Challenges of the Fight against Terrorism in Africa – Statement by Mr Gérard Araud, Permanent Representative of France to the United Nations', 13 May 2013, https://onu.delegfrance.org/13-May-2013-Security-Council-The, accessed 16 August 2020; Martin Briens, 'Threats to International Peace and Security Caused by Terrorist Acts – Statement by Mr Martin Briens, Deputy Permanent Representative of France to the United Nations', 15 January 2013, https://onu.delegfrance.org/15 January-2013-Security-Council, accessed 16 August 2020; Alexis Lamek, 'Peace and Security in Sahel – Statement by Mr. Alexis Lamek, Deputy Representative of France to the United Nations', 25 November 2015, https://onu.delegfrance.org/France-committed-to-assisting-the-countries-of-the-Sahel-in-addressing-the, accessed 16 August 2020; François Delattre, 'Mali/MINUSMA – Statement by Mr. François Delattre, Permanent Representative of France to the United Nations Security Council', 19 October 2018, https://onu.delegfrance.org/Mali-a-positive-dynamic-but-still-much-progress-that-needs-to-be-made, accessed 16 August 2020.

103 International Crisis Group, 'CrisisWatch: Mali', 2020, https://www.crisisgroup.org/crisiswatch/print?page=1&location%5B0%5D=26&date_range=cust&t=CrisisWatch+Database+Filter, accessed 16 August 2020.

clashes and cycles of reprisals.[104] The *problem* of countering violent extremism and jihadist armed groups was fairly clear and has endured.

All the Security Council responses to date can be understood to enshrine the counter-terrorism *value* of defending and buttressing state sovereignty. The logic underpinning MINUSMA, in particular, is supporting the host state in stabilising the situation, including through the extension of state authority and redeployment of the Malians Defence and Security Forces (MDSF) throughout the country.

The UN has been at pains to reiterate that MINUSMA is not a counter-terrorism force and it has not engaged in kinetic offensive operations against jihadist groups. It is nevertheless authorised 'to take active steps to anticipate, deter and effectively respond to threats to the civilian population, notably in the North and Center of Mali … [and] … to prevent the return of active armed elements to key population centres and other areas where civilians are at risk, engaging in direct operations pursuant only to serious and credible threats'[105] (presumably including jihadist groups). Furthermore, as mentioned above, MINUSMA is instructed to 'ensure adequate coordination, exchange of information and, when applicable, support, within their respective mandates and through existing mechanisms, between MINUSMA … the FC-G5S, [and] the French Forces'.[106]

The fact it is also tasked with supporting the host government in terms of stabilisation means there are a number of ways in which MINUSMA can be understood as part of the counter-terrorism constellation in Mali. However, regular attacks resulting in high levels of fatalities have led to the 'bunkerisation' of the mission.[107] This begins to illustrate the highly unstable environment in which

104 Natasja Rupesinghe, Mikael Hiberg Naghizadeh, and Corentin Cohen, 'Reviewing Jihadist Governance in the Sahel', *NUPI Working Paper, 894* (Oslo: NUPI, 2021). See also Tor A. Benjaminsen and Boubacar Ba, 'Why Do Pastoralists in Mali Join Jihadist Groups? A Political Ecological Explanation', *The Journal of Peasant Studies,* 46(1) 1–20 (2019); Adam Sandor, *Insecurity, the Breakdown of Social Trust, and Armed Actor Governance in Central and Northern Mali'*(Montréal: Centre FrancoPaix de la Chaire Raoul-Dandurand, 2017); Tor A. Benjaminsen and Boubacar Ba, 'Fulani-Dogon Killings in Mali: Farmer-Herder Conflicts as Insurgency and Counterinsurgency', *African Security,* 14(1) 4–26 (2021).

105 S/RES/2480, 28 June 2019, para. 28(c)(ii). NB: Similar formulation included in all mandates since beginning of the mission.

106 S/RES/2480, 28 June 2019, para. 30. NB: Similar formulation included in all mandates since beginning of the mission.

107 Mali has been labelled the 'most dangerous country in the world for UN peacekeepers'. See, for instance, Ruth Maclean and Dan Sabbagh, 'Dangerous, Complex, Vast: UK Troops' Challenges in Mali', *The Guardian,* 8 August 2019, https://www.theguardian.com

MINUSMA personnel are operating as a result, in part, of the emergence and proliferation of terrorist groups.[108]

4 The Interaction between PoC, R2P, and Counter-terrorism in Mali

The evidence of PoC, R2P, and counter-terrorism in Mali raises questions over their interaction, influence, and whether they carry equal weight as part of a human protection norm cluster. Let us first consider PoC and R2P. According to MINUSMA's official website, the mission's PoC 'responsibility is understood to be complementary to that of the host government, which has the primary responsibility to protect its own population'.[109] If it is generally accepted that part of this assistance is to protect the population from atrocity crimes, then this could equally be interpreted through an R2P lens under Pillar Two. Similarly, following the escalation of violence against civilians in 2019 a joint statement by the UN's Special Advisers on genocide and R2P called on actors in Mali 'to fulfil their responsibility to protect to prevent atrocity crimes and protect civilians'.[110] While it is plausible to argue that this language demonstrates important overlap between PoC and R2P, this is not acknowledged in these statements.

Some have argued this reflects the reality that these norms (in a human protection norm cluster) are in a co-evolutionary relationship where the implementation of one feeds back on and shapes the other. Given their shared foundations discussed above this is perhaps inevitable.[111] For critics, however, this language reflects the emergence of a 'responsibility to protect civilians'

/uk-news/2019/aug/08/britain-to-join-uns-mission-in-mali-in-effort-to-quell-violence, accessed 16 August 2020.

108 UNSC, *The Situation in Mali: Report of the Secretary-General on the Situation in Mali*, S/2020/952, 29 September 2020.

109 MINUSMA, 'Protection of Civilians', 2020, https://minusma.unmissions.org/en/protection-civilians, accessed 16 August 2020.

110 Office of the Special Representative of the Secretary-General, 'Joint Statement by the UN Special Advisers on the Prevention of Genocide and the R2P. Children and Armed Conflict', 15 October 2019, https://www.un.org/sg/en/content/sg/note-correspondents/2019-10-15/note-correspondents-joint-statement-adama-dieng-united-nations-special-adviser-the-prevention-of-genocide-and-karen-smith-united-nations-special-adviser-the, accessed 16 August 2020.

111 Charles T. Hunt, 'The Responsibility to Protect and the Protection of Civilians in UN Peace Operations: Interaction, Feedback and Co-evolution' in Charles T. Hunt and Paul Orchard (eds.), *Constructing the Responsibility to Protect: Contestation and Consolidation* (Abingdon: Routledge, 2020), pp. 89–112.

that conflates two distinct norms.[112] This exact language is explicit in successive UN resolutions on the crisis in Mali, which first appeared in Resolution 2100 and 'reiterates that the transitional authorities of Mali have primary responsibility to protect civilians in Mali'.[113] To draw on Lantis and Wunderlich, in Mali we therefore see potential 'conflicts that result from different understandings of a norm's meaning'.[114] The result of which are statements such as the responsibility to protect civilians where two distinct protection norms are presented as one. As we argued earlier however, PoC and R2P are distinct. R2P is framed more narrowly according to the four atrocity crimes and three pillars, while PoC is a much broader norm encompassing a wide range of subsequent values and behaviours. Simply assuming that PoC and R2P are two sides of the same coin thus neglects attempts to recognise their distinctiveness.[115]

Alongside the potential tensions between PoC and R2P is the additional contestation regarding 'disputes about the relative weight of a norm'.[116] While PoC has been identified as core to MINUSMA's mandate, there is a lack of explicit references to the R2P in official UN documents beyond Pillar One references in resolutions 2085, 2227, 2295, 2364, and 2375, and one explicit reference to Pillar Two in Resolution 2085.[117] As established, PoC has been a central component of MINUSMA's protection mandate since the mission's inception in 2013. Conversely, aside from the joint statement by the Special Advisers on genocide and R2P, one would be hard pressed to find an explicit reference to R2P in official UN documents beyond UNSC resolutions on Mali. When considering the explicit reference to alleged R2P crimes being committed in Mali, it is notable that little attempt has been made by the UN to apply an R2P lens in framing its response. This in turn conveys the impression that R2P is peripheral in Mali. As we have argued, the allegations of atrocity crimes and the assistance provided by MINUSMA are reflective of R2P's Pillar Two. Yet, in overlooking R2P in Mali, this does not bode well for attempts from the UN and its member states to translate R2P rhetoric into tangible action in relevant crises.

---

112 Tardy, 'The Dangerous Liaisons of the Responsibility to Protect and the Protection of Civilians in Peacekeeping Operations', p. 424.

113 UNSC Res. 2100, 25 April 2013, p. 9; UNSC Res. 2164, 25 June 2014, p. 10; UNSC Res. 2227, 29 June 2015, p. 11; UNSC Res. 2295, 29 June 2016, p. 12; UNSC Res. 2364, 29 June 2017, p. 13; UNSC Res. 2423, 28 June 2018, p. 16; UNSC Res. 2480, 28 June 2019, p. 13; UNSC Res. 2351, 29 June 2020, p. 15.

114 Lantis and Wunderlich, 'Resiliency Dynamics of Norm Clusters', p. 573.

115 Tardy, 'The Dangerous Liaisons of the Responsibility to Protect and the Protection of Civilians in Peacekeeping Operations'.

116 Lantis and Wunderlich, 'Resiliency Dynamics of Norm Clusters', p. 573.

117 UNSC Res. 2085, 20 December 2012; UNSC Res. 2227, 29 June 2015; UNSC Res. 2295, 29 June 2016; UNSC Res. 2364, 29 June 2017; UNSC Res. 2374, 5 September 2017.

On closer inspection however, even though the R2P is peripheral in Mali, MINUSMA's PoC mandate in some UN resolutions refers to R2P values and behaviours. For example, resolutions 2295, 2364, 2432, 2480, and 2351 refer explicitly to the role of early warning in order to protect civilians, which was identified in section one as being one of the four behaviours in the R2P norm cluster (see Figure 3).[118] In addition, MINUSMA's mandate in these resolutions authorises the use of force under Chapter VII to protect civilians, which is also an important R2P-type behaviour. This is an important finding because it shows how, in spite of the limited references to R2P beyond Pillar One, core behaviours in the R2P norm cluster are being implemented and pursued as part of MINUSMA's mandate. This raises broader questions as to why the PoC appears to have greater weight than R2P in Mali, despite there being clear grounds for the R2P's implementation and evidence of its values and behaviours being cited in MINUSMA's mandate.[119] As suggested in section one, research suggests that R2P has become an important part of the Security Council's discourse – being frequently mentioned in its resolutions.[120] In Mali, however, the PoC is at the core of the human protection response, with the R2P existing indirectly through inclusion of its values and behaviours rather than explicit references beyond Pillar One. R2P's peripheral role thus shows a gap between the proliferation of R2P rhetoric at the UN level and the practice of R2P in human protection crises such as in Mali.

Returning to Lantis and Wunderlich, the evidence of PoC and R2P values and behaviours in Mali demonstrates their overarching concern for human protection and therefore their inclusion in the human protection norm cluster. However, there are also clear differences in the relative weight of each norm and in interpretations of what the norms mean in relation to the situation in Mali. As this section shows, the PoC is at the core of the human protection norm cluster in Mali, while the R2P is peripheral. This is despite references to R2P values and behaviours, but limited direct references to explicit R2P action. This shows that even when norms form a cluster in order to address an overarching concern, these norms do not necessarily play an equal role even when there is evidence of the values and behaviours of different norms being invoked.

The interaction between PoC and R2P is further complicated by their relationship with counter-terrorism. At this point, it is important to reiterate that

118 UNSC Res. 2295, 29 June 2016; UNSC Res. 2364, 29 June 2017; UNSC Res. 2423, 28 June 2018; UNSC Res. 2480, 28 June 2019; UNSC Res. 2351, 29 June 2020.

119 Gallagher, 'The Promise of Pillar II'; Karlsrud, 'Mali'.

120 Gifkins, 'R2P in the UN Security Council'.

since its inception MINUSMA has been operating alongside counter-terrorism forces, including the French Operation Barkhane and the regional G5-Sahel Joint Force. While the UN Secretary-General acknowledges that MINUSMA does not have 'a counter-terrorism mandate',[121] the missions do 'pool some resources'.[122] Analysts claim that 'it is an open secret that MINUSMA shares intelligence and analysis with the parallel forces deployed in Mali'.[123] It is therefore unsurprising that 'the MINUSMA mandate could be interpreted as giving wide latitude for counterterrorism activities'.[124]

MINUSMA's mandate is also unclear on the relationship with the parallel counter-terrorism forces. One of MINUSMA's responsibilities under Resolution 2295 (2016) is 'to anticipate, deter and *counter threats,* including *asymmetric threats,* and to take *robust and active steps to protect civilians*' and 'engaging in direct operations pursuant only to *serious* and *credible threats*'.[125] What constitutes an asymmetric threat is highly ambiguous and it is plausible to argue that terrorist attacks on peacekeepers and civilians constitute both *asymmetric attacks* and *serious and credible threats*, especially to MINUSMA's mandate to protect civilians. Notably, both MINUSMA and Operation Barkhane have worked together in 'tracking down members of the terrorist networks'.[126] For France, this shows that 'both operationally and logistically, MINUSMA and Operation Barkhane are closely interlinked and mutually reinforcing'.[127]

Our concern is that even if one accepts the view that MINUSMA and Operation Barkhane are mutually reinforcing, this does not necessarily mean that counter-terrorism, PoC, and R2P reinforce one another. Interesting, however, is the extent to which the peripheral norm of counter-terrorism is impacting on the core norm of PoC. This is illustrated through the perceived mutual relationship between parallel enforcement operations targeting jihadist groups (counter-terrorism) and MINUSMA (PoC). A close association with counter-terrorism efforts risks MINUSMA being interpreted by parties to the conflict as being at war, which is said to 'undermine the legitimacy

121 UNSC, *Situation in Mali: Report of the Secretary-General*, S/2019/983, 30 December 2019, p. 17.

122 Yvan Guichaoua, 'The Bitter Harvest of French Interventionism in the Sahel', *International Affairs*, 96(4) 895–911 (2020), p. 899.

123 Charbonneau, 'The Military Intervention in Mali and Beyond'.

124 Karlsrud, 'From Liberal Peacebuilding to Stabilization and Counterterrorism', p. 12.

125 UNSC Res. 2295, 29 June 2016, p. 8, emphasis added.

126 Permanent Mission of France to the UN, 'France Stands by Mali's Side in Fighting Terrorism: The Example of Operation Fildjo in Gao', 19 July 2018, https://onu.delegfrance.org/Fight-Against-Terrorism-in-Mali-the-operation-Fildjo, accessed 16 August 2020.

127 Le Drian, 'Mali'.

of not only MINUSMA itself, but also the tool of peacekeeping'.[128] We share the concern that the loss of impartiality for peacekeepers responsible for implementing PoC makes them a target for terrorist groups. This can be counter-productive in that the importance of impartiality is that the goal of 'UN peacekeepers is to work *with*, not against, the parties to any conflict'.[129] The 2020 UN Peacekeeping Handbook on PoC suggests that peacekeeping missions 'must proceed with caution if the actions of those [counter-terrorism] forces directly or indirectly cause threats or harm to civilians or if association with them [counter-terrorism] affects the populations' perception of the mission'.[130] The UN thus recognises the implications for civilian harm and loss of impartiality if missions implementing PoC develop a relationship with counter-terrorism forces.[131] When viewed as an example of the human protection norm cluster, the crisis in Mali is significant in illustrating how the peripheral norm of counter-terrorism can have a detrimental impact on implementation of the core norm of PoC through the relationship between operations focusing on the two different norms, respectively.[132]

The Mali case thus shows that even though the three norms have been invoked alongside one another, they do not carry equal weight and influence on the response to the crisis. PoC is core to MINUSMA, while counter-terrorism efforts are peripheral, yet still potentially detrimental for the pursuit of PoC given MINUSMA's close links to parallel counter-terrorism forces. In comparison, the R2P's peripheral role in Mali raises questions about UN attempts to translate its rhetoric into action to demonstrate the added value and tangible influence of the norm on the ground. Given its protection focus, R2P would appear more suited to MINUSMA with regards to international assistance, and yet, counter-terrorism is having more of an impact upon the core PoC norm.

128 Karlsrud, 'Towards UN Counter-terrorism Operations?', p. 1225.

129 Louise R. Andersen, 'The HIPPO in the Room: The Pragmatic Push-back from the UN Peace Bureaucracy against the Militarization of UN Peacekeeping', *International Affairs*, 94(2) 343–361 (2018), p. 351.

130 UN Department of Peace Operations, 'The Protection of Civilians in United Nations Peacekeeping Handbook', p. 19.

131 For elaboration on this argument, see Hunt, 'All Necessary Means to What Ends?'

132 See also L. W. Moe, 'The Dark Side of Institutional Collaboration: How Peacekeeping-Counterterrorism Convergences Weaken the Protection of Civilians in Mali', *International Peacekeeping* 28(1) 1–29 (2021).

5 Conclusion

Mass violence in the 1990s saw the new norms of PoC and R2P emerge to become part of common human protection discourse at the Security Council. These norms, in and of themselves, have seen an exponential growth in academic study which has gone to great lengths to highlight the internal complexities, as well as the commonalities and differences, between them. Amidst these ongoing debates, mass violence in the twenty-first century has seen another level of complexity added as PoC and R2P are increasingly invoked alongside counter-terrorism. As far as the authors are aware, this is the first study to analyse the relationship between these three norms. To do this, it utilised two studies on 'norm clusters' which are notably different despite the fact that they use the same term. Section one drew on Winston's use of 'norm clusters' to explain the internal problem-value-behaviour structure embodied within the three norms in question.[133] Section two used Lantis and Wunderlich's understanding of 'norm clusters' to analyse the linkages between them.[134] Drawing these two together, we argue that because these three norms embody a commitment to 'the value' of human protection in order to solve 'the problem' of threats to civilians it helps shed light on why viewing these norms as separate independent areas of implementation is limited and limiting for our understanding of what pertains overall and the work being done by each norm. As a result, we argue these norms should be viewed as a 'human protection norm cluster'. Whereas some academics and policymakers have called for these norms to be treated as separate, we draw on Wight to propose that they cannot be viewed as 'parallel railroad tracks' and instead, we need to better understand the 'eddies and cross-currents' as they sometimes interlace.

Situating the human protection norms cluster within the context of Mali, the research findings show that first, even though the norms are invoked alongside one another this should not lead one to conclude that they are on an equal footing. Different norms have had different weight at different points in time. Counter-terrorism, and to lesser extent the R2P, were more influential in shaping AFISMA/French interventions. Even in its early stages, MINUSMA was really about state-support and only rhetorically interested in PoC until the threats to civilians changed post-2016, which saw PoC become the core norm. Second, despite these three norms embodying a human protection value they should not be viewed as mutually reinforcing. Third, even though

133 Winston, 'Norm Structure, Diffusion and Evolution'.

134 Lantis and Wunderlich, 'Resiliency Dynamics of Norm Clusters'.

counter-terrorism plays a more peripheral role, it has a detrimental impact upon PoC. Here we uphold the view that perceptions of peacekeeper partiality makes missions such as MINUSMA a target for terrorist groups which limits their PoC effectiveness.

Going forward, there is a need for more research on the three norms in question and we welcome other case study analysis in the future. Karlsrud foresees that future missions in countries such as Libya, Syria, and Yemen may face the same challenges as MINUSMA, thus creating an urgent need to better understand the norm dynamics at play.[135] At a broader level, norm orientated research needs to consider how different norms within norm clusters impact upon one another. The fact that a norm at the margins can have a detrimental impact upon a norm at the centre needs to be investigated in other contexts as we strive to make sense of the complexities embodied in norm dynamics.

135 Karlsrud, 'UN Peace Operations, Terrorism, and Violent Extremism', p. 159.

CHAPTER 5

Civilian Protection: Integrating Community Self-Protection with the Responsibility to Protect and the UN Global Counter-terrorism Strategy

Wisdom Oghosa Iyekekpolo | ORCID: 0000-0002-5957-3976
Faculty Member, Department of Politics and International Relations, University of Auckland, Auckland, New Zealand
w.iyekekpolo@auckland.ac.nz

Abstract

How do we achieve the protection of vulnerable civilians from violent non-state actors in Nigeria? This chapter argues that despite the seemingly different approaches of Responsibility to Protect (R2P) and the UN Global Counter-Terrorism Strategy, both can align at an intrastate implementation level to protect exposed communities from armed groups. The UN's adoption of a people-centric approach to counter-terrorism (CT) and the preventive measures against heinous crimes instituted in pillars one and two of R2P creates the space for this cooperation. This chapter further shows how practitioners can integrate both regimes with local networks to provide a holistic civilian protection strategy. This approach encompasses international, state, and local agency in halting the proliferation and activities of violent non-state groups. I espouse a framework for the protection of vulnerable Nigerian populations based on three factors – community self-protection, economic well-being, and ideological reorientation.

Keywords

R2P – counter-terrorism – Nigeria – self-protection – Boko Haram – insurgency – bandits – Fulani extremists – herders-farmers conflict

 | DOI:10.1163/9789004548114_007

1 Introduction

The persistent terror threats and armed attacks in northern Nigeria have placed the region's people as one of the most terrorised in the world. The Global Terrorism Database shows that Boko Haram and the Fulani extremist groups account for most of the area's killings and abduction of vulnerable civilians.[1] These armed groups have shown no discrimination between attacks on security officers and the civilian population. Soft targets have become the hallmark of their attacks. They have demonstrated their capacity in armed rebellion against Nigeria and their tendency to selectively abduct people for ransom or kill those who are either opposed to their ideology or of a different ethnoreligious group.[2] The failure of the state and the international community to ensure the protection of these vulnerable populations has resulted in calls and implementation of several forms of community self-protection initiatives, including armed community self-protection – with dire consequences.[3] This community involvement in civilian protection is begging for an overhaul and a more holistic integration into the overall countering of violent non-state actors.

Recent studies on countering these armed non-state actors in Nigeria have either emphasised more effective counter-terrorism (CT) measures or called on the state to invite international intervention through the doctrine of responsibility to protect (R2P).[4] However, emphasising these regimes without recognising and incorporating the vital role of local agency will inhibit and defeat the pursuit of a people-centric civilian protection approach. When it comes

1 Institute for Economics & Peace, 'Global Terrorism Index 2020: Measuring the Impact of Terrorism', Sydney, November 2020. Available from: http://visionofhumanity.org/reports, accessed from 18 May 2021.

2 Bolaji Omitola et al., 'The Triangle of Terror: Boko Haram, Fulani Herdsmen, Bandits and Organised Insecurity in Nigeria', *Studia Securitatis*, 15(1) 21–33 (2021); Global Centre for the Responsibility to Protect, '35,000 People Killed since 2009 Due to Violence and Insecurity Caused by Boko Haram', updated 31 May 2021, https://www.globalr2p.org/countries/nigeria/, accessed 31 May 2021.

3 Abubakar Ahmadu Maishanu, 'Terrorism: Buy Guns, Defend Yourselves, Zamfara Govt Tells Residents', 26 June 2022. https://www.premiumtimesng.com/news/headlines/539237-terrorism-buy-guns-defend-yourselves-zamfara-govt-tells-residents.html, accessed 26 June 2022.

4 Surulola Eke, 'Population-Centric Counterinsurgency in the Age of Salafi-Driven Insurgencies', *Journal of Global Security Studies* 5(1) 196–215 (2020); Chijioke Egwu Ekumaoko and Kingsley Emeka Ezemenaka, 'Responsibility to Protect: External Intervention on Boko Haram Terrorism in Nigeria', *Security Journal*, 33(3) 493–513 (2020); Emeka Thaddues Njoku, 'Merchants of Terror: Neo-Patrimonialism, Counterterrorism Economy, and Expansion of Terrorism in Nigeria', *African Conflict and Peacebuilding Review*, 10(2) 83–107 (2020);

to implementation, studies have shown the complexities of environments and challenges when the external interpretation of protection does not resonate well with local realities.[5] Hence, there is the need to identify when both regimes can align and how best they can support the resilience of communities exposed to incessant armed attacks. Integrating local support, knowledge, and the communication network with a combination of CT and R2P norms would provide a holistic civilian protection measure that incorporates the international community, the state, and local agency.

How do we achieve the protection of vulnerable civilians from violent non-state actors in Nigeria? There is no doubt that both CT and R2P aim to protect helpless civilians. However, while the CT regime seems state-centric and focuses on the coercive crackdown on terrorist groups, the R2P norm emphasises the international and state responsibility to protect the civilian population in conflict zones against four cardinal crimes perpetuated by the state or armed non-state groups. In analysing the convergence between CT and R2P, scholars have sought to understand if CT is a state obligation under R2P.[6] However, Shannon Zimmerman's study of the Tamil Tigers conflict in Sri Lanka and the Islamic State insurgency in Iraq and Syria emphasises that subject to interpretation and implementation, the norms could either support or oppose each other.[7] Zimmerman's study established that these regimes that approach the protection of vulnerable communities from international and state perspectives could support each other. Still, I argue for the augmentation of these with local knowledge and support. In essence, this chapter argues that while the R2P and CT regimes need to support each other in countering the activities of non-state armed groups, they need to align their measures with an increased capacity of the vulnerable communities to remain resilient.

Daniel Kofi Banini, 'Security Sector Corruption and Military Effectiveness: The Influence of Corruption on Countermeasures against Boko Haram in Nigeria', *Small Wars & Insurgencies*, 31(1) 131–158 (2020); Sehlule Sibanda, 'Terrorism and Military Intervention under the Principle of the Responsibility to Protect: The Case of Boko Haram', (2020); Oyeniyi Ajigboye, 'International Law and the Responsibility to Protect: Legal and Theoretical Basis for International Intervention in Nigeria', *Journal of Sustainable Development Law and Policy*, 3(1) 87–98 (2014); D. U. M. Suffoletta, 'Combating the Boko Haram Insurgency', Canadian Forces College, JCSP 40, 2016, https://www.cfc.forces.gc.ca/259/290/301/305/suffoletta.pdf, accessed 31 May 2021.

5 Aditi Gorur and Nils Carstensen, 'Community Self-Protection', *Protection of Civilians* (2016).

6 Kyle Matthews and Cedrick Mulcair, 'The Responsibility to Protect and Counter-Terrorism', Montreal Institute for Genocide and Human Rights Studies, Concordia University, 2015.

7 Shannon Zimmerman, 'Strange Bedfellows: Terrorism/Counter-Terrorism and the Responsibility to Protect', in Charles T. Hunt and Phil Orchard (eds.), *Constructing the Responsibility to Protect: Contestation and Consolidation* (London: Routledge, 2020).

The adoption of R2P no doubt significantly refocused intervention from its emphasis on protecting the state to that of vulnerable people against the four mass atrocity crimes. However, one of the apparent challenges with adopting R2P against armed groups in Nigeria is the norm's core focus on countering a state's use of violence against its people without emphasising the violence of armed non-state groups. Alex Bellamy considers this as an oversight in the conceptual business of R2P that requires addressing with a clear statement.[8] The rise of armed groups like those in Nigeria which perpetrate heinous crimes speaks to the need for this explicit statement. However, there is no doubt that R2P encompasses the form of violent attacks by Boko Haram and the Fulani extremist groups in Nigeria.

This study advances the debate on which framework is more appropriate in countering armed groups in Nigeria and Zimmerman's findings that both CT and R2P can reinforce each other by posing the research sub-question: When can CT and R2P regimes coalesce to counter the terror of armed non-state groups in Nigeria? This chapter further seeks to integrate a linked version of CT and R2P with community self-protection approaches, economic well-being, and ideological orientation in redesigning and implementing a holistic civilian protection mechanism. Hence, another research sub-question is: How can local agency and knowledge of self-protection be integrated with a reinforced CT-R2P measure? Based on these questions and my desire to limit the incessant killing of civilians in conflict regions in Nigeria, I approached this study from an interpretive ontological and epistemological outlook. Although I started this study with some significant knowledge of Nigeria, this was insufficient for me to answer the research question due to the multiple and divergent natures of the rise of armed groups and the vulnerability of civilians. Hence, I utilised a qualitative method for data collection.

This chapter shows that despite these seeming conflicting CT and R2P regimes, they could align at an intrastate implementation level. The United Nations' adoption of a people-centric approach to CT and the preventive measures against heinous crimes instituted in Pillars One and Two of R2P creates the space for cooperative implementation of actions that would significantly protect vulnerable populations from violence and prevent the proliferation of armed groups in Nigeria. Furthermore, this chapter argues that civilian protection measures would be more effective if integrated with self-protection

8 Alex Bellamy, 'The Islamic State and the Case for Responsibility to Protect: Do Not Let Feelings toward Past Invasions in the Middle East Deter Us from Protecting Syrians and Iraqis.', *Open Canada*, 20 April 2015, https://opencanada.org/the-islamic-state-and-the-case-for-responsibility-to-protect/, accessed 31 May 2021.

measures, economic well-being, and ideological reorientation of vulnerable communities. Combining international, state, and community civilian protection approaches would increase the community's resilience and enhance the security of vulnerable populations from the activities of violent non-state actors.

This introductory section will precede a description of the emergence and activities of Boko Haram and the Fulani extremist groups. The chapter will then discuss the core pillars of the CT and R2P norms and analyse the point at which both regimes can align to terminate the activities of armed non-state actors. Another section will show how Nigeria can implement the reinforced parts of both models to protect the vulnerable population against violent non-state actors. The last segment will summarise the essence and findings of this study.

1.1 *Boko Haram Terror Groups*

The Boko Haram insurgency effectively started in July 2009 after the Nigerian special security force countered the unbecoming activities and road violations of the religious sect in Maiduguri, the capital city of Borno State. Scholars have traced the emergence of this armed rebellion to multiple factors, including grievances over sociopolitical and economic inequalities, state repression, transnational and domestic religious-ideological concerns, and the political opportunities created by the developing democratic processes.[9] Despite its relatively small beginning, Boko Haram has not only persisted for over a decade but increased in frequency and scale with resultant Internally Displaced People, abductions, and killings in the tens of thousands.[10]

The rebel group's initial violence focused on security officers, politicians, and perceived state informants. Soon, IED (improvised explosive device) and

---

9 Iro Aghedo and Oarhe Osumah, 'The Boko Haram Uprising: How Should Nigeria Respond?', *Third World Quarterly* 33(5) 853–869 (2012); Wisdom Oghosa Iyekekpolo, 'Boko Haram: Understanding the Context', *Third World Quarterly* 37(12) 2211–2228 (2016); Wisdom Oghosa Iyekekpolo, 'The Political Process of Boko Haram Insurgency Onset: A Political Relevance Model', *Critical Studies on Terrorism* 12(4) 673–692 (2019); Wisdom Oghosa Iyekekpolo, 'Political Elites and the Rise of the Boko Haram Insurgency in Nigeria', *Terrorism Political Violence* 32(4) 749–767 (2020); Jacob Zenn, *Unmasking Boko Haram: Exploring Global Jihad in Nigeria* (Lynne Rienner Publishers, 2020); Abdulbasit Kassim, 'Defining and Understanding the Religious Philosophy of Jihādī-Salafism and the Ideology of Boko Haram', *Politics, Religion & Ideology* 16(2–3) 173–200 (2015); Kyari Mohammed, 'The Message and the Methods of Boko Haram' in Marc-Antoine Perouse de Montclos (ed.), *Boko Haram: Islamism, Politics, Security and the State in Nigeria* (Leiden: African Studies Centre, 2014); Efehi Raymond Okoro, 'Terrorism and Governance Crisis: The Boko Haram Experience in Nigeria', *African Journal on Conflict Resolution* 14(2) 103–127 (2014).

10 Brendon Cannon and Wisdom Iyekekpolo, 'Explaining Transborder Terrorist Attacks: The Cases of Boko Haram and Al-Shabaab', *African Security* 11(4) 370–396 (2019).

suicide bombings at public places accompanied this initial targeted attack. Several violent attacks on villages and cities also resulted in mass killings and displacement of civilian populations in the group's attempt to establish a caliphate in north-east Nigeria. Boko Haram also sought affiliation with transnational terrorist organisations and developed similar propaganda mediums.[11] Some of the most well-known violence associated with the group – which now has two major factions, Jama'atu Ahlul Sunnah Lidda'awatu Wal-Jihad (JAS) and Islamic State's West Africa Province (ISWAP) – includes the suicide attack on the UN building and police headquarters in Abuja, the abduction of girls from Chibok and Dapchi, the bloody invasion of the towns Gwoza and Baga, and the slaughter of dozens of rice farmers in Zabarmari. The persistence of Boko Haram for this long is evidence that a gap exists in the Nigerian counter-strategy.[12]

1.2 *Fulani Extremist Groups*

The Fulani extremist groups are a complex mix of violent groups mainly emerging from the traditionally nomadic Muslim Fulani herders in northern Nigeria. There were initial debates on whether to designate these Fulani groups as terrorists,[13] but the federal government of Nigeria recently declared these groups terrorists after prolonged foot-dragging.[14] There is no doubt that the violent activities of these groups in vulnerable communities are hardly different from those of Boko Haram. The International Crisis Group reports that between 2011 and 2014, there was an upsurge in violence perpetrated by these violent groups, often referred to as 'Bandits' in Nigeria.[15]

---

11 Zenn, *Unmasking Boko Haram.*

12 The Soufan Center, 'IntelBrief: Boko Haram Massacre Indicates Frailty in Nigeria's Counterinsurgency Strategy', 9 December 2020, https://thesoufancenter.org/intelbrief-boko-haram-massacre-indicates-frailty-in-nigerias-counterinsurgency-strategy, accessed 28 Jun 2021.

13 M. O. M. Akpor-Robaro and F. O. Lanre-Babalola, 'Nomadic Fulani Herdsmen Turn Terrorists? Exploring the Situation and the Security Implications for Nigeria', *IOSR Journal of Humanities and Social Science* 23(7) 47–57 (2018); Cyril Anaele, 'Herdsmen Terror in Nigeria: The Identity Question and Classification Dilemma', *American Research Journal of Humanities & Social Science* (*ARJHSS*) 3(3) 10–25 (2020); Peter Duru, 'FG's Refusal to Declare Armed Fulani Herdsmen "Terrorists" Encourages Killings in Benue, Other States', *Vanguard Nigeria*, 7 August 2021, https://www.vanguardngr.com/2021/08/fgs-refusal-to-declare-armed-fulani-herdsmen-terrorists-encourages-killings-in-benue-other-states/, accessed 16 Jan 2022.

14 Ameh Ochojila, 'At Last, FG Declares Bandits as Terrorists', *The Guardian*, 6 January 2022, https://guardian.ng/news/at-last-fg-declares-bandits-as-terrorists/, accessed 16 Jan 2022.

15 International Crisis Group (ICG), *Violence in Nigeria's North West: Rolling Back the Mayhem*, Afric Report No. 288 (Belgium: ICG, 18 May 2020).

Studies trace the emergence of bandits to the struggle over scarce resources between nomadic herders who seek food for their cattle and farmers who seek to protect their land from invasion by these herders and their cattle.[16] The struggle escalated to the level of each side forming militias for attack and defence against the other. However, some of them have gone rogue and become criminal gangs engaged in extensive extortion, robbery, and abduction for ransom. There are even indications of some form of alliance between the bandits and the Boko Haram group.[17] These autonomous armed groups spread over northern Nigerian forests such as Kamuku, Falgore, Dansadau, and Davin Rugu. They target both rich and poor individuals and groups in various communities.[18]

The violence of these Fulani militias initially focused on opposing farmers and their communities. However, with the abundance of illegal small and light weapons in the country, they have become formidable against even the Nigerian security forces. The armed non-state actors now carry out coordinated attacks against communities and schools to kidnap people and demand huge sums of money for ransom. They have now spread southward, causing the south-western and south-eastern geopolitical zones to establish regional community protection groups – the Western Nigeria Security Network (WNSN) codenamed Operation Amotekun and the Ebubeagu regional security in the south-east. Some of the most well-known violence and abduction associated with bandit groups include the 2021 abduction of 136 students at an Islamic school in Niger State,[19] the 2019 killing of 85 people in Kaduna,[20] the 2021

16 Oludayo Tade, 'What's Triggered New Conflict between Farmers and Herders in Nigeria', *The Conversation*, 2 September 2020, https://theconversation.com/whats-triggered-new-conflict-between-farmers-and-herders-in-nigeria-145055, accessed 16 Jan 2022; Sallek Yaks Musa, 'Nigeria's 'Bandits' Are Not "Unknown Gunmen": Why the Label Matters', *The Conversation*, 19 October 2021, https://theconversation.com/nigerias-bandits-are-not-unknown-gunmen-why-the-label-matters-166997, accessed 16 Jan 2022.

17 James Barnett, 'Boko Haram Isn't Nigeria's Biggest Problem', *Foreign Policy*, 4 June 2021, https://foreignpolicy.com/2021/06/04/boko-haram-bandits-nigeria-buhari-biggest-problem/, accessed 16 Jan 2022; Malik Samuel, 'Boko Haram Teams up with Bandits in Nigeria', *Institute for Security Studies*, 2021.

18 ICG, *Violence in Nigeria's North West*; International Crisis Group, *Stopping Nigeria's Spiralling Farmer-Herder Violence*, Africa Report No. 262 (26 July 2018).

19 Jamilu Mohammed, 'Nigerian State Government Confirms 136 Children Abducted in Niger State', Reuters, 2 June 2021, https://www.reuters.com/world/africa/nigerian-state-government-confirms-136-children-abducted-niger-state-2021-06-02/, accessed 17 Jan 2022.

20 John Shiklam, 'Herdsmen Kill 85 People in Kaduna Communities', This Day, 13 March 2019, https://www.thisdaylive.com/index.php/2019/03/13/herdsmen-kill-85-people-in-kaduna-communities/, accessed 17 Jan 2022.

kidnapping of 317 students in Zamfara,[21] and the 2021 kidnap of 165 Bethel Baptist High School students in Kaduna.[22] The persistence of these armed non-state actors despite the government's effort to eliminate them also shows a significant gap in the state's counter-measures.

2 The Reinforcing Role of Responsibility to Protect and Counter-terrorism

R2P resulted from the Independent International Commission on Intervention and State Sovereignty (ICISS). The ICISS was formed in 2000 by the Canadian government in response to the clarion call by the then UN Secretary-General, Kofi Annan, for the international community to counter the kind of mass murder and large-scale loss of lives like those of Srebrenica, Rwanda, and Kosovo.[23] World leaders at the 2005 World Summit unanimously agreed to the R2P principles that emphasise the responsibility of the state and the international community to protect vulnerable populations from genocide, war crimes, ethnic cleansing, and crimes against humanity.[24]

The first of the three pillars emphasises the responsibility of the state to protect its populations from atrocious crimes. World leaders agreed to use all necessary means to prevent mass killings and bring perpetrators to book. In the second pillar, the international community agreed to encourage and provide reasonable assistance to states that need the requisite capacity to perform this responsibility. When a state manifestly fails to perform this duty to its people, the third pillar bestows the burden on the international community. The UN can exercise this obligation through diplomacy and collective means.[25]

---

21 Emmanuel Akinwotu, 'Kidnappers Abduct 317 Schoolgirls in Nigeria in Armed Night-Time Raid', *The Guardian*, 26 February 2021, https://www.theguardian.com/world/2021/feb/26/kidnappers-abduct-schoolchildren-in-nigeria, accessed 17 Jan 2022.

22 Fred Muvunyi, 'Nigerian Kidnappings Reach Crisis Point', Deutsche Welle (DW), 6 July 2021, https://www.dw.com/en/nigerian-kidnappings-reach-crisis-point/a-56818981, accessed 17 Jan 2022.

23 International Commission on Intervention and State Sovereignty (ICISS), *The Responsibility to Protect* (Ottawa: IDRC, 2001); Alex J. Bellamy, *Responsibility to Protect: A Defense* (Oxford: Oxford University Press, 2014).

24 '2005 World Summit Outcome', UNGA Res. 60/1, 16 September 2005; UNSC Res. 1674, 28 April 2006; Bellamy, *Responsibility to Protect: A Defense*.

25 '2005 World Summit Outcome',; UN Office of Genocide Prevention and the Responsibility to Protect, 'About', 2005, https://www.un.org/en/genocideprevention/about-responsibility-to-protect.shtml, accessed 31 May 2021.

Similar to the adoption of R2P, the UN Global Counter-Terrorism Strategy was a reaction to evidence of state-sponsored killings of vulnerable people and the subsequent 11 September 2001 attack on the United States by Al Qaeda. Security Council Resolution 1638 highlighted the responsibility of states and the international community to prevent and bring perpetrators of terrorism to book. It emphasises the salience of individual and collective self-defence while expressing its readiness to apply all necessary measures to counter terrorist acts.[26] These responsibilities, especially those of the state, were further articulated in Resolution 1373.[27] Faced with how state-centric foreign armed interventions are justified using CT, as seen in the US-led 'war on terror' in Afghanistan and Iraq,[28] the UN General Assembly and Secretary-General canvassed a people-centred global CT strategy emphasising the root cause and the respect for human rights.[29]

World leaders agreed on the UN Global CT Strategy at the 60th General Assembly on 20 September 2006. The first pillar of the four-pillar CT measures advocates the need to address the conditions that facilitate the spread of terrorism. These include protracted conflicts, abuse of human rights, and perpetuation of inequalities. The second pillar focuses on combating terrorism by denying armed groups access to means of attacks. At the same time, the third pillar identifies the role of the UN in assisting states to enhance their capacity to prevent and combat terrorism. The fourth pillar reemphasises the promotion of human rights and the rule of law in countering terrorist activities.[30] The Counter-Terrorism Implementation Task Force (CTITF) was set up to facilitate this global strategy in collaboration with individual states.[31] Although the UN's attempt at CT did not start with this global strategy,[32] it is a profound effort to refocus CT measures on protecting vulnerable populations and not solely on the state. Sebastian von Einsiedel acknowledges that the challenges observed

26 UNSC Res, 1368: 12 September 2001.

27 UNSC Res. 1373, 28 September 2001.

28 Christine Chinkin and Mary Kaldor, *International Law and New Wars* (Cambridge: Cambridge University Press, 2017), pp. 129–174.

29 Sebastian von Einsiedel, 'Assessing the UN's Efforts to Counter Terrorism', United Nations University Centre for Policy Research, Occasional Paper no. 8, 2016.

30 UNGA Res. 60/288, 8 September 2006.

31 United Nations, 'The Counter-Terrorism Implementation Task Force (CTITF)', https://www.un.org/victimsofterrorism/en/about/ctitf, accessed 16 Aug 2021.

32 Mike Smith, 'Securing Our Future: A Decade of Counter-Terrorism Strategies', *UN Chronicle*, no. 2 (2011), https://www.un-ilibrary.org/content/journals/15643913/48/2/4/read, accessed 16 Aug 2021.

in the attempts to counter Islamic State through only security-based CT measures have resulted in efforts at operationalising this UN Global CT Strategy.[33]

Armed non-state groups expose civilian populations to forms of violence enunciated as crimes against humanity, hence the need for civilian protection, which is the state's primary responsibility. In essence, CT and R2P share the same core objective of protecting vulnerable people from violence; they are different ways of countering violence against civilian populations. 'The fact that a crisis can be described in terms of counter-terrorism does not mean that it is not also a challenge to R2P.'[34] Matthews and Mulcair support the argument that terrorist activities double as crimes against humanity.[35] This conclusion raises the question of when both CT and R2P regimes can coalesce to counter the terror of armed non-state groups.

Although some studies about R2P implementation have focused on preventing the emergence of armed groups and protecting exposed communities from violent attacks, their questions have centred around foreign troop intervention and appropriate forms of engagement.[36] These debates often gloss over the essence of Pillars One and Two of R2P. However, recent discussion at the UN has emphasised the importance of social inclusion, human rights, and development policies in protecting vulnerable communities.[37] Similarly, after the errors of the initial state-centric counter-terrorism strategy and the negative outcomes witnessed in its application in the 'war on terror', UN members agreed on a broader strategy that includes locals and non-governmental organisations (NGOs) in advancing necessary narratives and structural conditions in the prevention of armed non-state groups.[38]

The preventive measures now focus on people and structural conditions that enable the emergence of violent groups instead of the continued emphasis on military elimination of these actors and protecting the state.[39] With the growing focus on protecting local populations from violent non-state actors through forestalling structural conditions that enable the proliferation of such

33 von Einsiedel, 'Assessing the UN's Efforts to Counter Terrorism'.

34 Bellamy, 'The Islamic State and the Case for Responsibility to Protect'.

35 Matthews and Mulcair, 'The Responsibility to Protect and Counter-Terrorism'.

36 Isaac Taylor, 'State Responsibility and Counterterrorism', *Ethics & Global Politics* 9(1) 1–19 (2016), p. 2.

37 Spain MFA, 'Madrid Hosts 5th Meeting of Global Network of Responsibility to Protect (R2P) Focal Points', news release, 24 June 2015, http://www.exteriores.gob.es/Portal/en/SalaDePrensa/NotasdePrensa/Paginas/2015_NOTAS_P/20150624_NOTA156.aspx, accessed 31 May 2021.

38 UNSC Res. 2178, 24 September 2014, p. 16.

39 Zimmerman, 'Strange Bedfellows', p. 4; UNSC Res. 2178, 24 September 2014, p. 19.

groups, I argue in support of Zimmerman[40] that CT has converged with the objectives of Pillars One and Two of R2P.

In answering the question of when the CT and R2P regimes can merge to prevent the activities of armed groups, I argue that the proactive step enunciated in the UN Global CT Strategy that the international community should assist individual states to attain structural conditions that limit the emergence and proliferation of armed non-state actors is similar to that enunciated in pillars one and two of R2P. Josie Hornung's recent study of the protection of the Yazidis exposed to violence on Mount Sinjar exemplifies the significant convergence of R2P and CT.[41] I submit that the R2P and CT regimes align in three significant ways. One, they both acknowledge the primary responsibility of individual states to protect vulnerable communities against the emergence, proliferation, and violence of armed non-state actors. Two, this responsibility extends beyond the adoption of coercive force in countering the activities of violent groups to include the broader scope of maintaining structural conditions that mitigate the emergence of such armed non-state actors. Three, both regimes further agree on the initial responsibility of the international community to help maintain a just, equitable and stable economic, religious, and socio-political environment that would limit the rise of violent non-state actors.

3 Practical Integration of Local Agency in Civilian Protection

Having arrived at this convergence of the R2P and CT regimes, how can these shared principles improve the practical implementation of a people-centric approach to civilian protection against the emergence and activities of armed groups in Nigeria? In answering this question, this chapter argues that even a CT-R2P merger would require local knowledge, support, and a communication network. To achieve this civilian protection, I agree with recent studies advocating that civilian protection measures should give communities in conflict zones a sense of participation in their security.[42] Felicity Gray's study of South Sudan shows how much local agency is salient in the protection of civilians

40 Zimmerman, 'Strange Bedfellows', p. 14.

41 Josie Hornung, 'Terrorism and Pillar Two Protection Assistance: The Yazidis on Mount Sinjar', *Global Responsibility to Protect*, 14(2) 232–256 (2022).

42 Erin Baines and Emily Paddon, '"This Is How We Survived": Civilian Agency and Humanitarian Protection', *Security Dialogue*, 43(3) 231–247 (2012).

exposed to armed non-state actors.[43] Hence, the next section of this chapter advances a practical framework of how civilian protection can integrate local agency and the knowledge of self-protection with an aligned CT-R2P measure in countering armed groups in Nigeria. I present a three-step non-mutually exclusive framework of community self-protection, economic wellbeing, and ideology as a solution to the question: How do we achieve the protection of vulnerable civilians from violent non-state actors?

3.1 *Armed Community Self-Protection*

Despite the rhetoric of the UN Global CT Strategy and R2P, civilian populations worldwide remain vulnerable to armed groups. However, the limited research on armed self-protection has shown a significant divide among scholars over its salience and relevance. While some studies continue to show how the adoption of armed self-protection has and could fail, others advance its salience to populations in vulnerable communities.[44] However, no matter the salience of armed community self-protection, this chapter does not obscure the fact that individual states and the international community are primarily responsible for protecting the civilian population. Aditi Gorur and Nils Carstensen elucidated that 'while self-protection strategies may be necessary for survival, they do not in themselves provide the degree of safety, security, and dignity that people need and to which they are entitled'.[45]

The Nigerian government's counter-insurgency/banditry strategies have mostly glossed over the valuable contribution and importance of the civilians in conflict zones. This omission is evident in the continuous focus on engaging the violent non-state actors instead of interacting and drawing from the superior local knowledge of the population that needs protection. Louise Wiuff Moe and Markus-Michael Müller reflected on Thomas Edward Lawrence's argument that counter-insurgent forces must directly engage with indigenes

43 Felicity Gray, 'Relational R2P? Civilian-Led Prevention and Protection against Atrocity Crimes', *Global Responsibility to Protect*, 14(3) 313–338 (2022).

44 Deborah Mayersen, '"Is Help Coming?" Communal Self-Protection During Genocide', *Stability: International Journal of Security and Development*, 9(1) 1–17 (2020); Betcy Jose and Peace A. Medie, 'Understanding Why and How Civilians Resort to Self-Protection in Armed Conflict', *International Studies Review*, 17(4) 515–535 (2015); Betcy Jose and Peace A. Medie, 'Civilian Self-Protection and Civilian Targeting in Armed Conflicts: Who Protects Civilians?', in *Oxford Research Encyclopedia of Politics* (2016); Geraint Hughes and Christian Tripodi, 'Anatomy of a Surrogate: Historical Precedents and Implications for Contemporary Counter-Insurgency and Counter-Terrorism', *Small Wars & Insurgencies*, 20(1) 1–35 (2009).

45 Gorur and Carstensen, 'Community Self-Protection', p. 420.

of conflict zones because they possess superior local knowledge and practical skills more than the intervening forces.[46] In the same vein, David J. Kilcullen stressed the indigenes' superior knowledge in culture, actors, 'topography, economy, history, religion', 'road, village, population group, tribal leader and ancient grievance'.[47] The advantage of local knowledge was evident in the Philippines, where CAFGU (Citizen Armed Force Geographical Unit) provided the necessary grassroots information for the military. The same was the case in Oman's Dhofari insurgency and Turkish rebellion, where the knowledge of the local language, geography, relationships, and networks was significant in protecting the people against violent groups.[48]

The Nigerian government's CT strategy and desire for international intervention and assistance have primarily focused on military engagement. These coercive countering measures have been implemented, among others, by joining border countries to activate the Multinational Joint Taskforce, seeking military hardware and training from other foreign countries, and the involvement of private military companies. There has also been the creation of self-protection militias within the vulnerable communities to mostly patrol and sometimes join the security forces in attacking insurgent locations.[49] However, these measures have significantly failed to protect the civilian populations in locations where armed groups frequently operate.

Instead of this continuous focus on coercive strategy, this chapter argues for a strategic increase in the resilience of these vulnerable populations to stem the activities of armed groups. Andrew Bonwick contends that interventions in conflict zones rarely recognise the importance and resourcefulness of the vulnerable population in deciding how it could achieve better civilian protection. He argues that the leading player in civilian protection is the population itself.[50] This chapter focuses on advancing community resilience through developing the self-protection capabilities of these civilians during the significant time lag between an armed group attack and when military intervention arrives at a community under attack. How can the government and international

46 Louise Wiuff Moe and Markus-Michael Müller, 'Introduction: Complexity, Resilience and the "Local Turn" in Counterinsurgency' in *Reconfiguring Intervention* (Springer, 2017), pp. 4–5.

47 Kilcullen, David. *Counterinsurgency*. (Oxford University Press, 2010).

48 Goran Peic, 'Civilian Defense Forces, State Capacity, and Government Victory in Counterinsurgency Wars', *Studies in Conflict & Terrorism*, 37(2) 162–184 (2014), pp. 166–167.

49 Daniel E. Agbiboa, 'The Precariousness of Protection: Civilian Defense Groups Countering Boko Haram in Northeastern Nigeria', *African Studies Review* 64(1) 192–216 (2021).

50 Andrew Bonwick, 'Who Really Protects Civilians?', *Development in Practice* 16(3–4) 270–277 (2006).

community facilitate the self-protection of vulnerable communities in their effort to end constant attacks by armed groups?

It is crucial to enhance the resilience of the vulnerable communities to reduce the unresisted killings of civilians before military assistance arrives in an ongoing attack. Scholars have discussed various forms of civilian self-protection in different conflict locations.[51] Populations have used a variety of self-protection measures in conflict zones like Swat Valley, Nuba, northern Uganda, Abidjan, Darfur, and Sierra Leone because of the limitations of intervention forces.[52] Sanaullah Sanaullah explains that the civilian population tends to take the initiative to protect themselves when they have the capacity. The researcher observed that those in the Swat Valley challenged the Taliban through armed resistance, among other initiatives.[53] Paul D. Williams argues that 'in the inevitable gap between a crisis erupting and outside help arrival (if it does at all), civilians have to make provision for their protection by escaping violence, protecting their property and reducing threats'.[54] In that case, it is salient to harness the endogenous sources of protection and the agency of civilians, acquired through local knowledge and networks, in enhancing their community self-protection.[55]

Pew Research has shown that most Nigerians view armed non-state groups unfavourably.[56] Based on this, I argue that vulnerable communities should be *reasonably armed* to resist the unsophisticated killings before the arrival of the military intervention. As shown earlier, this call is not entirely new as it has been implemented at various levels in Nigerian communities. Governments at subnational levels have facilitated the emergence of armed militias in some communities, which has helped in the coercive approach. However, analysts have accused the Civilian Joint Task Force (CJTF) of working for politicians,

51 Alex J. Bellamy and Paul D. Williams, 'Protecting Civilians in Uncivil Wars' in Sara E. Davies and Luke Glanville (eds.), *Protecting the Displaced: Deepening the Responsibility to Protect* (Leiden: Martinus Nijhoff, 2010).

52 Jose and Medie, 'Understanding Why and How Civilians Resort to Self-Protection in Armed Conflict.'; Justin Corbett, 'Learning from the Nuba: Civilian Resilience & Self-Protection During Conflict', Local to Global Protection, October 2011.

53 Sanaullah Sanaullah, 'Civilians' Survival Strategies During the Taliban's Insurgency (2007–9), Pakistan: A Look at the Consequences', *Small Wars & Insurgencies* online, (10 November 2020).

54 Paul D Williams, 'Protection, Resilience and Empowerment: United Nations Peacekeeping and Violence against Civilians in Contemporary War Zones', *Politics* 33(4) 287–298 (2013), p. 292.

55 Baines and Paddon, '"This Is How We Survived"'.

56 Richard Wike and Jacob Poushter, *Concerns About Islamic Extremism on the Rise in the Middle East: Negative Opinions of Al Qaeda, Hamas and Hezbollah Widespread* (Washington DC: Pew Research Center, 2014).

engaging in a war economy, recruiting child soldiers, extra-judicial killings, rape of women, arson, and other human rights abuses.[57]

The Minister of Defence recently encouraged Nigerians to defend themselves against armed groups.[58] Similarly, Governor Samuel Ortom of Benue State has advocated the arming of *responsible individuals* to stem the tide of armed group attacks on communities in Nigeria. His counterpart, Governor Aminu Masari of Katsina State, the home state of President Muhamadu Buhari, asserted that

> *One must rise to defend himself, his family, and assets.* ... It's surprising how a bandit would own a gun while a good man trying to defend himself and his family does not have one. ... We'll support those who come with the initiative to procure arms because residents need to also complement the efforts of security agencies [emphasis added].[59]

In the most recent development, the Zamfara State government has gone further by directing 'the state commissioner of police to issue (gun) licenses to *people who are qualified* and willing to use the guns'.[60] Analysts and scholars alike have argued against arming the civilian population.[61] However, to counter the excesses observed in the CJTF and the possible challenges in arming the civilian population, I draw on the traditional role of the family heads in these Nigerian communities, as in Masari's statement that *one must rise in defence of the family*. I define this 'one' as the family heads locally regarded as *responsible*

57 Idayat Hassan and Zacharias Pieri, 'The Rise and Risks of Nigeria's Civilian Joint Task Force: Implications for Post-Conflict Recovery in Northeastern Nigeria' in Jacob Zenn (ed.), *Boko Haram Beyond the Headlines: Analyses of Africa's Enduring Conflict* (Combating Terrorism Center, West Point, May 2018).

58 Nwafor Sunday, 'Breaking: Let 'Responsible Citizens' Carry Guns, Others – Ortom Begs FG', *Vanguard*, 12 August 2020, https://www.vanguardngr.com/2020/08/breaking-let-responsible-citizens-carry-guns-others-ortom-begs-fg/, accessed 17 Aug 2021; Segun Adewole, 'Bandits: Defend Yourselves, Minister Tells Nigerians', *Punch Newspaper*, 17 February 2021, https://punchng.com/bandits-defend-yourselves-minister-tells-nigerians/?utm_medium=Social&utm_source=Twitter#Echobox=1613590511, accessed 17 Aug 2021.

59 Mohammed Babangida, 'Insecurity: Buy Guns, Defend Yourselves, Nigerian Governor Tells Residents', *Premium Times*, 29 December 2021, https://www.premiumtimesng.com/news/headlines/503013-insecurity-buy-guns-defend-yourselves-nigerian-governor-tells-residents.html, accessed 5 Jan 2022.

60 Maishanu, 'Terrorism: Buy Guns, Defend Yourselves'.

61 Folahanmi Aina, 'Arming Civilians in Northern Nigeria Is a Bad Idea', Foreign Policy (FP), 20 July 2022, https://foreignpolicy.com/2022/07/20/zamfara-nigeria-bandits-small-arms-civilians-bad-idea/, accessed 21 July 2022.

individuals and *qualified* in these communities, phrases used by the governments of Benue and Zamfara States above. In essence, *I do not argue in favour of giving weapons to young males in the community but instead for arming family heads whose traditional role has always included defending their families.*

These comments by such influential individuals recognise the importance of arming the right people for self-protection, which would eventually be for the defence of the community. Hence, I argue in support of the idea that the government should train and arm the heads of each home or choose a person who would hold the responsibility of defending the family in an eventual attack. This method of protecting a family is not new to a traditional Nigerian society where the family leader mobilises to protect the lives and property affiliated with the family. Communities in the recent past have organised security against armed robbers through combined armed response from family heads using weapons appropriately licensed by the state in collaboration with the police. *Practical adoption of this strategy is the acquisition and licensing of guns with GPS tracking devices for each family head adequately recognised by the leaders of their communities.*

The law enforcement agents should train these family heads or their designated household members on the rudiments of defending their households. Suppose every home can defend itself for some hours before the arrival of military intervention. The resistance will minimise the unfettered access of armed non-state groups and, at the very least, their rudimentary mass killings and abductions. At the time of armed group attacks, every house should be able to respond with gunfire against the sources of armed threats. One of the core reasons why violent non-state actors can indiscriminately carry out killings and adoptions is because of the weapons they wield. The proliferation of illegal small arms and light weapons gives armed groups immediate superiority over the civilian population who abide by the law that deprives them of the ability to access weapons.

The possible militarisation of the communities and other challenges of arming a small group of young males has become evident since the introduction of the CJTF. However, its replacement with family heads who are more likely to be motivated by the desire to protect their families and property will augur better for these vulnerable communities. Unlike the usual selection of a group of boys with violent tendencies to pursue community protection, *established heads of families* will be much more purposeful in providing leadership in this armed community self-protection strategy. However, arming the family heads in these communities does not give them the primary responsibility for civilian protection. The state and the international community are primarily responsible for protecting vulnerable communities. However, a limited form of armed self-protection before military mobilisation is necessary in a place like Nigeria that cannot guarantee civilian safety, partly due to infrastructural and logistics reasons.

Another aspect that requires deliberate and practical measures in protecting vulnerable communities is countering the flow of illegal small arms and light weapons in Nigeria. This challenge is not only local but also an international one. Weapons used by these armed groups are both illegally fabricated locally and internationally sourced. A recent study by SB Morgen (SBM) shows that non-state actors smuggle illegal ammunition into the country through the international waters off the Gulf of Guinea from a least 21 countries, including Israel, Iran, Turkey, Poland, Brazil, Iran, United States, Czech Republic, Algeria, and Egypt.[62] Particularly notorious land borders for the entry of these illegal weapons are at Idi-Iroko in Ogun State and Seme in Lagos State, and the north-east borders with Niger and Cameroon in Adamawa, Borno, and Yobe States.[63] Local non-state actors manufacture a significant percentage of Nigeria's illegal arms and light weapons. SBM found that locally fabricated weapons account for more than half of the country's violent attacks in the north-central geopolitical zone.[64] *Countering this flow of arms would require the support of these originating and transiting countries and a deliberate and significant investment into international and local intelligence to prosecute the illegal arms dealers. Incentives like one-off payments to informants could motivate individuals to provide the necessary information to counter arms proliferation. Local knowledge and networks would be salient in locating places of both illegal local fabrication and international smuggling.*

It is also essential to enhance the speed of military intervention in attacks by providing communication equipment to the communities. In conflict zones, accurate and timely information often defines the success or failure of attacks. Therefore, insiders and outsiders must disseminate knowledge of the local portfolio of self-protection strategies.[65] Bellamy and Hunt observed that communities in the Democratic Republic of Congo (DRC) established Community Alert Networks and Community Liaison Assistants (CLA) to enhance information sharing between vulnerable communities and UN peacekeepers. The CLAs

62 SBM, *Report on Small Arms, Mass Atrocities & Migration in Nigeria*, (SB Morgen and OSIWA, April 2020), pp. 9 and 21, https://www.sbmintel.com/wp-content/uploads/2021/02/202005_SALWMAIM.pdf, accessed 31 May 2021.

63 Jennifer M. Hazen and Jonas Horner, *Small Arms, Armed Violence, and Insecurity in Nigeria: The Niger Delta in Perspective*, The Small Arms Survey (Geneva, Switzerland: The Small Arms Survey, December 2007).

64 SBM, *Report on Small Arms, Mass Atrocities & Migration in Nigeria*, p. 9.

65 Williams, 'Protection, Resilience and Empowerment', p. 293.

are individuals who facilitate communication with the security actors and the communities. They became a core source of early warning information.[66]

Just as training on safe gun use and the procurement of guns installed with GPS devices are provided for the family heads, *trackable phones, including satellite or UHF phones with direct access to different levels of both political and military authorities should be provided to family heads to expedite intervening coercive action.* Several individuals in a community should have these *phones installed with speed-dial* numbers of the responsible intervening military commanders and several of their superior officers. They should also have access to call the local government chairpersons, parliamentarians, police, and governors when an attack is imminent or commences. This initiative would ensure that within a minute of an attack, information is transmitted far and wide to those individuals and institutions primarily responsible for the security of the people. At the same time, the armed self-protection strategy helps to push the armed groups back in anticipation of external intervention. This initiative will improve the communities' trust in the government's commitment to their security. There would also be fewer civilians joining the ranks of the armed bandits and insurgents because of their need for security. Further, this measure would make it difficult for the armed groups to invade a community to kill or abduct civilians as fighters or sex slaves.

It is salient to highlight armed gangs' possible infiltration of these information networks, informants, and family heads. Access to these networks by armed militants could misinform the community leadership, security agencies, government, and the international community. However, this should not stop this strategic effort as the reality of rogue security agents has not necessitated the discontinuation of state security agencies. 'The practical limitations of local resilience are not a reason to abandon the project.'[67] Instead, civilian protection strategists should further their strategic efforts to avert or limit the possible infiltration of these networks. That explains why I advocate the selection of established family heads recognised and respected in each community. The state should install GPS tracking devices in the firearms and UHF phones to make them traceable. This technology would serve two core purposes. First, it would prevent misuse as locations used can be tracked. Second, if violent non-state groups steal the guns, it would enable tracking of their movement and locations. Furthermore, the fears of possible gun proliferation may be

66 Alex J Bellamy and Charles T Hunt, 'Twenty-First Century Un Peace Operations: Protection, Force and the Changing Security Environment', *International Affairs*, 91(6) 1277–1298 (2015), p. 1292.

67 Williams, 'Protection, Resilience and Empowerment', p. 292.

unfounded as studies show that licensing guns to individuals does not necessarily imply the proliferation of small and light weapons.[68]

This framework proposes the individualisation of the armament. Guns should be allocated to family heads and not a group of young men, as has been the case. As shown in previous studies, this strategy limits the possibility of state militia turning in arms against the government.[69] However, this selective arming does not eliminate the likely coercive incorporation of these local and security individuals into bandit/insurgent networks. So, a further check could be the deliberate calibration of information dissemination within the community and security networks on a need-to-know basis, only supplying security information of happenings that directly relate to family heads and security operatives. Also, government agents must sufficiently confirm information from individuals in the community and treat all necessary security concerns.

3.2 *Community Economic Well-being*

Another factor that requires the government's attention in its attempt to halt the rise and proliferation of armed groups in Nigeria is the economic well-being of the civilian population. Research has shown that most deaths in war result from the population's inability to satisfy their economic welfare. This economic welfare refers to needs like food, medicine, and accommodation, which they initially enjoyed, at least on a subsistence level before the conflict.

Their displacement by armed groups and sometimes forced movement to Internally Displaced Persons' camps worsened the sustenance ability of the people.[70] In a survey of 1,200 young males in Russia's North Caucasus, researchers found that socio-economic woes necessitated by bad governance exposed the populace to armed group recruitment more than other concerns. It is also salient to mention that locals pledged their support to the side of the belligerent that met this economic need.[71] Williams argues that a community should be able to function enough to sustain the livelihood of its people to protect its civilian population from joining armed groups. He argues that the protection of economic livelihood ensures that other resilience-building mechanisms are

68 John R. Lott, *More Guns, Less Crime: Understanding Crime and Gun Control Laws* (Chicago: University of Chicago Press, 2013), p. 1.

69 Iyekekpolo, 'The Political Process of Boko Haram Insurgency Onset'; Iyekekpolo, 'Political Elites and the Rise of the Boko Haram Insurgency in Nigeria'.

70 Bellamy and Williams, 'Protecting Civilians in Uncivil Wars'.

71 Theodore P. Gerber and Sarah E. Mendelson, 'Security through Sociology: The North Caucasus and the Global Counterinsurgency Paradigm', *Studies in Conflict & Terrorism*, 32(9) 831–851 (2009).

effective.[72] Similarly, Andrew Beath, Fotini Christia, and Rueben Enikolopov argue that providing development projects to those communities vulnerable to violent non-state actors will reduce their exposure to joining those groups. Their study of Afghanistan reveals that economic support to a community increases the population's support for the government. The population's support could be through providing information necessary for government forces. Economic sufficiency could also dissuade the civilian population from yielding to the call of armed groups to take weapons against vulnerable communities, ethnicities, or even the state.[73] In a similar study of Iraq, researchers found that the satisfaction of socio-economic needs of civilians in a conflict zone could enhance their information sharing about violent non-state actors and reduce their joining of these groups. They emphasise that to deprive the insurgents of recruits and support, the government should satisfy the well-being of the people.[74] Studies also found that the rising optimism of a better livelihood shifted the Iraqi Sunni Arab minority from a state of violent opposition to supporting the government.[75]

Based on these studies, I argue that a more effective strategy to end the activities of armed groups should include a concerted effort to alleviate the challenging economic situation and galvanise a return of the civilian population in vulnerable communities to a resemblance of normalcy. However, this satisfaction of the economic need that should at least return the people to their usual ability to fend for themselves must be developed based on the first stage of the self-protection capacity of the people. How can the economic welfare of the vulnerable people in Nigeria be achieved to counter the proliferation of violent non-state actors?

The primary occupations of the indigenes of northern Nigeria are agriculture and commerce. Their agricultural endeavour includes farming and breeding animals that partly cater to Nigeria and other countries, especially in the Sahel and other parts of Africa. However, the insecurity has displaced over 6,000 farming households, and millions of indigenes face a severe food

72 Williams, 'Protection, Resilience and Empowerment', p. 293.

73 Andrew Beath, Fotini Christia, and Ruben Enikolopov, *Winning Hearts and Minds through Development? Evidence from a Field Experiment in Afghanistan*, Policy Research Working Paper; No. 6129 (Washington, DC: World Bank, 2012).

74 Eli Berman, Jacob N. Shapiro, and Joseph H. Felter, 'Can Hearts and Minds Be Bought? The Economics of Counterinsurgency in Iraq', *Journal of Political Economy*, 119(4) 766–819 (2011).

75 Christoph Mikulaschek, Saurabh Pant, and Beza Tesfaye, 'Winning Hearts and Minds in Civil Wars: Governance, Leadership Change, and Support for Violent Groups in Iraq', *American Journal of Political Science*, 64(4) 773–790 (2020).

security risk in the north-east alone.[76] Farmers are killed on their farms, as evident in November 2020 in a violent incident involving over 40 individuals.[77] Herders have similarly suffered from bandits and insurgents who perpetrate cattle-rustling.[78] These have drastically reduced the income from agriculture and the wages paid to the worker in the sector.[79]

Indigenes involved in commerce also provided significant trading activities that served Nigeria and other countries in the Sahel.[80] However, armed groups now control the usual busy trade routes. Remadji Hoinathy observed that even boat drivers who are central to transnational trade between north-east Nigeria and other countries in the Sahel had abandoned usual trade routes because of the activities of these violent groups.[81] Ahmad Salkida reports on how Boko Haram has taken control of the lucrative transnational fish and red pepper trade in the Lake Chad basin. The armed non-state actor created a new regime of levies and took charge of the trading route for these commodities, which hitherto accounted for tens of millions of euros and employment for over 300,000 people.[82] The resultant loss of income and jobs creates a bigger pool of recruits for the violent non-state groups.

Any effort to halt the emergence and activities of armed groups must target this economic challenge that drives young men to embrace this life of violence. There is room again for a collaborative effort between Nigeria and the international community. *There should be a deliberate attempt by government forces to protect farmers and traders in a way that would ensure they return to a semblance of their pre-violence economic status.* The international community

76 Eka Ikpe, 'Counting the Development Costs of the Conflict in North-Eastern Nigeria: The Economic Impact of the Boko Haram-Led Insurgency', *Conflict, Security & Development*, 17(5) 381–409 (2017).

77 Haruna Umar, 'Suspected Extremists Kill at Least 40 Farmers in Nigeria', Associated Press, 30 November 2020, https://apnews.com/article/international-news-rice-farming-local-governments-militant-groups-nigeria-83dabb4dc772e6f09aab862e0677ff25, accessed 31 May 2021.

78 Al Chukwuma Okoli, 'Cows, Cash and Terror', *Africa Development/Afrique et Développement*, 44(2) 53–76 (2019).

79 Adesoji Adelaja and Justin George, 'Effects of Conflict on Agriculture: Evidence from the Boko Haram Insurgency', *World Development*, 117, 184–195 (2019).

80 Ikpe, 'Counting the Development Costs of the Conflict in North-Eastern Nigeria'.

81 Remadji Hoinathy, *Boko Haram Blocks Lake Chad Trade Routes*, Institute for Security Studies, 11 January 2021, https://issafrica.org/iss-today/boko-haram-blocks-lake-chad-trade-routes, accessed 31 May 2021.

82 Ahmad Salkida, 'How Boko Haram Sustain Operations through International Trade in Smoked Fish', *Premium Times*, 26 April 2020, https://www.premiumtimesng.com/news/headlines/389916-how-boko-haram-sustain-operations-through-international-trade-in-smoked-fish.html, accessed 31 May 2021.

can then assist these local communities back on their feet with empowerment programs spearheaded by international non-government organisations. In addition, there should be a deployment of police to protect farmers in such ways that would not allow a few violent individuals to walk into a rice farm and slit the throat of tens of farm workers. I further propose that in collaboration with foreign nations, Nigeria should thoughtfully deploy soldiers and naval vessels to protect trade routes. Through this collaborative effort, the protection of agricultural and commercial activities will guarantee that indigenes satisfy their economic needs to the level they experienced before the group's violent actions. This concerted effort to return the local economy to business as usual will discourage those who would have contemplated the need to join armed groups to make ends meet. The smaller the pool for new fighters, the faster any coercive means would achieve its target of ending the proliferation of armed groups. Hence the need to reapproach the fight against violent non-state actors by countering the economic needs of the vulnerable civilian populations.

3.3 *Community Ideology*

Another factor that must be considered in the struggle to halt the activities of armed groups is the ideology which drives the non-material commitment to the values of militant groups. Since the trajectory of an insurgency is significantly concerned with winning the trust and support of the vulnerable population, ideology constitutes a core part of mobilisation for both the rebels and state forces.[83] Plakoudas avers that 'counterinsurgency must properly understand the narrative of the insurgents and the society and then propagandize a narrative that explains their intentions and effectively appeals to the population'.[84]

A number of historical background factors have shaped the rise of armed non-state actors in northern Nigeria. Some armed groups originated and shaped their canons on these pre-existing opportunities and constraints. For example, the views advocated by Boko Haram predate the group's rise and are not unfamiliar in the region. We must understand these factors to decipher why young people in this region would feel the need to identify with an ideology that leads to a life of violence. These influences include the historical development of sharia and its role in politics, the sacred purging role of jihad, and the evolution of hatred for Western education in northern Nigeria. These factors' influence cut across Nigeria's pre-colonial, colonial, and post-colonial eras. Very salient to the ideology Boko Haram professes is the argument that

83 Spyridon Plakoudas, 'Strategy in Counterinsurgency: A Distilled Approach', *Studies in Conflict & Terrorism*, 38(2) 132–145 (2015).

84 *ibid.* 138.

any form of government outside the rule of God or employment under such government is a sin. The violent non-state actor contends that if political leaders fail to adopt the sharia legal system, it is right to declare jihad to cleanse the society of this *taghut* and earthly tyrannical government. Also, any form of education, such as Western education, that does not conform to the teachings of Islam and the Quran is sinful.[85]

Contention over the role and implementation of sharia as the official law of northern Nigeria is not new. Individuals and groups in the region have historically pursued the course of sharia in society. The Pew Research Center found in 2013 that 71 per cent of Muslims in Nigeria support sharia as the law of the country.[86] However, the majority of Muslims in Nigeria are non-violent; in fact, 80 per cent of Muslims in Nigeria have an unfavourable opinion of Boko Haram.[87] We must understand that sharia in northern Nigeria dates back at least to the rule of Uthman Dan Fodio of the Sokoto Caliphate in the early nineteenth century. But sharia lost its critical societal role in the region's politics with the advent of colonial rule in the early twentieth century. Several attempts to re-establish its dominance over the English legal system have not yielded the desired fruit. On this basis, some armed groups anchored their values on implementing sharia. Such groups have expanded based on this high support for sharia implementation in the northern region. These armed actors' connection with existing normative ideologies ensured they continued mobilising armed fighters.

An armed group like Boko Haram also espouses a core ideology that any form of Western education that does not conform to the Quran is sinful. Nonmembers nicknamed the group 'Boko Haram' (Western education is sinful) to reflect this core belief. Yet this belief is neither new to northern Nigeria nor introduced by Boko Haram and dates back to the British colonisation of northern Nigeria and the subjugation of its people's values to those of Europeans. However, the group's association with the idea that European education is sinful mobilises members who imbibe this idea. Maintaining this view created an opportunity for group formation, and the group's activities are further constrained to the idea because many of the members share this value.

Another principle closely related to sharia that helped shape Boko Haram's formation is jihad. Although jihad rhetoric became more significant in the group's evolution into an insurgent one, it harnessed jihad as a valuable tool

85 Mohammed, 'The Message and the Methods of Boko Haram', p. 16.

86 Luis Lugo et al., *The World's Muslims: Religion, Politics and Society*, The Pew Research Center's Forum on Religion & Public Life (2013), p. 46.

87 Wike and Poushter, *Concerns About Islamic Extremism on the Rise in the Middle East*, p. 5.

to legitimise its existence. Boko Haram draws from the Quran and Hadith to justify the essence of jihad as a means to cleanse the political leadership of infidels. The violent non-state actor admonishes the population on the importance, reward, and need to respond to a call to jihad affirmatively. The jihad rhetoric resonates and mobilises followers for the group because it is not new to northern Nigeria. The ability to interpret its essence in a way that links the holy book, historic jihads, and the present instability of the polity endears some people to the group.[88] Some Boko Haram fighters who wilfully join the group are motivated by the moral need to identify with these ideas. Scott Atran found that some Al Qaeda and ISIS (Islamic State in Iraq and Syria) fighters are young people with limited knowledge of the religion and cause with which they have identified.[89] Interestingly, the Nigerian CT measures focus less on these issues of identity and ideology.[90]

Any attempt to end ideologically mobilised armed groups like Boko Haram should counter the falsification of existing ideology to cater to violent behaviour. The insurgents have emphasised aspects of the Islamic religion to pursue their recruitment needs. While the government speaks and implements programs on deradicalisation, it has focused on repentant militants as part of its current CT approach. The combined CT measures of killing the insurgents and deradicalising repentant militants, over a decade, has not ended the violent rebellion. Insurgency will not end if the group has this space to recruit more youths as fighters. Atran argues that the panacea would be to offer youth a future they can realise through their effort and initiative.[91] Although this is important, as has been shown in the section on economic welfare, more is needed to stop youths from the desire to identify with dangerous ideologies.

The government should refocus on those vulnerable civilians who are potential recruits instead of focusing solely on those who are already members. The state should make considerable effort to counter the existing ideology in the communities that makes the civilian population prone to recruitment. This displacement of the wrong doctrine will significantly reduce the wilful joining of the armed group. Not only is the content of the counter-narrative salient, but the transmitter is also essential.[92] A promising way to change these

88 Abdulbasit Kassim and Michael Nwankpa, *The Boko Haram Reader: From Nigerian Preachers to the Islamic State* (London: Oxford University Press, 2018).

89 Scott Atran, 'The Role of Youth in Countering Violent Extremism and Promoting Peace', Address to UN Security Council Ministerial Debate, 23 April 2015.

90 Heather S. Gregg, 'Identity Wars: Collective Identity Building in Insurgency and Counterinsurgency', *Small Wars & Insurgencies*, 31(2) 381–401 (2020).

91 Atran, 'The Role of Youth in Countering Violent Extremism and Promoting Peace'.

92 Plakoudas, 'Strategy in Counterinsurgency: A Distilled Approach'.

pervasive ideas in northern Nigeria is through religious and traditional leaders in specific communities.[93] These leaders are revered and are the custodians of values in their communities. *These leaders should be trained and retrained on how to re-engineer the ideological values of their communities. R2P and CT measures should support community leaders with the necessary resources, especially with the other factors of self-protection and economic rejuvenation.* When these are in place, the success of the community leaders in changing the pervasive ideology is more guaranteed.

4 Conclusion

The unravelling of significant overlap between the two regimes of Responsibility to Protect and the United Nations Global Counter-Terrorism Strategy reinforces the pursuit of a people-centric approach aimed at protecting local communities exposed to the violence of armed non-state actors. This chapter has highlighted points of R2P-CT interactions that can significantly shift Nigeria's current approach to ending the activities of armed groups from its focus on military elimination to engaging with the vulnerable populations in ways that shore up their resilience. This study further canvasses the integration of local agency with a merged R2P-CT measure. In this way, we can achieve a holistic approach covering the agency of the local populations, state, and international community in civilian protection. Specifically, I further canvass a framework that would integrate local efforts in Nigerian conflict-prone communities with R2P-CT measures. I propose a non-mutually exclusive three-step framework of community self-protection, economic well-being, and ideological reorientation.

I argue in line with (but not in total conformity) the calls for and steps aimed at implementing armed community self-protection by highly placed individuals like the governors of Benue, Katsina, and Zamfara States of Nigeria. Although this measure is different from those currently canvassed, it is not new to the traditional Nigerian community. While armed militias are already in use, and several analysts and government officials have proposed arming individuals in vulnerable communities, my framework advances the arming and training of established heads of households. The head of the traditional

93 Chigozie Ifekwe Okonkwo, Onuigbo Richard Amechi, Okechukwu Innocent Eme, and Ezinwanne Ekekwe, 'Traditional Rulers and Community Security in Nigeria: Challenges and Prospects', *International Journal of Innovative Social Sciences & Humanities Research*, 7(2) 145–159 (2019).

Nigerian family is the first line of defence for the members and property of the home. This household protection has been achieved through different means over the years, including applying crude implements and sometimes bearing arms, mainly to ward off armed robbers. A redesign of this traditional process to enable individual households to resist armed groups before the arrival of the intervening forces would reduce the constant mass slaughter easily perpetrated by armed groups in vulnerable communities. I must restate that this measure does not advocate that civilian protection becomes the primary responsibility of the local population but only as a form of resistance before the arrival of the intervention forces. I have further proposed measures to protect vulnerable populations' economic well-being to prevent them from joining armed groups to meet basic economic needs. We need the collaboration of local, national, and international security actors in protecting farms and commercial places, including trade routes. The final factor discussed pertains to how local leaders can reorientate the communities against historically perverted ideology.

This chapter primarily argues that we can better achieve the protection of vulnerable populations if we integrate the agency of locals in conflict-prone communities with a bridged version of the people-centric first two pillars of R2P and the UN Global CT measures. This holistic approach will incorporate the views and interpretation of civilian protection from international, state, and local actors. It would further shift the civilian protection strategy from the focus on existing armed groups and their members to an emphasis on building the resilience of the vulnerable populations who are exposed to abduction, maiming, killing, and joining armed non-state groups.

CHAPTER 6

Terrorism and Pillar Two Protection Assistance: The Yazidis on Mount Sinjar

Josie Hornung
Ph.D. Candidate in International Relations, University of Queensland, Queensland, Australia
j.hornung@uq.edu.au

Abstract

The last decade has seen an overall increase in mass atrocity crimes being committed by non-state actors, including terrorist groups. A key strength of R2P Pillar Two Protection Assistance lies in its potential for addressing imminent threats of mass atrocity posed by such groups. This chapter discusses the scope and legitimacy of R2P Pillar Two, its application to non-state actors, and the conditions that enabled limited protection assistance action to be effectively rendered in response to the impending genocide of 40,000 Yazidis trapped on Mount Sinjar in northern Iraq in 2014.

Keywords

terrorism – R2P – mass atrocity – Pillar Two – protection assistance – Yazidi

1 Context[1]

In 2015 Adrian Gallagher wrote that 'Pillar II remains the most overlooked and under-researched of the three pillars' and that there is 'a striking disconnect

1 This piece started its life as my Master's thesis at the Coral Bell School of the Australian National University under the supervision of Dr Cecilia Jacob. Without her unwavering encouragement and support I would not be in academia today. Heartfelt thanks also go to my current supervisors at the University of Queensland, Professors Christian Reus-Smit and Alex Bellamy, both of whom read earlier versions of this piece. I am very grateful, too, for the sharp and insightful comments of the anonymous reviewers.

 | DOI:10.1163/9789004548114_008

between the importance of Pillar II on the one hand, and the lack of research into it on the other'.[2] Seven years on, this remains the case.[3] This is despite the fact that Pillar Two has particular relevance in cases involving non-state actors, including terrorist groups,[4] who pose a growing threat worldwide. This chapter seeks to illuminate the capacity of R2P Pillar Two 'Protection Assistance' action to be taken to assist states in their efforts to prevent atrocities being perpetrated by such groups, and to discuss the scope and legitimacy of this type of action.

It will examine the 2014 Protection Assistance action led by the United States (US) in response to a call from the Iraqi government to assist it in fulfilling its responsibility to protect populations at imminent risk of genocide, in this case at the hands of the Islamic State in Iraq and the Levant (ISIL), a United Nations (UN) designated terrorist group.[5] In doing so, it will seek to establish that, although the response did not prevent all genocidal acts by ISIL, the Protection Assistance actions, when examined in isolation, did nevertheless prevent the likely genocide of approximately 40,000 Yazidis trapped on Mount Sinjar in northern Iraq. It will show that the military and humanitarian assistance provided at Iraq's request helped reduce casualties and allowed local forces to evacuate the trapped members of the Yazidi ethno-religious minority group into Syria and away from the imminent risk posed. It will argue that the US' actions should therefore be viewed as an example of Pillar Two Protection Assistance effectively rendered. Further, through an analysis of the case, the conditions that enabled the US' limited response to be effective will be discussed, and claims against its effectiveness weighed.

---

2 Adrian Gallagher, 'The Promise of Pillar II: Analysing International Assistance under the Responsibility to Protect', *International Affairs*, 91(6) 1259–1275 (2015), pp. 1260, 1274, doi:10.1111/1468-2346.12459.

3 The author notes the importance of the in-process research project 'Explaining Non-State Perpetration of Mass Atrocity Crimes' being led by Adrian Gallagher and Kaisa Hinkkainen. This project should usefully identify what drives non-state armed groups to perpetrate mass atrocities, and will go some way to addressing the identified 'lacuna'. Smaller scale research into the link between terrorism and mass atrocities is also underway or has been completed. However, the mechanisms with which, and circumstances under which, such threats might be effectively responded to is an area that still warrants further attention.

4 Ban Ki-moon, *Fulfilling Our Collective Responsibility: International Assistance and the Responsibility to Protect*, A/68/947–S/2014/449, 11 July 2014, para. 76; Ban Ki-moon, *Implementing the Responsibility to Protect*, A/63/677, 12 January 2009, paras. 29 and 40; Ramesh Thakur, 'The Responsibility to Protect at 15', *International Affairs*, 92(2) 415–434 (2016), p. 424.

5 United Nations, 'Security Council Al-Qaida Sanctions Committee Amends Entry of One Entity on Its Sanctions List', Press Release, SC/11019, 30 May 2013.

1.1 *Protection Assistance and Terrorist Threats*

The last decade has seen a 'dramatic resurgence' in violent conflict involving non-state actors,[6] including terrorist groups, who 'represent a powerful new threat to established international norms'.[7] A key strength of R2P Pillar Two lies in its potential for addressing the rising threat of mass atrocities posed within the context of such conflict.[8] Indeed, as UN Secretary-General (UNSG) Ban Ki-moon observed in his 2014 Report on R2P, 'Pillar II emphasizes assistance to States [which] is particularly relevant in cases where a non-state actor is preying upon the civilian population'.[9] Pillar Two, as Gallagher puts it, allows us to re-conceptualise how we think about responses to mass atrocities, since it implies 'quite simply [that] the state does not hold a monopoly over the perpetration of mass violence'.[10]

Under R2P Pillar Two, there are three main types of assistance that states can provide to help other states uphold their Pillar One responsibilities: Encouragement, Capacity Building, and Protection Assistance.[11] Each type of assistance is intended to reinforce, rather than undermine, state sovereignty.[12] In this way, Pillar Two action can be distinguished from Pillar Three action in that it is not appropriate in situations where national authorities are manifestly failing to protect at-risk populations, or are engaging in the commission of atrocity crimes themselves.[13] Rather, it is intended to be provided when the state in question requires help to implement efforts to uphold its own responsibility to protect.

Within the literature, the potential of Pillar Two to combat violence by non-state actors remains largely unexplored.[14] This is despite the fact that in the inaugural UNSG report on R2P, in which Ban Ki-moon first articulated the three pillars, he noted that Pillar Two Protection Assistance action may be suitable

---

6 UN and World Bank, *Pathways for Peace: Inclusive Approaches to Preventing Violent Conflict* (Washington DC: World Bank, 2018); Stanley Foundation, 'Violent Nonstate Actors as Perpetrators and Enablers of Atrocity Crimes', *Policy Dialogue Brief*, 56th Annual Strategy for Peace Conference, October 2015, Warrenton Virginia, p. 5.

7 A/69/981–S/2015/500, 13 July 2015, para. 46.

8 Gallagher, 'The Promise of Pillar II', p. 1269. See also: Ki-moon, *Implementing the Responsibility to Protect*, paras. 29 and 40.

9 A/68/947–S/2014/449, 11 July 2014, para. 76.

10 Gallagher, 'The Promise of Pillar II', p. 1272.

11 Ki-moon, *Fulfilling Our Collective Responsibility*, para. 70; Ki-moon, *Implementing the Responsibility to Protect*, para. 28.

12 Ki-moon, *Fulfilling Our Collective Responsibility*, para. 12; Ki-moon, *Implementing the Responsibility to Protect*, para. 40.

13 *ibid.*, paras. 11 and 29.

14 Gallagher, 'The Promise of Pillar II', p. 1260; Thakur, 'The Responsibility to Protect at 15', p. 424.

where 'with the host Government's consent ... military units [are] employed ... to counter armed groups'.[15]

When the application of R2P to non-state actors has been discussed in the literature, the focus tends to have been on whether a collective responsibility to protect includes them, or whether they possess Pillar One responsibilities.[16] As the Yazidi case and the rapid rise of groups like ISIL and Boko Haram show, however, host governments often require assistance to combat threats from non-state actors. It is in just such situations, provided the host government has requested assistance to prevent 'egregious crimes relating to the responsibility to protect', that the 'targeted and restrained use of international military assets and armed forces' under R2P Pillar Two seems appropriate.[17] Pillar Two Protection Assistance offers a clear mechanism through which the rising mass atrocity threat posed by non-state actors, including terrorist groups, can be combated.

1.2 *The Scope of Protection Assistance*

In Ban Ki-moon's 2014 report on R2P, he reiterated that the scope of support rendered under Pillar Two should be '"narrow but deep": narrow because it is restricted to the protection of populations from atrocity crimes, but deep given the array of measures required for its implementation'.[18] Protection Assistance rendered in response to an imminent threat is the last line of defence in this 'deep array of measures'. Unlike most Encouragement or Capacity Building efforts, it generally has a short-term operational focus, rather than a long-term root cause one; that is, it is generally 'targeted and restrained'.[19]

In this sense, the scope of Pillar Two responses tends to align with most R2P informed protection approaches that have historically taken place. That is, they are intended to de-escalate an imminent mass atrocity risk, rather than to implement more 'genuinely preventative commitments'.[20] It is worth noting that one criticism of such short-term approaches is that while they may help to address the immediate threat, they do not address the risk factors behind

15 Ki-moon, *Implementing the Responsibility to Protect*, para. 40.

16 Shannon Zimmerman, 'Strange Bedfellows: Terrorism/Counter-terrorism and the Responsibility to Protect' in Charles T. Hunt and Phil Orchard (eds.), *Contestation and Consolidation* (London: Routledge, 2020), p.11; Stanley Foundation, 'Violent Nonstate Actors as Perpetrators and Enablers of Atrocity Crimes', p. 2.

17 Ki-moon, *Implementing the Responsibility to Protect*, para. 40.

18 A/68/947–S/2014/449, 13 August 2014, para. 79.

19 Ki-moon, *Implementing the Responsibility to Protect*, para. 40.

20 Alexandra Bohm and Garrett Wallace Brown, 'R2P and Prevention: The International Community and Its Role in the Determinants of Mass Atrocity', *Global Responsibility to Protect*, 13(1) 60–95 (2020), p. 71.

that threat. In the words of Bohm and Brown, such responses remain a 'necessary but insufficient'[21] means to combat mass atrocities, and do not address the 'externally driven systemic determinates' of atrocity crime.[22] It is beyond the scope of this chapter to engage at length with this criticism. Suffice to say, however, that Protection Assistance will rarely be sufficient on its own where a conflict or tensions pose an ongoing mass atrocity risk. Complex causes simply cannot be addressed by short-term operational measures. This does not in itself entail that such responses ought not be taken to protect populations at risk, or that such actions fall outside the scope of legitimate R2P action. In the case of the assistance rendered to Iraq in 2014, although it did not prevent all acts of genocide involved in ISIL's spread through northern Iraq and Syria, this does not mean that it was pointless, that it was not a case of Pillar Two Protection Assistance effectively rendered, or that it is not a case worthy of further examination within the context of R2P.

1.3 *The Legitimacy of Protection Assistance*

Despite the UN's repeated insistence to the contrary,[23] sceptics of the doctrine of R2P have raised concerns that, like the doctrine of Humanitarian Intervention before it, it could be used as a neo-colonial 'Trojan horse';[24] an illegitimate rhetorical vehicle for increased self-interested actions by powerful international actors.

If such concerns turned out to be true, there would be little point in furthering the research agenda in regard to Pillar Two. Nonetheless, it is true that since Protection Assistance action necessarily involves weighing and balancing the responsibility to protect populations at risk against the potential for success and other more practical political and economic imperatives, it will often result in what either is – or appears to be – selective implementation. As Gareth Evans puts it, R2P is a doctrine for 'pragmatists not purists', and any state that pursues R2P Protection Assistance faces 'myriad and complicated' impediments to acting,[25] especially in an environment characterised by imperfect information. The existence of a pragmatic dimension to the decision

21 *ibid.*, p. 75.

22 *ibid.*, p. 94.

23 A/RES/60/1, 6 September 2005, para. 5; Ki-moon, *Implementing the Responsibility to Protect*, para. 10; Ki-moon, *Fulfilling Our Collective Responsibility*, para. 12.

24 Alex J. Bellamy, 'Responsibility to Protect or Trojan Horse? The Crisis in Darfur and Humanitarian Intervention after Iraq', *Ethics & International Affairs*, 19(2) 31–54 (2005).

25 Gareth Evans, 'R2P: The Next Ten Years' in Alex J. Bellamy and Tim Dunne (eds.), *The Oxford Handbook of the Responsibility to Protect*, vol. 1 (Oxford: Oxford University Press, 2016), p. 913.

to render assistance does not, in itself, undermine the legitimacy of the assistance provided in situations where these impediments have been able to be successfully navigated.

For the US, as with other major powers, finding the point of balance between fulfilling their responsibilities while avoiding accusations of purely self-interested implementation[26] is still difficult, however. R2P situations can put pressure on the 'culture of neutrality' that has generally guided the UN's approach to conflict prevention and resolution since its inception.[27] Gallagher confronts this view with the claim that 'clearly Pillar II is about assisting a preferred actor and does not set out to be impartial'.[28] Nonetheless, making the choice to support a side in any given conflict, even one that involves a designated terrorist organisation like ISIL, is a practical and moral minefield, and can cause unforeseen consequences or an exacerbation of conflict. Perhaps more than blanket scepticism of R2P, it is these practical and moral concerns that require addressing before any claimed case of Protection Assistance can be considered legitimate rather than purely self-interested.

The threshold for what constitutes a mass atrocity – or a risk thereof – and, therefore, for when R2P Pillar Two Protection Assistance ought to be able to be rendered, is not defined anywhere.[29] This presents the first practical concern for states considering assistance. If the threshold is interpreted too expansively, states risk accusations of meddling in sovereignty by assisting, particularly if that assistance involves military action. An over-expansive interpretation additionally runs the risk of recreating the problem that faced humanitarian intervention throughout the 1990s; that is, the 'moral hazard' dilemma.[30] Conversely, if the threshold for action is too restrictive, it is arguably not going to be robust enough to protect those most at risk. Shifting this threshold too far

---

26 Ben Brumfield and Jim Sciutto, 'Why U.S. Intervenes in Iraq but not Syria?', *CNN World*, 14 August 2014; Adam Taylor, 'Why U.S. Bombs Are Falling on Iraq and not Syria', *Washington Post*, 8 August 2014.

27 Alex J. Bellamy, *Global Politics and the Responsibility to Protect: From Words to Deeds* (New York: Routledge, 2011), p. 8; Ruben Reike, 'Conflict Prevention and R2P' in Alex J. Bellamy and Tim Dunne (eds.), *The Oxford Handbook of the Responsibility to Protect*, vol. 1 (Oxford: Oxford University Press, 2016).

28 Gallagher, 'The Promise of Pillar II', p. 1262.

29 Anna Khalfaoui, 'Mass Atrocities: Definition and Relationship with Development' in Walter Leal Filho, Anabela Marisa Azul, Luciana Brandli, Pinar Gökcin Özuyar, and Tony Wall. (eds.), *Peace, Justice and Strong Institutions* (Cham: Springer Nature, 2021), pp. 539–540.

30 Alex J. Bellamy and Paul D. Williams, 'On the Limits of Moral Hazard: The "Responsibility to Protect", Armed Conflict and Mass Atrocities', *European Journal of International Relations*, 18(3) 539–571 (2012).

in either direction could allow real or perceived cases of selective implementation based on self-interested motivations, and could thus undermine the legitimacy, or perceived legitimacy, of Protection Assistance action.

The decision to render Protection Assistance is also inevitably made within the context of multiple competing situations of ongoing or potential atrocities, and a lack of clear principles or frameworks at hand with which to prioritise who ought to be assisted and to what extent. As Alex Bellamy puts it, there are simply too many cases to commit to, while the resources that can be committed are finite.[31] This 'prioritisation dilemma' poses an additional practical concern for states considering Protection Assistance. Since not all atrocity threats can be responded to, any response that is made will necessarily be selective, but the criteria used to determine when to act need not be arbitrary or purely self-interested. Glanville and Pattison usefully break down the legitimate criteria a state may consider into 'atrocity-specific' and 'response specific'.[32] According to this dichotomy, response specific criteria would concern, for example, the likely effectiveness of the action, the risk of civilian harm, and the risk of damaging the R2P norm, while atrocity specific criteria would concern the likely severity of the action, the imminency of the threat, the degree to which the response risks exacerbating harms, and the wider consequences of action or inaction.[33] Many of these areas of concern echo those canvassed in the International Commission on Intervention and State Sovereignty's 2001 report (the ICISS Report) on R2P, which invoked the just war principles of proportionality and reasonable prospects for success as relevant determinants of when to act.[34]

Another criterion not considered in the ICISS Report, but worthy of consideration from a moral point of view, is whether the assisting state owes a reparative duty to the host state.[35] In the context of the 2014 Mount Sinjar case, the relevant question would be whether the US' actions during the 2003 invasion of Iraq and their subsequent military campaign contributed to the

---

31 Alex Bellamy, *The Responsibility to Protect: A Defence* (Oxford: Oxford University Press, 2015), p. 138.

32 Luke Glanville and James Pattison, 'Where to Protect? Prioritization and the Responsibility to Protect', *Ethics & International Affairs*, 35(2) 213–225 (2021), pp. 219–220.

33 *ibid.*, pp. 219 and 221.

34 International Commission on Intervention and State Sovereignty (ICISS), *The Responsibility to Protect: Report of the ISCISS* (Ottawa: International Development Research Centre, 2001), p. 47.

35 Cécile Fabre, *Cosmopolitan War* (Oxford: Oxford University Press, 2012), pp. 181 and 189–191; Garrett Wallace Brown and Alexandra Bohm, 'Introducing *Jus ante Bellum* as a Cosmopolitan Approach to Humanitarian Intervention', *European Journal of International Relations*, 22(4) 897–919 (2016); Glanville and Pattison, 'Where to Protect?', p. 219.

risk of atrocity in the region, and whether, as a consequence, they should have prioritised 'responding to atrocities ... in that region rather than in others'.[36] Where such a reparative duty exists, it may be one of the few factors that leads to an increase, rather than a decrease, in the perceived legitimacy of Protection Assistance. On the other hand, assisting states must be mindful of the risk of exacerbating the underlying problem, particularly where the assistance rendered involves military action. As President Obama observed in his speech authorising airstrikes in Sinjar, there may be 'no military solution to the larger crisis'[37] that underpins a situation of imminent risk. In this context, it seems an important precondition of legitimacy that military assistance measures under Pillar Two be reserved for 'support to States facing imminent or ongoing atrocity crimes',[38] though it has also been suggested that some UN Peacekeeping actions of a more long-term nature might also be counted as legitimate Pillar Two Protection Assistance.[39]

In a context where Protection Assistance rendered under R2P Pillar Two does involve a military dimension, it attracts a further challenge to its legitimacy in the form of conforming with the established traditions governing state-sanctioned uses of force. In an attempt to clarify when and how such force may be used ethically, Michael Walzer draws a distinction between *jus ad vim* (the rightfulness of force short of war) and *jus ad bellum* (the rightfulness of war).[40] Walzer lists possible measures of rightful force in response to a threat of violence as including strategies such as the implementation of no-fly zones, conducting pinpoint air/missile strikes, and conducting small-scale foreign-operative missions.[41] Acts such as ground invasions and large-scale bombing campaigns are not justified under *jus ad vim*.[42] The rise in non-state actors like ISIL, and advancements in precision weapons technologies such as drones, may have made the shift from *jus ad bellum* to *jus ad vim* seem unremarkable. Nonetheless, Walzer's distinction remains a contentious one, and even evokes

---

36 *ibid.*

37 Barack Obama, 'Statement by the President', Obama White House Office of the Press Secretary, Press Release, 7 August 2014.

38 Ki-moon, *Fulfilling Our Collective Responsibility*, para. 11.

39 Gallagher, 'The Promise of Pillar II', p. 1262; Global Centre for the Responsibility to Protect, 'The Relationship between the Responsibility to Protect and the Protection of Civilians in Armed Conflict', Policy Brief, 9 May 2011.

40 Michael Walzer, 'Preface to the Fourth Edition' in *Just and Unjust Wars: A Moral Argument with Historical Illustrations* (New York: Basic Books, 2006).

41 *ibid.*

42 Daniel Brunstetter and Megan Braun, 'From *Jus ad Bellum* to *Jus ad Vim*: Recalibrating Our Understanding of the Moral Use of Force', *Ethics & International Affairs*, 27(1) 87–106 (2013).

outright hostility from some scholars.[43] While it is beyond the scope of this chapter to engage with the debate surrounding this distinction, it is important to note that Walzer's work marked a shift in the traditional state-centric thinking surrounding the use of force, towards a recognition of the more complicated nature of modern warfare, including the need to respond to threats posed by non-state actors such as terrorist groups. In the context of R2P Pillar Two, *jus ad vim* allows for greater moral clarity about when and how Protection Assistance might be legitimately rendered.

With or without the additional legitimacy that *jus ad vim* lends to small-scale uses of force that seek to prevent mass atrocities, it remains an established norm that any use of force must be consented to – either by the international community or the state being assisted – in order to be considered legitimate.[44] The alignment of Protection Assistance with this norm, in that it requires the consent of the host government and, therefore, does not undermine state sovereignty, is a key factor adding to the legitimacy of assistance rendered in accordance with Pillar Two.[45]

2 Case Study: The Yazidis on Mount Sinjar

In August 2014, approximately 40,000 Yazidis faced an impending mass atrocity at the hands of ISIL, who had surrounded them as they sought refuge on Mount Sinjar in northern Iraq. In response to their imminent genocide, and at the request of the Iraqi government, the US conducted a drone attack and airstrikes on key ISIL targets, provided much needed humanitarian assistance to the trapped civilians, and resupplied the local forces who created a path for the Yazidis to escape. This Protection Assistance action helped to avert the immediate risk of genocide faced by the ethno-religious minority group.[46]

A closer study of the details of the case will provide further insight into the potential of Pillar Two Protection Assistance to be effectively rendered in the context of mass atrocity threats posed by terrorist groups such as ISIL. It will

43 C. A. J. Coady, *Morality and Political Violence* (New York: Cambridge University Press, 2008).

44 Ian Clark, *Legitimacy in International Society* (Oxford: Oxford University Press, 2007), p. 3; Adrian M. Gallagher, 'A System, Society, and Community Perspective on Genocide', *Genocide Studies and Prevention*, 7(2/3) 166–183 (2012), p. 174; Gallagher, 'The Promise of Pillar II', p. 1265.

45 *ibid.*, p. 1264.

46 UN Assistance Mission for Iraq (UNAMI), *Report on the Protection of Civilians in Armed Conflict in Iraq: 6 July – 10 September 2014*, 26 September 2014, p. 3.

begin by outlining the events that preceded the Protection Assistance action on Mount Sinjar, as well as the initial response to the atrocity threat. It will then examine four conditions that enabled Protection Assistance to be effectively rendered in this case: the clarity and imminence of the threat; the existing operational relationship between the assisting state and host government; the alignment of the Protection Assistance action with the assisting state's domestic and foreign policy agenda, and; the broad support for the Protection Assistance action provided by the international community. Finally, criticism of the effectiveness of the Protection Assistance action will be considered and responded to.

2.1 *Events Preceding the Protection Assistance Action and Initial Response*

ISIL advanced through the Nineveh region of northern Iraq during the 'Nineveh Offensive' beginning June 2014.[47] On 10 June 2014, ISIL successfully captured the region's capital, Mosul, amid mass surrenders and desertions by Iraqi Security Forces (ISF).[48] The ISF collapse left the defence of Nineveh to local Kurdish forces, including the Peshmerga, who had anticipated an ISIL expansion into Nineveh.[49] After taking control of Mosul, ISIL made multiple small-scale attacks on Yazidis in Nineveh.[50] It was clear that the Yazidi population who occupied the small towns and villages within the Sinjar District of Nineveh were being intentionally targeted by ISIL on the basis of their religion.[51]

Sinjar Town, the capital of the Sinjar District, lies approximately five kilometres to the south of the 100-kilometre-long Mount Sinjar, along what was in 2014 a major ISIL east–west supply route connecting Mosul (in Iraq) and Raqqa (in Syria), both of which ISIL considered strategically important outposts.[52] Fifty-three days after taking Mosul, on the night of 3 August 2014, ISIL conducted a coordinated attack on five small villages to the south of Sinjar Town, before eventually taking the town itself.[53] They encountered little resistance

47 Rick Burns, 'Battle for Sinjar, Iraq', Threat Action Report, US Army, 25 April 2016.

48 Kenneth Katzman, Carla E. Humud, Christopher M. Blanchard, Rhoda Margesson, and Alex Tiersky, *Iraq Crisis and U.S. Policy*, R43612 (Washington DC: United States Congressional Research Service, 2014), p. 19.

49 Ned Parker, Peter Graff, and Reuters Staff, 'Kurds Realize Dream as Baghdad Loses Grip on North Iraq', *Reuters*, 13 June 2014.

50 UNITAD Iraq, 'The Crimes of ISIL against the Yazidi Community in Sinjar with English Subtitles', video, 14 May 2021.

51 A/HRC/28/18, 27 March 2015, para. 5.

52 Burns, 'Battle for Sinjar'.

53 UNITAD Iraq, 'The Crimes of ISIL against the Yazidi Community in Sinjar'.

from the Peshmerga, who had reportedly withdrawn prior to the attacks.[54] The Peshmerga's decision was not effectively communicated to locals, and no evacuation orders were issued.[55] Many Yazidis were captured by ISIL, and the remaining population was left defenceless.[56]

ISIL took control of the main roads and strategic junctions outside Sinjar Town, blocking the easiest path of escape.[57] Those who fled the town and its surrounds early enough took refuge on the upper plateau of Mount Sinjar, with UN reports indicating that approximately 40,000 civilians became trapped there, in the middle of what was, by then, ISIL-controlled territory.[58] For the trapped Yazidis, the situation was dire. In a report filed on 7 August, Deputy Special Representative of the UNSG for Iraq Gyorgy Busztin stated: The United Nations is deeply worried by the humanitarian situation of civilians in areas under [ISIL] control. Many are in locations that are inaccessible, including those who have been trapped for over 5 days on Jabal Sinjar Mountain ... Without the delivery of urgent life-saving items ... the lives of thousands of these civilians is now at serious risk.[59]

Besieged on the mountain, the tens of thousands of Yazidis could not access adequate water, food, or medical care.[60] The situation intensified as temperatures reached up to 50 degrees Celsius, without any available shelter.[61] US, Iraqi, British and Australian forces were involved in airdropping aid to the trapped Yazidis, but ISIL fighters actively shot at their planes, and at helicopters attempting to evacuate the most vulnerable civilians.[62] Hundreds of Yazidis – primarily infants and young children – died during the Mount Sinjar siege.[63]

---

54 A/HRC/32/CRP.2, 15 June 2016, para. 24; Tracey Shelton, 'If It Wasn't for the Kurdish Fighters, We Would Have Died Up There', *The World*, 29 August 2014; Vicken Cheterian, 'ISIS Genocide against the Yazidis and Mass Violence in the Middle East', *British Journal of Middle Eastern Studies*, 48(4) 629–641 (2021), p. 632.

55 Burns, 'Battle for Sinjar', p. 3; Naomi Kikoler, '"Our Generation Is Gone": The Islamic State's Targeting of Iraqi Minorities in Ninewa', *Bearing Witness Trip Report*, November 2015, United States Holocaust Memorial Museum, pp. 13–14.

56 A/HRC/32/CRP.2, 15 June 2016, paras. 23–25.

57 *ibid.*, para. 26.

58 UNAMI, *Report on the Protection of Civilians in Armed Conflict in Iraq*.

59 UNAMI, 'UN Gravely Concerned about Situation in Northern Iraq; Calls for Urgent Response', UNAMI Public Information Office, Press Release, 7 August 2014.

60 UNAMI, *Report on the Protection of Civilians in Armed Conflict in Iraq*, p. 4; ABC, 'US Aircraft Strike Islamic State Positions in Iraq: Pentagon', *ABC News*, 11 August 2014.

61 A/HRC/32/CRP.2, 15 June 2016, paras. 27–28.

62 *ibid.*

63 *ibid.*; Valeria Cetorelli and Sareta Ashraph, 'A Demographic Documentation of ISIS's Attack on the Yazidi Village of Kocho', LSE Middle East Centre Report, June 2019, p. 9.

2.2 *Clarity and Imminence of the Threat*

In early 2014, UN officials warned that minorities in Iraq faced a grave risk of mass atrocity.[64] All warning signs indicated that if ISIL expanded into Northern Iraq, it would continue its pattern of perpetrating mass atrocities against minority communities, including the Yazidis, in an effort to 'supress, expel or eliminate' them.[65] On 25 June 2014, following the fall of Mosul to ISIL, Iraq sent a letter to the UN Security Council requesting international assistance.[66] In this letter, the scale of the atrocities faced was made clear, with ISIL described as 'terrorising civilians, carrying out mass executions, persecuting minorities and women, and destroying religious buildings'.[67] Intelligence further suggested that the Sinjar District would be targeted next by ISIL in order to create a strategic passageway between Mosul and Raqqa.[68]

Despite the accuracy of this intelligence, ISIL's actions in Sinjar were not motivated solely by geostrategic aims. It was clear from their statements and the strategies they employed that ISIL was intentionally targeting the Yazidi population for religious reasons.[69] In ISIL's own English-language publication and 'official mouth piece', *Dabiq*, the Yazidis were not only marked out as infidels (along with Christians and Jews), but also as pagans whose existence could not be tolerated within the 'caliphate'.[70] ISIL proclaimed that the killing or forced conversion of Yazidis fulfilled a deliberate policy in accordance with its extremist ideology.[71] They specifically noted that captured Yazidis should not be offered the same options that 'people of the book' – such as Jews or Christians – were.[72] Unlike these groups, the Yazidis were not to be given the option to pay a tax (*jizya*) to avoid death or forced conversion.[73] ISIL's stance on these matters, as well as its destruction of sacred religious sites and monuments,[74] demonstrates that its actions in Sinjar were calculated with the intent of annihilating Yazidism and its followers.[75] Critically, ISIL's views on

64 Kikoler, '"Our Generation Is Gone"', p. 12.
65 *ibid.*
66 S/2014/440, 25 June 2014.
67 *ibid.*
68 Kikoler, '"Our Generation Is Gone"', p. 12.
69 UNITAD Iraq, 'The Crimes of ISIL against the Yazidi Community in Sinjar'.
70 ISIL, 'The Revival of Slavery before the Hour', *Dabiq*, 4(12) 14–16 (2014), p. 15; Cetorelli and Ashraph, 'A Demographic Documentation', p. 8; Cheterian, 'ISIS Genocide against the Yazidis', p. 635.
71 Kikoler, '"Our Generation Is Gone"', p. 21.
72 ISIL, 'The Revival of Slavery before the Hour', p. 15.
73 *ibid.*
74 UNITAD Iraq, 'The Crimes of ISIL against the Yazidi Community in Sinjar'.
75 Kikoler, '"Our Generation Is Gone"', p. 21; Cheterian, 'ISIS Genocide against the Yazidis', p. 632.

the Yazidis were known prior to the Protection Assistance action taken in Sinjar.[76] It has been argued that ISIL's position on the Yazidis shows their premeditated genocidal intent; that they 'came to destroy'[77] the Yazidi population on account of their religion.[78]

That the Yazidis trapped on Mount Sinjar faced a clear threat of genocide is further substantiated by the atrocities committed in the wider Sinjar District on those Yazidis who failed to escape the initial attacks. A recent demographic documentation of violations committed in the village of Kocho, for example, shows that ISIL's attack was directed against the village's entire population, not just its military aged males.[79] While at least 17 mass graves holding the remains of men and boys aged 12 and above have been discovered there,[80] reports also indicate that those Yazidis captured during ISIL's initial advance into the Sinjar District were separated during their captivity in Kocho into two other distinct groups, after which they were systematically subjected to violations that appeared designed to destroy their Yazidism.[81] Apart from men and boys aged 12 and above, the other two groups targeted by ISIL were boys aged 7–12, and women and children.[82]

Reports of violence in villages other then Kocho indicate that ISIL summarily executed men and boys throughout the Sinjar District who refused to convert to Islam.[83] Up to 35 mass graves[84] containing men and boys from the Sinjar District (estimated to be at least 5,000)[85] have been reported, with efforts to identify the victims ongoing.[86] Further to these executions, boys aged 7–12 were separated from their mothers, and sent to training centres where they were re-educated, given new Islamic names, and treated as ISIL recruits.[87]

76 George Packer, 'A Friend Flees the Horror of ISIS', *The New Yorker*, 6 August 2014; UNITAD Iraq, 'The Crimes of ISIL against the Yazidi Community in Sinjar'; Human Rights Watch (HRW), 'Iraq: ISIS Abducting, Killing, Expelling Minorities', HRW, Press Release, 19 July 2014; HRW, 'On Vulnerable Ground: Violence against Minority Communities in Nineveh Province's Disputed Territories' (New York: HRW, 2009), p. 41.

77 A/HRC/32/CRP.2, 15 June 2016.

78 Cheterian, 'ISIS Genocide against the Yazidis', p. 635.

79 Cetorelli and Ashraph, 'A Demographic Documentation', p. 21.

80 UNITAD Iraq, 'The Crimes of ISIL against the Yazidi Community in Sinjar'.

81 A/HRC/32/CRP.2, 15 June 2016, paras. 31–97.

82 *ibid.*

83 UNITAD Iraq, 'The Crimes of ISIL against the Yazidi Community in Sinjar'; Burns, 'Battle for Sinjar', p. 4.

84 Matthew Barber, *Mass Graves of Yazidis Killed by the Islamic State Organisation or Local Affiliates on or After August 3, 2014* (Erbil: Yazda, 2016), pp. 7–20; HRW, 'Iraq: Protect Mass Graves', HRW, Press Release, 30 January 2016.

85 Burns, 'Battle for Sinjar', p. 3.

86 UNITAD Iraq, 'The Crimes of ISIL against the Yazidi Community in Sinjar'.

87 A/HRC/32/CRP.2, 15 June 2016, para. 94.

Captured Yazidi women and children (including girls as young as nine) were systematically sold to ISIL fighters, and often forced into sexual slavery and domestic servitude.[88] As early as 12 August 2014, the UN Special Rapporteur on Violence Against Women, Rashida Manjoo, stated that the UN had 'reports that strongly suggest that hundreds of women and children have been kidnapped – many of the teenagers have been sexually assaulted, and women have been assigned or sold to [ISIL] fighters as "malak yamiin" or slaves'.[89] The Human Rights Council report on crimes against the Yazidis states that the enforced sexual slavery of Yazidi women constituted a crime against humanity, as defined by Article 7(1)(g) of the Rome Statute.[90]

To establish that the Yazidis trapped on Mount Sinjar faced a clear mass atrocity threat, it must be shown that ISIL intended to commit one or more of the prohibited acts listed in Article 2 of the Genocide Convention,[91] or related articles of the Rome Statute.[92] This means, in regard to a claim of genocide, that their intent to destroy the Yazidis as an ethnic or religious group, in whole or in part, needed to be established,[93] or, in regard to a claim of crimes against humanity, that they were genuinely contemplating 'widespread and systematic attacks' against Yazidi civilians. Importantly, in the context of the aforementioned forced conversions, rapes, sexual violence, enslavement and transferring of children into ISIL training camps, these acts could constitute genocide if they could be shown to have been carried out with genocidal intent.[94] ISIL's own words repeatedly made it explicit that they intended to 'kill or convert' any infidels, including Yazidis. Indeed, ISIL's public statements on the matter provide 'an invaluable resource directly demonstrative of its intent'.[95] Since, if it had been able to fulfil its intent completely, ISIL would effectively have destroyed the Yazidis as a religious group, and given that they did destroy them in part, it seems beyond doubt that a clear threat of genocide was posed.

Although much of the hard evidence of mass graves and systematic sexual slavery against the Yazidis did not appear until after the siege on Mount Sinjar,[96]

---

88 *ibid.*, paras. 54 and 72.

89 Office of the United Nations High Commissioner for Human Rights (OHCHR), '"Iraq: Immediate Action Needed to Protect Human Rights of Yazidis in Grave Danger" – UN Experts', OHCHR, Press Release, 12 August 2014.

90 A/HRC/32/CRP.2, 15 June 2016, para. 116; A/CONF.183/9, 17 July 1998.

91 A/RES/260(iii), 9 December 1948.

92 A/CONF.183/9, 17 July 1998, articles. 5–7.

93 A/RES/260(iii), 9 December 1948.

94 *The Prosecutor v. Jean-Paul Akayesu*, ICTR-96-4-A, 1 June 2001.

95 A/HRC/32/CRP.2, 15 June 2016, para. 151.

96 S/2021/419, 1 May 2021.

it was still abundantly clear at the time that ISIL held a genocidal intent, and would have committed genocidal acts upon the Yazidis trapped on Mount Sinjar had they not escaped.[97] It was also clear early on during the siege that the UN and the international community was aware that atrocities were being committed against the Yazidis who had failed to escape Sinjar Town and its surrounding villages. In a press release on 7 August 2014, the Deputy Special Representative of the UNSG for Iraq stated that he thought ISIL's actions appeared to fulfil 'a widespread and systematic policy aimed at cleansing non-Sunni ethnic and religious communities from areas under its control'.[98]

Not only was the threat of genocide posed by ISIL against the Yazidis on Mount Sinjar clear, so too was the imminence of the threat. On 6 August 2014, Vian Dakhil, the only Yazidi member of the Iraqi parliament, made an impassioned plea for urgent international assistance.[99] She accused ISIL of genocide and claimed that 'there is a collective attempt to exterminate the Yazidi people'.[100] The following day, the UNSG issued a statement condemning ISIL's attacks and their impact on vulnerable minority groups,[101] and the Security Council issued a statement calling on the international community to assist the Iraqi government.[102] The Security Council statement condemned the attacks against the Yazidis, who it said were in immediate need of humanitarian assistance.[103] Further, it warned that any systematic attacks against Yazidi civilians on the basis of their religion may constitute an atrocity crime.[104] The *Wall Street Journal* also reported on that day that US officials had received a formal request for assistance from the Iraqi government.[105] The US decision to assist was announced that night, at 9:30 pm Washington time.[106]

---

97 ISIL, 'The Revival of Slavery before the Hour'; HRW, 'Iraq: ISIS Abducting, Killing, Expelling Minorities'; UNAMI, *Report on the Protection of Civilians in Armed Conflict in Iraq*; Packer, 'A Friend Flees the Horror of ISIS'.

98 UNAMI, 'UN Gravely Concerned about Situation in Northern Iraq'.

99 Laura Smith-Spark, 'Iraqi Yazidi Lawmaker: "Hundreds of My People Are Being Slaughtered"', *CNN World*, 6 August 2014.

100 *ibid.*

101 Stéphane Dujarric, 'Statement Attributable to the Spokesman for the Secretary-General on Attacks on Yezidis and Other Minority Groups in Iraq', United Nations Department of Public Information, Press Release, 7 August 2014.

102 SC/11515–IK/683, 7 August 2014.

103 *ibid.*

104 *ibid.*

105 Julian E. Barnes, Jeffrey Sparshott, and Nour Malas, 'Barack Obama Approves Airstrikes on Iraq, Airdrops Aid', *Wall Street Journal*, 8 August 2014.

106 Obama, 'Statement by the President'.

In the days that followed, despite the efforts of the US and local forces, the atrocity threat did not subside. On 12 August 2014, just one day prior to the US airstrikes that assisted to evacuate the majority of the remaining trapped civilians[107] and to, in the words of the Pentagon 'end the siege' on Mount Sinjar,[108] six UN Special Rapporteurs issued a joint statement calling for immediate action to protect the Yazidis.[109] The UN Special Rapporteur on the Rights of Minorities, Rita Izsák, stated that 'all possible measures must be taken urgently to avoid a mass atrocity and potential genocide within days or hours'.[110] She further cautioned that 'the responsibility to protect populations at risk of atrocity crimes falls both on the Iraqi government and the international community'.[111] The UN Special Rapporteur on Summary Executions, Christof Heyns, stated that the UN had received verified reports that ISIL was systematically targeting minority groups, and that 'International actors must do all in their power to support those on the ground with the capacity to protect lives'.[112]

The threat of genocide posed by ISIL to the Yazidis trapped on Mount Sinjar was clear, as was the imminency of the threat. Information emerging on the ground from multiple credible sources allowed this to be substantiated prior to the decision to assist being made, and then again prior to the final assistance action being rendered. This was a crucial enabling condition for Protection Assistance to be effectively provided in this case.

2.3 *Operational Relationship between the Assisting State and Host Government*

On 7 August 2014, President Obama announced US' Protection Assistance 'to help Iraqis push back against ISIL'.[113] From 7 to 12 August 2014, the US conducted at least 15 targeted airstrikes which 'helped check the advances of ISIL

107 It should be noted that although the US-led Protection Assistance efforts were rendered at the request of the Iraqi government and involved coordination with Iraqi forces, soldiers from the Kurdish People's Protection Unit and Kurdish Workers' Party based in Syria were responsible for opening the corridor off the mountain and into Syria that allowed the Yazidis to escape. See: UNAMI and OHCHR, *A Call for Accountability and Protection: Yezidi Survivors of Atrocities Committed by ISIL*, Human Rights Report, 12 August 2016, p. 8.

108 Helene Cooper and Michael D. Shear, '"Militants"' Siege on Mountain in Iraq Is Over, Pentagon Says', *The New York Times*, 13 August 2014.

109 OHCHR, 'Iraq: "Immediate Action Needed"'.

110 *ibid.*

111 *ibid.*

112 *ibid.*

113 Obama, 'Statement by the President'.

forces' in Northern Iraq.[114] They also provided five airdrops of aid to Yazidis stranded on Mount Sinjar.[115] On 13 August they launched a drone strike on an ISIL mortar position that was attacking local forces, followed by a resupply of those forces and 'airstrikes in and around Mount Sinjar' that 'absolutely had an impact on ISIL's ability to place direct fire on those on Mount Sinjar'.[116] The Obama administration's response to the situation unfolding on Mount Sinjar was decisive. Not only did this decisiveness reflect the clear prioritisation of mass atrocity prevention by the administration, and their belief that there was a clear cause for action, but also that there were pre-existing operational conditions that made such decisive action possible. In this case, a major element of those conditions was the ability of the US and host government forces to coordinate and communicate effectively based on years of experience working together.

One Pentagon official, speaking on the condition of anonymity, revealed that US forces were in constant communication with Iraqi officials from 'day one' about how they could 'help co-ordinate additional relief, enhance [Iraqi] efforts, and provide direct assistance wherever possible'.[117] In addition to its airstrikes and airdrops of aid, the US conducted 50–60 'Intelligence, Surveillance and Reconnaissance' flights over the Nineveh region per day throughout the siege, providing vital strategic information to local ground forces who lacked these unique capabilities.[118] The local forces in turn fed information back to the US that allowed them to precisely target airstrikes.[119] On 13 August 2014, the Pentagon announced that the siege on Mount Sinjar was broken. The Pentagon Press Secretary, John Kirby, credited US airstrikes and humanitarian airdrops, as well as the efforts of the local forces on the ground, for 'allowing thousands of Yazidis to evacuate from the mountain each night over the last several days'.[120] Without the level of coordination between the assisting state and host

114 Claudette Roulo, 'Humanitarian Assistance Continues in Iraq', *DoD News*, 11 August 2014.

115 *ibid.*; US Central Command, 'U.S. Continues Humanitarian Airdrops in Northern Iraq', *DoD News*, 12 August 2014.

116 US Central Command, 'U.S. Provides Aid to Yezidis, Strikes ISIL Mortar Position', *DoD News*, 13 August 2014; Tyrone C. Marshall Jr, 'Speed Necessary for Iraq Assessments, DoD Spokesman Says', *DoD News*, 13 August 2014.

117 Spencer Ackerman, Martin Chulov, and Julian Borger, 'US Carries Out Air Drops to Help Iraqis Trapped on Mountain by ISIS', *The Guardian*, 7 August 2014.

118 Gordon Lubold and Kate Brannen, 'Sinjar Surprise: How the U.S. May Have Misjudged the Refugee Situation in Iraq', *Foreign Policy*, 15 August 2014; Roulo, 'Humanitarian Assistance Continues in Iraq'.

119 Helene Cooper and Michael D. Shear, '"Militants"' Siege on Mountain in Iraq Is Over, Pentagon Says', *The New York Times*, 13 August 2014.

120 *ibid.*

government that this Protection Assistance action clearly demonstrated, it seems unlikely that the local ground forces would have been able to help as many civilians escape from Mount Sinjar as they did.

The fact that the assisting state and host government forces had such a close relationship, based on years of experience working together, allowed for a clarity of communication and degree of coordination that was crucial to the timeliness and effectiveness of the Protection Assistance action.

2.4 *Alignment with Assisting State's Domestic Political and Foreign Policy Agenda*

The language in President Obama's statement authorising airstrikes on 7 August was consistent with R2P Pillar Two, which indicates the degree to which atrocity prevention had, by that time, been effectively mainstreamed into US foreign policy.

> I've said before, the United States cannot and should not intervene every time there's a crisis in the world. So let me be clear about why we must act, and act now. When we face a situation like we do on that mountain – with innocent people facing the prospect of violence on a horrific scale, when we have a mandate to help – in this case, a request from the Iraqi government – and when we have the unique capabilities to help avert a massacre, then I believe the United States of America cannot turn a blind eye. We can act, carefully and responsibly, to prevent a potential act of genocide. That's what we're doing on that mountain.[121]

The components of this justification – strategic responsibility, a legitimate mandate for action, the unique capabilities of the US to prevent an imminent genocide, and the responsibility of the US to act in such a situation – are significant in the context of this study. Obama also claimed in this speech that it was the US' responsibility to act to prevent a potential genocide,[122] which directly reflects the language and spirit of R2P.

In terms of the decisiveness of their action, President Obama explained the situation on Mount Sinjar in great detail and made a clear case for the urgency of action based on the imminency of the threat. He stated that ISIL's actions towards religious minorities were 'particularly barbaric' and informed his audience that ISIL had 'called for the systematic destruction of the entire Yazidi people, which would constitute genocide'.[123]

121 Obama, 'Statement by the President'.

122 *ibid.*

123 *ibid.*

In a press call on 8 August 2014, following Obama's speech, senior administration officials echoed his position, and spelled out how the actions of the US would be consistent with international law, since they were at the request of the Iraqi government.[124] This was a key enabling condition for their assistance to be effectively rendered in line with Pillar Two. It reflected an alignment with the US' foreign policy agenda, and a willingness to comply with the R2P doctrine.[125]

Equally noteworthy, President Obama's statement that the US 'can't and won't intervene in every crisis' appeared designed to differentiate the actions taken to prevent genocide on Mount Sinjar from the previous 'pre-emptive' actions taken by the US in Iraq.[126] Obama referenced working to 'assist', 'empower' and 'help' Iraqis push back against ISIL, and made clear that no combat troops would be deployed as part of the limited mission.[127] This provided an important degree of reassurance to US voters.[128] It aligned the action taken with the administration's previously articulated domestic political agenda of 'welcoming troops home' and not being 'dragged into another war'.[129] This alignment was an important condition that enabled the US to take Protection Assistance action in this case.

2.5 *Support from the International Community*

There was widespread endorsement of the US' Protection Assistance action in 2014 from the international advocacy community, leading R2P scholars, and states. The International Coalition for the Responsibility to Protect reported that 'many hailed the move as a necessary measure to prevent the imminent genocide of the Yazidi population, and as a clear example of upholding the Second Pillar of R2P'.[130] Prominent R2P scholars reiterated the appropriateness of the response. For example, Gareth Evans wrote that it was 'completely consistent with the principles' of R2P, touched 'on all the necessary bases of

124 Barack Obama, 'Background Briefing by Senior Administration Officials on Iraq', The American Presidency Project, 7 August 2014.

125 Further evidence of the degree to which the Obama administration had mainstreamed atrocity prevention into their foreign policy by 2014 can be found in their 2011 Presidential Study Directive on Mass Atrocities, which established an interagency 'Atrocity Prevention Board', as well as in their 2012 Defence Strategic Guidance and their development and adoption of a Mass Atrocity Response Operations handbook for military personnel.

126 Barnes, Sparshott, and Malas, 'Barack Obama Approves Airstrikes on Iraq, Airdrops Aid'.

127 Obama, 'Statement by the President'.

128 Katzman, et al., *Iraq Crisis and U.S. Policy*, pp. 6–7.

129 Obama, 'Statement by the President'.

130 The International Coalition for the Responsibility to Protect, '"Convert, Pay, Flee, or Be Killed" Iraq's Minorities Under Threat', 15 August 2014.

legality, legitimacy and likely effectiveness', and deserved 'unconditional support' from the international community.[131] In turn Alex Bellamy clarified that the US' actions aligned with R2P Pillar Two since they were 'in response to a specific request for assistance from a member state', which helped 'fulfil its R2P' by assisting Iraq while it was 'under stress', satisfying paragraphs 138 and 139 of the World Summit Outcome Document on R2P.[132] Support for the need to act in ways compatible with the US' Protection Assistance efforts was also provided by a diverse range of international leaders. The United Kingdom (UK) Prime Minister, David Cameron, said, 'I welcome president Obama's decision ... to conduct targeted US airstrikes'.[133] UNSG Ban Ki-moon welcomed the US' 'decisive and firm commitment' and stated that he thought the 'air strike and military operation, which was done at the request of the Government of Iraq, was able to help ... save a lot of human lives'.[134] The Security Council, following its Resolution 2170, 'urging all parties to protect the civilian population ... affected by the violent activities of ISIL', called on the international community to assist 'in association with local and regional authorities, to combat the terrorist threat facing all Iraqis ... notably Yazidis'.[135] Rwandan Minister for Foreign Affairs Louise Mushikiwabo said that 'ISIL ... has committed mass and gross atrocities' and that while 'the effort against that organization should be nationally led and owned ... we acknowledge the active role played by the United States'.[136] Spanish Foreign Affairs Minister José Manuel García Margallo offered even stronger support, saying that 'we cannot remain impassive before the systematic elimination of entire communities and religious minorities ... resolution 2170 ... makes unequivocally clear the will to act [and] provides legitimacy beyond any question'.[137] The Gulf Cooperation Council, through the *Jeddah Communique*, resolved to support 'all Iraqis in combating ISIL' and confirmed their 'commitment to implement UN Security Council Resolution 2170'.[138] Perhaps the most representative endorsement of the style of action taken by the US came from the landmark Paris Conference on Peace and

---

131 Gareth Evans, 'The Right Iraqi Invasion', *The Sydney Morning Herald*, 12 August 2014; Gareth Evans, 'A Legitimate, Humane Mission in Iraq to Halt Islamic State Extremism', *The Australian*, 2 September 2014.

132 Alex Bellamy, 'Aiding Iraqis Meets Responsibility to Protect and Could Lead to Common Ground on Syria', *IPI Global Observatory*, 11 August 2014.

133 Georgia Graham, 'David Cameron Condemns "Barbaric" Islamic State Attacks but Will Not Match US Promise of Airstrikes', *The Telegraph*, 8 August 2014.

134 SG/SM/16150, 16 September 2014.

135 *ibid.*; S/RES/2170, 15 August 2014.

136 S/PV.7271, 19 September 2014.

137 *ibid.*

138 US Department of State (USDOS), *Jeddah Communique*, 11 September 2014.

Security. The conference was held in September 2014, and involved representatives from over 29 countries, including Russia, China, and multiple countries from the Arab League. All participants at the conference, many of whom might normally have been expected to oppose any US military action on foreign soil, agreed that they were 'committed to supporting the new Iraqi government in its fight against [ISIL] by any means necessary, including appropriate military assistance'.[139] It is clear that the Protection Assistance actions undertaken by the US enjoyed widespread support from the international community.

In addition to rhetorical support, many states supported the US-led assistance efforts in Sinjar by offering support in the form of humanitarian aid or 'providing arms, equipment, training, or advi[ce]'.[140] For example, the Netherlands sent a C-130 Hercules transport aircraft 'fully loaded' with humanitarian aid to Mount Sinjar.[141] The UK supplied financial and non-lethal military support to the Peshmerga forces defending the Yazidis, while Czechoslovakia provided arms, and Germany supplied logistical support.[142] Australia, the UK, and Canada all assisted, at first by supporting the aid drops on Mount Sinjar, and eventually by joining the military coalition.[143] By the end of 2014, six Western governments had joined the US in conducting air strikes against ISIL.[144] Though a significant proportion of this support was only offered after Protection Assistance action had already been taken on Mount Sinjar, it reflects the widespread support from the international community that the US had as an assisting state. This support was a key condition enabling Protection Assistance to be effectively rendered.

2.6 *Criticisms of the Effectiveness of the Protection Assistance Rendered*

Criticisms of the effectiveness of the Protection Assistance provided by the US in this case generally fall into one of four categories: the inappropriateness

139 France Diplomatie, 'International Conference on Peace and Security in Iraq', Press Release, 15 September 2014.

140 David Villars and Laurence Norman, 'EU Prepares to Scale Up Iraq Involvement', *Wall Street Journal*, 15 August 2014; US Department of State (USDOS), 'Building International Support to Counter ISIL', Press Release, 19 September 2014.

141 USDOS, 'International Efforts to Counter ISIL', Press Release, 23 September 2014.

142 Lawrence Norman and David Villars, 'EU Prepares to Scale Up Iraq Involvement', *Wall Street Journal*, 13 August 2014.

143 Global Centre for R2P, 'R2P Monitor', Issue 24, 15 November 2015, p. 4; Katharine Murphy, 'Australian Troops Complete First Humanitarian Mission in Northern Iraq', *The Guardian*, 14 August 2014; Ian M. Phedran and Paul Toohey, 'Bullets Delivered to Kurdish Fighters', *Daily Telegraph*, 5 September 2014.

144 Jason Ralph and James Souter, 'A Special Responsibility to Protect: The UK, Australia and the Rise of Islamic State', *International Affairs*, 91(4) 709–723 (2015), p. 709.

of the response, the inauthenticity of the response, the inability of the response to absolve the US of its culpability for the conditions that gave rise to the threat, and the inadequacy of the response. Each of these categories of criticism will be considered in turn, before the overall effectiveness of the Protection Assistance action is weighed.

In her opening address to the 69th session of the UN General Assembly, the Brazilian President Dilma Rousseff reiterated the statements she had made minutes earlier to the press outside the UN that 'bombing ISIL' could not lead to peace.[145] As she put it in her more formal address, 'it is impossible to eliminate the underlying causes of conflict through the use of force. That has been made clear by the ... tragic national fragmentation of Iraq'.[146] She further explained her views on the inappropriateness of military action as a response to an atrocity threat by claiming that 'instead of leading to peace, every military intervention has worsened ... conflicts'.[147] Brazil's Foreign Minister, Luiz Alberto Figueiredo, also criticised the appropriateness of the US' actions, stating that there is 'no military solution to ISIL', and that 'the best way to peace will always be dialogue and diplomacy'.[148]

China's position on the US' Protection Assistance was officially 'neutral'.[149] It took 'an open attitude towards actions that facilitate ensuring security and stability', so long as there was 'respect in place for Iraq's sovereignty'.[150] Chinese state media outlets were less tactful than this, dismissing the US' humanitarian protection claims as an inauthentic guise to garner domestic support and international approval for an intervention that was ultimately economically motivated.[151] Many states have echoed China's concerns about the authenticity of the use of R2P's military dimensions more broadly,[152] as canvassed in the legitimacy section of this chapter.

---

145 Eduardo Simões, 'Dilma critica ação contra Estado Islâmico e diz que bombardeios não levam à paz', *Reuters*, 25 September 2014.

146 A/69/PV.6, 24 September 2014, p. 8.

147 *ibid.*

148 Rafael Moraes, 'Dilma quer diálogo com comunidade internacional, não com terroristas, diz ministro – Política', *Estadão*, 25 September 2014.

149 Shannon Tiezzi, 'US Airstrikes in Iraq: A Win-Win Situation for China', *The Diplomat*, 8 August 2014.

150 Zhang Yunubi, 'China Responds to US Airstrikes in Iraq', *China Daily*, 8 August 2014.

151 Mu Dong and Liang Youchang, 'Why Did the U.S. Finally Start in Iraq?', *Xinhua*, 8 August 2014.

152 Bellamy, 'Responsibility to Protect or Trojan Horse?'; Edward Luck, 'Sovereignty, Choice, and the Responsibility to Protect', *Global Responsibility to Protect*, 1(1) 10–21 (2009), pp. 12–20; Noam Chomsky, 'Statement to the United Nations General Assembly Thematic Dialogue on the Responsibility to Protect', United Nations, 2009, pp. 20–26; Thomas G. Weiss, 'Military Humanitarianism: Syria Hasn't Killed It', *The Washington Quarterly*, 37(1) 7–20 (2014), p.8.

Argentina noted the culpability of the US for the atrocity threat being responded to when it added to Security Council debates with the observation that 'ISIL … finds its origins in the turbulent years that followed the invasion suffered by the country in 2003'. It added that ISIL 'must not be the pretext for unilateral actions, which have shown that they generate more problems than they solve'.[153] A different line of argument regarding culpability was made in the UK parliament when it was contemplating participation in the US-led operation. Opposition leader, Edward Miliband, argued that 'while some would say our [2003] intervention in Iraq means we should not intervene in this case, I think there is a heightened responsibility for us precisely because we did'.[154] Whether of the view that any further military action would do more harm than good, or that a special 'reparative' duty to protect existed, critics of the US' Protection Assistance efforts in 2014 on the grounds that they were culpable for the conditions giving rise to the threat appear to agree that their actions were unable to absolve them of this culpability.

Perhaps the most frequently levelled criticism of the US' actions in this case is that they were not adequate to protect the population at risk. As the UN Investigative Team to Promote Accountability for Crimes Committed by Da'esh/ISIL (UNITAD) has now established, acts of genocide were committed by ISIL against the Yazidis both before and after the US led Protection Assistance efforts. If the US had intended to save all the Yazidis at risk of mass atrocity in 2014, then it is clear that its Protection Assistance efforts did not come soon enough, or go far enough, to protect the population at risk beyond the confines of Mount Sinjar.

Evaluating the effectiveness of the Protection Assistance rendered in light of these criticisms is no easy task, and whatever the result, further research into the US' actions in this case, including into their effectiveness, is welcomed. Nonetheless, it is the contention of this chapter that the US' actions did constitute an example of Protection Assistance effectively rendered, so these criticisms will now be briefly weighed.

Regarding the criticism that the Protection Assistance effort – particularly its use of military measures – was inappropriate, the suitability of the use of military measures in situations of impending mass atrocity has repeatedly been agreed to by the international community. Further, it has been reiterated by the UNSG in multiple reports that military measures lie within the scope of

153 S/PV.7271, 19 September 2014, p. 15.

154 Edward Miliband, 'Speech to the House of Commons', 26 September 2014, *Parliamentary Debates*, Vol. 585, Col. 1271.

appropriate responses under R2P Pillar Two, so long as the assistance provided is as the request of the host nation, as it was in this case.

In relation to the criticism that the response reflected an inauthentic invocation of R2P, while there is no denying that the Obama administration framed the action to appeal to a domestic political audience, the fact that action was taken at all is still noteworthy given how unpopular any further involvement in Iraq was with American voters. Moreover, the US did not appear to gain anything strategically or financially from the action outside of its ability to claim good global citizenship, and to potentially fulfil a reparative duty.

In terms of the criticism that the US' reparative duty reflected a culpability for the underlying conditions of risk that it was unable to absolve itself of through its Protection Assistance actions, one wonders if there is anything the US could ever do that would absolve it of such responsibility (if indeed a direct causal connection between its military campaign in Iraq and ISIL's commission of atrocities could be established). While it is true that more genuinely preventative measures ought to enjoy a greater focus for states wishing to fulfil their responsibility to protect, and that the responsibility to rebuild is an often overlooked dimension of R2P that may be of relevance to the US–Iraq relationship, the present chapter does not seek to contribute to this discussion. Suffice to say that, within the confines of the limited actions that were taken, it appears the US was able to effectively render assistance in response to Iraq's request.

Regarding the claim that the US' response was inadequate, it should be noted that, from a Yazidi perspective, some Protection Assistance must have been infinitely preferable to no Protection Assistance. Further, the US' limited actions did help to avert an impending mass atrocity.[155] As a paper on the Yazidi case published by the Simon-Skjodt Center for the Prevention of Genocide notes, an 'important takeaway from the Mt. Sinjar case is that in the face of a single mass atrocity event, even the limited use of force can prevent significant loss of life'.[156] Given the dearth of domestic voter support for more extensive US military action at the time,[157] criticisms that the US did not do enough seem to lack a pragmatic dimension.

Despite the various criticisms contemplated, the Protection Assistance provided by the US at the request of Iraq in 2014 helped to prevent the imminent

155 Yazda, 'Yazidis Urge International Community to Raise Yazidi Genocide Issue at International Criminal Court', Press Release, 2 August 2016.

156 Colin Thomas-Jensen, 'Fighting Fire with Fire', Simon-Skjodt Center for the Prevention of Genocide, Series of Occasional Papers, No. 8, February 2018, p. 12.

157 CBS, 'Poll: Many Americans Wary of U.S. Role in Iraq', *CBS News*, 23 June 2014.

genocide of 40,000 Yazidis. Notwithstanding the limited scope of the action, and its failure to prevent the genocide of all Yazidis at the hands of ISIL in Sinjar, it still stands as an example of Pillar Two Protection Assistance effectively rendered.

3 Conclusion

The US' actions in Iraq in 2014 helped to prevent the genocide of 40,000 Yazidis trapped on Mount Sinjar. It provides a clear example of a state rendering R2P Pillar Two Protection Assistance effectively, in this case in response to an atrocity threat posed by a non-state terrorist group. As UNITAD continues to release its sobering findings into ISIL's mass atrocity crimes 2013–2017, and as terrorist groups continue to pose mass atrocity threats around the world, cases like this deserve increased attention, particularly within the context of the ability of R2P Pillar Two to provide a legitimate means through which to respond to such threats.[158] R2P Pillar Two contemplates a 'narrow but deep' array of measures, of which responses to imminent risks are but a small part. Further research into the applicability of R2P to atrocity threats posed by non-state actors, like the threat posed by ISIL to the Yazidis in 2014, should be considered.

158 Threats worthy of particular mention in this context include those in Afghanistan and Nigeria, where serious mass atrocity risks are posed by ISIL-affiliated terrorist groups. Although Al-Qaeda also poses a mass atrocity threat in Syria, the manifest failure of national authorities there to protect at-risk populations makes it a case more suitable for consideration under Pillar Three.

Index

www.ingramcontent.com/pod-product-compliance
Lightning Source LLC
Chambersburg PA
CBHW031325230926
51848CB00001B/98
9789004548114